TRUE CRIME CASE HISTORIES

VOLUMES 4, 5, & 6

JASON NEAL

AKAMAI PUBLISHING

More books by Jason Neal

Looking for more?? I am constantly adding new volumes of True Crime Case Histories. The series **can be read in any order**, and all books are available in paperback, hardcover, and audiobook.

Check out the complete series at:

https://amazon.com/author/jason-neal

or

http://jasonnealbooks.com

All Jason Neal books are also available in **AudioBook format at Audible.com.** Enjoy a **Free Audiobook** when you signup for a 30-Day trial using this link:

https://geni.us/AudibleTrueCrime

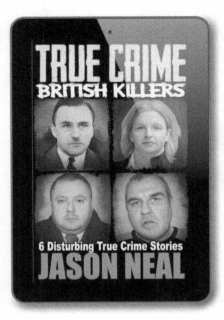

FREE BONUS EBOOK
FOR MY READERS

As my way of saying "Thank you" for downloading, I'm giving away a FREE True Crime e-book I think you'll enjoy.

https://TrueCrimeCaseHistories.com

Just visit the link above to let me know where to send your free book!

CONTENTS

TRUE CRIME CASE HISTORIES
VOLUME 4

Introduction	3
1. The Broomstick Killer	7
2. Bloodthirsty Parolee	23
3. The Body in the Bag	39
4. Mr. Mom Killer	55
5. The Incest Killer	75
6. The Copper Gulch Killer	85
7. Taking a Chance	95
8. The Tiger Parents	107
9. Mom, I'm a Monster	121
10. A Grisly New Orleans Tale	133
11. The Alligator Theory	143
12. The Kičevo Monster	155

TRUE CRIME CASE HISTORIES
VOLUME 5

Introduction	167
1. The Homeschoolers	171
2. The Submarine Case	183
3. Unlucky 13	195
4. Divine Justice	211
5. The Amish Killer	221
6. Cold Storage Killer	229
7. Coercive Control	241
8. The Werewolf Butcher	251
9. The Black Widow	261
10. The Crossbow Killer	269
11. Murder in the Sacristy	279
12. Devious Dixie	287

TRUE CRIME CASE HISTORIES
VOLUME 6

Introduction		301
1. Lost in the Desert		305
2. Consumed by Desire		315
3. Gay Panic		323
4. Saving a Soul		333
5. The Jacksonville Monster		341
6. Dead in the Water		351
7. The Carnival Cult		367
8. The Mousse Can Killer		375
9. A Glitzy Cowboy Tale		385
10. Blue Mist #22		397
11. The Crybaby Killer		409
12. The Darlington Cannibal		419
Online Appendix		429
Thank You!		431
Also by Jason Neal		433
Free Bonus Book		435
About the Author		437

TRUE CRIME CASE HISTORIES

VOLUME 4

TRUE CRIME
CASE HISTORIES

12 Disturbing True Crime Stories
JASON NEAL

INTRODUCTION

If you've read the previous volumes of the True Crime Case Histories series, you know that I like to start with a brief word of warning. The stories included in this book are truly depraved and shocking. They are not for the squeamish. Many true crime television shows and news articles often leave out the gruesome details, simply because they may be too much for the average viewer or reader. With my books, I try not to leave out the details, no matter how vicious they may be. My intention is not to shock, but to provide a clear and accurate description of some of the most evil minds of the world. Though the stories are brief, I do my best to include enough detail so that the reader can get a better look into the demented mind of the killer.

This volume features twelve of the most incomprehensible stories of the last sixty years. Trying to understand the motivation behind murders like these can be an exercise in futility. But one thing is for sure—the stories in this volume will keep you turning pages.

In this book you'll encounter a story that has haunted me since I was a little kid growing up in southwest Washington. I lived a normal American life where I could ride my bike around my small town from dusk till dawn without a care in the world. When I was twelve years old, a boy in my neighborhood just a year older than I disappeared and was later found murdered. At the time I didn't know many of the details, but after researching the story all these years later and realizing that monsters like Tommy Ragan were roaming my tiny town, I may not have felt quite so secure.

In this volume you'll also read of how the Texas justice system grossly failed to protect the people of Texas. The result of their leniency was that a brutal killer of three teenagers was allowed back on the streets to kill as many as eleven more women.

Several of the stories include familial killings: There's the husband that killed his successful wife because he was jealous of her career, the wife that killed her husband so she could marry his best friend and collect insurance money, the young New Orleans man that survived Hurricane Katrina only to kill and cook his girlfriend, the young girl that hired hitmen to kill her parents, and the man that married his teenage daughter before hunting her down and killing her.

Though all the killings are senseless, some are particularly perplexing: One example is the story of the newspaper reporter who kidnapped, tortured, and butchered women who resembled his mother, then wrote stories of the killings in his newspaper articles. There's also the unthinkable story of a teenage boy obsessed with decomposition, who kidnapped, raped, and dismembered a young innocent girl.

The stories in this volume are revolting and disconcerting, but they're true. These things really happen in the world. Though we will never fully understand the criminal mind, at least we can be better informed.

Lastly, please join my mailing list for discounts, updates, and a free book. You can sign up for that at

TrueCrimeCaseHistories.com

You can also purchase paperbacks, hardcovers, and signed copies of my books directly from me at:

JasonNealBooks.com

Additional photos, videos, and documents pertaining to the cases in this volume can be found on the accompanying web page:

https://TrueCrimeCaseHistories.com/vol4/

Thank you for reading. I sincerely hope you gain some insight from this volume of True Crime Case Histories.

- Jason

CHAPTER 1
THE BROOMSTICK KILLER

The tale of The Broomstick Killer is easily one of the most sinister stories in Texan history. Kenneth McDuff was a bloodthirsty killer who was granted unprecedented leniency by a justice system that allowed him to continue killing even after he had shown that he was a sadistic psychopath.

The tiny town of Rosebud in central Texas was the home of a notoriously strange family: the McDuffs. J.A. McDuff, the father, owned a cement finishing business that did quite well during the building boom of the late seventies, and the family was well-off by small town standards. The mother, Addie McDuff, ran the laundromat across from their home and doted over her six children. She was a large, headstrong woman known for being over-protective of her children, and would come running if they ever encountered trouble.

Addie was notoriously known to carry a gun in her purse and was referred to as the "Pistol-Packin' Mama" by the locals in Rosebud. Her children's teachers feared her because she would storm into the school in a huff any time one of her children was accused of misconduct. To

Addie, her children could do no wrong whatsoever, and if someone accused them of anything, the school was likely to blame.

The eldest son, Lonnie, was the bully of the family. He once pulled a knife on the school principal who subsequently threw him down a flight of stairs. Lonnie spoke with a speech impediment and referred to himself as "Wuff and Tuff Wonnie McDuff."

Addie McDuff was particularly fond of her youngest son, Kenneth. Though technically he wasn't the youngest of the children, she fawned over him as her "baby boy." Even in his early teens when Kenneth started getting into trouble, somebody else was always to blame in her eyes.

Kenneth was a known troublemaker and a bully like his older brother Lonnie. He was always the kid with a pocketful of money, and new clothes, and he rode a loud motorcycle to school. Though he had an average IQ, he didn't do well in school. Kenneth didn't seem to care about school and his only genuine friend was his brother Lonnie.

By the fall of 1964 Kenneth was seventeen and spent most of his time causing trouble. He broke into businesses and homes looking for things to steal and drove around town looking for girls. But he wasn't looking for a girl to date: He was looking for a girl to rape. McDuff confided in his brother that he had once raped a woman, slit her throat, and left her dying. Whether the story was authentic is uncertain, as the crime was never reported.

Even at an early age, local law enforcement was all too familiar with Kenneth McDuff. Inevitably he was arrested in 1965 for a string of more than a dozen burglaries. The sentence for his crimes totaled fifty-two years, but because he was only eighteen the judge was lenient. McDuff was allowed to serve his time concurrently instead of consecutively. The fifty-two years of prison was reduced to a meager three years, and he only ended up serving ten months before they released him.

The brief sentence gave McDuff a sense of invincibility and just eight months later he moved on to much more heinous crimes.

On a hot August night in 1966, McDuff and his new friend Roy Dale Green were on their way to Fort Worth. Roy assumed they were on their way to drink some beer and look for girls, but McDuff had much more diabolical plans in mind.

Roy Dale Green was a skinny eighteen-year-old who was impressed with, and excited to be hanging out with twenty-year-old McDuff. Green knew that McDuff was a troublemaker, but when Kenneth told him he wanted to rape a girl that night, Roy didn't take him seriously. When McDuff pulled into the parking lot of the baseball field in Everman, Texas, Roy had no idea what a mess he had got himself into.

McDuff pulled his car up next to a parked car near the baseball diamond; he could see there were three teenagers inside the car. He reached under the seat and pulled out a Colt .38 revolver, got out of the car, and walked up to the driver's side door of the parked car.

Pointing the revolver at the window, McDuff ordered the three teens out of the car. Inside the car was sixteen-year-old Edna Louise Sullivan, her boyfriend seventeen-year-old Robert Brand, and his fifteen-year-old cousin Mark Dunham. McDuff led them to the trunk of the car and commanded them to get in. The three teens climbed in, and he closed the lid.

Mark Dunham, Robert Brand & Edna Sullivan

McDuff drove their car while Roy Green followed in McDuff's car to an isolated area where they stopped. McDuff and Green got out of the cars and McDuff turned to Green and said, "We're gonna have to knock 'em off." Kenneth then opened the trunk and pulled Edna out. The teen girl screamed as he dragged her away from her friends to his own car and locked her in his trunk. He then went back over to the young boys. Unable to see, Edna's terror only intensified when she heard six gunshots. McDuff had emptied the revolver into the two other boys' bodies. When he could not close the trunk, McDuff became frustrated and backed the car up to a fence and abandoned it with the boy's bodies hanging out of the back.

Roy Green was in shock. They both got back in to McDuff's car and drove to another location where McDuff pulled Edna out of the back of the car and raped her. After he raped her, McDuff ordered Green to rape her too. Then McDuff yelled to Green, "Find something for me to strangle her with." Green pulled the belt off of his pants and handed it to him, but McDuff found something he liked better. He had a broom in the back of his car. He raped her with the broomstick, then sat on her chest and held it across her neck. He leaned forward on the broom-stick, putting more and more pressure on her neck until he crushed her throat. McDuff threw her body over his shoulder, walked to the side of the dirt road and tossed her body into the nearby bushes; the two drove away.

The next day Roy Green was consumed with guilt and told his friend's mother what they had done. His friend's mother went to Green's mother, who subsequently convinced him to turn himself in.

Green was arrested and led the police to the bodies, and McDuff was quickly arrested as well. Green gave the police the gun that McDuff had buried next to his garage.

During the trial, a terrified Roy Green stuttered and stammered as he testified against McDuff. McDuff was cocky and nonchalant, taking the stand in his own defense, but it didn't help his case.

Kenneth McDuff mugshots

In November 1966 a jury found Kenneth McDuff guilty on three counts of murder. Roy Green served eleven years in prison for his part in the murders, while McDuff was handed three death sentences in the electric chair. In a normal world, this would be the end of the story, but it was nowhere near over.

On June 29, 1972 after six years on death row, the US Supreme Court decided that the death penalty, as it was then written, was a cruel and unusual punishment and was therefore unconstitutional under the Eighth and Fourteenth Amendments. In an extraordinary event, all death penalty cases in the United States were commuted to life sentences.

McDuff was now eligible for parole and applied for it every time he was allowed. He was convicted of such heinous crimes; it was unimaginable that he would ever be paroled. The residents of Central Texas thought that such a vicious killer could never be paroled. Over and over he applied, and he was repeatedly denied.

Fifteen years later in 1987, McDuff saw his chance. The Texas Federal Court ruled that the prisons of Texas were far too overcrowded, violating the civil rights of the inmates. Rather than spend money building more prisons, the courts set population limits in the prisons which led to a massive backlog of inmates being held in county jails across the state.

Texas Governor Bill Clements made an unthinkable deal with the parole board. In order to reduce prison population, they were required to release 150 inmates per day. Initially, the white-collar crimes were released, then the minor drug offenses. Within two years the only people left in the prisons were murderers. This is when McDuff saw his chance.

Each time he applied for parole, McDuff still had to appear before a parole board of three members, plead his case, and get two out of three votes in his favor. He had tried several times and was denied each time. In one instance he actually received two votes, but it was ultimately denied when an unknown party argued against his release. In another instance he tried to bribe a parole board official by offering him $10,000. Each time he was denied, but it didn't deter him.

Outside of the prison, McDuff's mother was busy doing her part. She hired two well-known attorneys from Huntsville, paying them $2,200 to try to find a way to get her beloved son released from prison.

Unbelievably, in 1989, after serving twenty-three years in prison, McDuff was paroled. The two members of the parole board that voted to release him were James Granberry and Chris Mealy. Mealy later blamed the tremendous pressure he was under from the government. Granberry was later charged with perjury in an unrelated case and ordered to serve six months in a halfway house.

During those years, the Texas parole board set free 127 murderers and twenty death row inmates.

The people of Rosebud were in shock at the news of McDuff's release. Some put bars over their windows and many feared walking the streets of the tiny town without a gun.

Immediately after his release, McDuff was required to visit his parole officer in Temple, Texas. After their first visit, the parole officer told police,

 "I don't know if it'll be next week or next month or next year, but one of these days, dead girls are gonna start turning up, and when that happens, the man you need to look for is Kenneth McDuff."

The parole officer was right. Just three days after his release, the body of twenty-nine-year-old Sarafia Parker was found in a field twenty-five miles west of Rosebud in Temple, the town that McDuff's parents had moved to while he was in prison. Though they had no evidence, police suspected McDuff was responsible for the killing.

McDuff was known as a racist. Just seven months after his release he harassed a young black man in Rosebud, yelling racial slurs at him, and pulled a knife on him. This violated his parole, and he was quickly sent back to prison, but McDuff knew how the prison system worked. He knew about the overcrowding issues and he was back on the streets just two months later.

After his release from prison, McDuff enrolled at Texas State Technical College in Waco and briefly got a job as a cashier at a convenience store called Quik-Pak. But working for a lowly $4 an hour did not satisfy him, and he quit after only a month.

By the summer of 1991, McDuff had given up his feeble attempts at the straight-and-narrow life and continued his life of crime. Living in the college dorms, he started dealing and using drugs. He knew this violated his parole, but he didn't care. He spent his spare time picking up prostitutes in Waco and used them to satisfy his need for violent sex.

In the late hours of October 10, 1991, McDuff picked up a young crack-addicted prostitute from Waco, Brenda Thompson, intent on killing her. McDuff had Brenda tied up in the passenger seat of his red pickup truck when he noticed a police checkpoint up ahead. Brenda saw her opportunity and screamed as she raised her legs up to the windshield and began kicking, cracking the windshield several times. When the police ran toward his truck McDuff hit the gas and crashed the road-block. Several police officers had to jump out of the way to avoid being run over.

McDuff led police on a high-speed chase but escaped into the night by turning off his lights and driving the wrong way down one-way streets. After he escaped, he took Brenda Thompson down an old abandoned road into a wooded area near Route 84 where he raped, tortured, and murdered her. Her body wasn't found until seven years later.

Just a week later McDuff picked up another Waco prostitute. Seven-teen-year-old Regina DeAnne Moore was last seen arguing outside a motel with McDuff on the night of October 17. Again, McDuff tied her arms and legs with her own stockings, then took her to a remote area where he raped and murdered her. Her remains were not found until 1998.

Two months later in Austin, twenty-eight-year-old Colleen Reed was washing her shiny new Mazda Miata convertible at a self-serve car wash.

One thing that McDuff learned in prison was to find a malleable side-kick. That evening he was driving around Austin with his latest side-kick, Alva Hank Worley. As they drove past the car wash McDuff spotted Colleen and made a quick U-turn.

McDuff pulled his tan Thunderbird into the bay next to hers, got out of the car and walked into Colleen's stall. Without a word, McDuff grabbed her around the neck and lifted the tiny girl off the ground. When Colleen screamed, neighbors behind the car wash came out to see what was happening. They watched as McDuff threw Colleen in his car and he and Worley drove away, again driving the wrong way on a one-way street.

The witnesses got a good look at Worley and alerted the police of his description and the type and color of the vehicle that sped away. Right away police suspected that McDuff was behind the abduction.

When police got the description of Worley, they began looking through McDuff's known associates and noticed Hank Worley immediately as one of his known drinking buddies. Like Roy Dale Green, Worley was timid and easily influenced by McDuff.

Worley wasn't hard to find, living in a motel with his fourteen-year-old daughter. When police knocked on his door, he was already terrified with guilt.

Though his guilt consumed him, he feared McDuff and wasn't quite ready to point a finger at him. On the first visit to his motel room, Worley claimed he barely knew McDuff. It took a few visits to his motel room for police to persuade him to admit to what had happened that night. They stopped by while he was having a barbecue by the motel pool with his daughter, and Detective Mike McNamara whispered in his ear,

"Hank, you're hiding a kid killer, you know that? You're protecting a man who raped and brutalized and strangled a girl not much older than your daughter over there. Picture her on the ground, a broomstick across her throat, crying out for you to help, begging you to speak out, to do what's right, to save the life of some young girl, to..."

McNamara couldn't finish his sentence before Worley screamed. He was ready to talk. When investigators got him into the interrogation room, he told the complete story of the night of Colleen's abduction.

Worley said he and McDuff were in Austin looking for drugs when McDuff saw Colleen washing her car. When McDuff lifted her off the ground by her throat she screamed "Please, not me! Not me!" He then threw her in the back of their car and told Worley to hold her down as they sped off.

When they got a few miles out of Austin McDuff got in the back with Colleen and commanded Worley to keep driving out of town. McDuff tied her hands behind her back with her shoelaces, then took his cigarette and put it out between her legs as she screamed. He beat her and raped her. When he finished, he told Worley to change places with him and Worley raped her while McDuff drove.

 Worley recalled, "I didn't want to have sex with her but if I didn't have sex with her, I knew that he was gonna get back there with her and beat her up some more and burn her with cigarettes. He was taking the cigarettes and getting the fire real hot and burning her down there in the wrong spots."

When they got near the town of Belton, McDuff pulled onto a secluded dirt road and raped her again.

 "He turned around, and he hit her. Slapped her real hard and knocked her backwards. Then he took another cigarette, and he lit it, and got the fire real hot and he burned her like that again."

When she was able to stand Worley claimed Colleen put her head on his shoulder and said "Please don't let him hurt me anymore." McDuff was having none of that. He grabbed her by the neck and stuffed her into the trunk of the car and turned to Worley and said, "I'm gonna use her up." McDuff used the term often to mean that he was going to terminate her life.

 "Then he put her in the trunk of the car, closed the trunk down and he takes me home. On the way home he asked me for my pocketknife and I told him I don't know where it is."

"Then he asked me, 'Well, I need a shovel. Let me borrow a shovel.' And I said, 'I ain't got one.' He didn't say what he was going to do with it, but I knew what he was gonna do with it. He wanted to kill her with it."

"Ain't nothin' I could do. Real scary being like that. If you can't help yourself, there ain't no way you gonna help anybody else. I wasn't even sure if I was gonna make it outta that."

"I'll always have a tear for that girl. I'll always cry for her, for what she went through. Nobody should be put through that type of torture."

McDuff was nowhere to be found, but police knew he was still in the area the following February when they found the body of another young prostitute. Twenty-two-year-old Valencia Joshua, a student at the same college that McDuff had attended was found on a golf course near the school. She had been strangled. The last time anyone had seen her, she was looking for Kenneth McDuff on the campus of their school.

Then on March 1, 1992, Melissa Northrup was working the night-shift at the Quik-Pak convenience store. She was a pregnant mother of two who knew the dangers of working the night shift, but needed to pay the bills. She would regularly call her husband during her shift to let him know she was okay.

Late that night McDuff was cruising the streets looking for drugs when his tan Thunderbird broke down just 100 yards from the Quik-Pak. This was the same store that McDuff had worked for only a month. McDuff knew that the store was open twenty-four hours a day and had no security to speak of. He also knew that there was a cute twenty-three-year-old who worked the night shift and had told friends that the place could easily be robbed.

When Melissa's husband didn't hear from her at 4:00 a.m. that night he got worried and called the store. He repeatedly got no answer so he drove to the store, but there was no sign of his wife.

When police found McDuff's car abandoned at the New Road Inn just 100 yards away, their suspicions were confirmed. McDuff was on a killing spree, and they started a massive nationwide manhunt.

Knowing how close McDuff was with his family, they started by questioning his parents. As always, his mother stood by her beloved son and claimed he was innocent but didn't know where he was. His father, however, was less loving,

 "I don't know where he is. If you find him, you can kill him if you want to."

On April 26, the badly decomposed body of Quik-Pak employee Melissa Northrup was found floating in a gravel quarry in Dallas County. Her hands were still tied behind her back with shoelaces - a signature of Kenneth McDuff.

The big break came on May 1 when the manhunt was aired on America's Most Wanted. The TV show was massively popular; through the years it has helped capture 1,200 fugitives. This airing was no exception. Shortly after it aired a man called from Kansas City, Missouri claiming that McDuff worked for a trash company under the assumed name Richard Fowler.

Texas police called Kansas City police who looked up the name Richard Fowler in their records. Someone had been using the name and had been arrested and fingerprinted for soliciting prostitutes. The fingerprints matched that of Kenneth McDuff. McDuff was arrested on May 4, 1992 as he was driving a trash truck to a landfill.

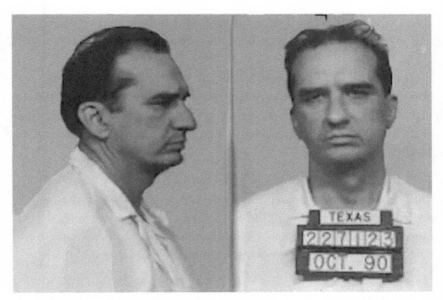

McDuff 1990 Mugshot

When he was brought back to Texas, crowds of angry people gathered outside of the courthouse. McDuff embraced the media and professed his innocence to the mob of cameras outside, often claiming that his trial was unfair.

Prosecutors had their strongest evidence against him for the abduction and murder of Melissa Northrup, so they decided to try that case first and worry about the rest later.

Addie McDuff, who was now seventy-seven years old, was called as a hostile witness to testify against her son. She confirmed that her son used her credit card near the Quik-Pak store on the night of the abduction, putting him near the scene of the crime when it happened.

McDuff was livid that his own mother was being used by the prosecution to testify against him, but there was more to come. The prosecution called two of his friends to testify that he had tried to enlist them in his plans to rob the Quik-Pak store.

At one point McDuff directed his anger at his own attorneys when he screamed at them,

"Why don't you get up and go sit on the prosecution's side! You're helping them more than you are me!"

The murder of Colleen Reed had not been tried yet, and the prosecution called Hank Worley to testify to show that there was a signature to McDuff's killings. Worley was brought to the courthouse in handcuffs. From his visible shaking, it was clear that just being in the presence of McDuff again terrified him.

The ultimate nail in the coffin for McDuff was when he insisted on testifying on his own behalf despite his defense team's wishes. They explained to him that under the rules of evidence, his past 1966 murders couldn't be mentioned in court if he wasn't on the stand, but if he took the stand, the prosecution could use that against him. McDuff wouldn't listen.

McDuff took the stand for two hours rambling a nonsensical story of his whereabouts on the night of the murder. Meanwhile, the prosecution took advantage of their opportunity and the jury heard the complete story of his brutal killings of the teenagers in 1966.

The jury took four hours to return their guilty verdict on February 16, 1993. His defense team requested leniency and asked for a life sentence, but the jury only took one hour to decide that Kenneth McDuff should die by lethal injection.

McDuff's trial for the murder of Colleen Reed started in 1994. Although the body had still not been found, he was given a second death sentence.

In television interviews from prison awaiting his death sentence, McDuff continued to profess his innocence, even for the 1966 killings.

In the months before his execution, investigators enlisted the help of a jailhouse informant to try to get McDuff to give up the locations of the bodies. Their plan worked.

In September 1998, the body of Regina DeAnne Moore was found beneath a bridge on the side of a highway. McDuff had buried her in a shallow grave. Her hands were still tied behind her back with shoelaces, and her ankles were bound with stockings.

The body of Brenda Thompson, who kicked McDuff's windshield as he crashed through the roadblock, was found in a grouping of trees outside of Waco. She had been tied up, raped, and tortured.

McDuff only had two weeks before his execution, but he wasn't giving up the location of Colleen Reed. He told the informant that he didn't want to tell the cops because it was the last body and if he gave them everything they needed they would "take away my commissary rights, and won't treat me right." With only two weeks to live, McDuff's only concern was his own diminished rights and had no regard for the closure of his victim's families.

Police met with prison officials and arranged to take none of his prison rights away. Presented with the assurance, McDuff finally gave them directions to where he had buried Colleen Reed's body.

Despite digging for hours exactly where he told them, they were unable to locate her body. That afternoon, in a covert arrangement, McDuff was brought to the dig site. The body of Colleen Reed was found on October 6, 1998.

In McDuff's final days investigator John Moriarty spent over forty hours interviewing him, trying to gain a deeper understanding of the psychopath's mind. In the time he spent with him, though he showed no remorse at all, McDuff admitted to all eight murders and alluded that there may have been many more.

Kenneth McDuff was executed on November 17, 1998. His family didn't claim his body, and he was buried in the Huntsville prison graveyard with a tombstone that displayed only his death row number X999055 and the day of execution.

As a result of the mayhem that McDuff caused and an outcry from the public, the Texas parole system was completely overhauled and the state spent $2 billion building more prisons.

CHAPTER 2
BLOODTHIRSTY PAROLEE

Anyone who has driven the 180 mile stretch of Interstate 5 from Portland, Oregon to Seattle, Washington possibly remembers the small town of Centralia, Washington. Not because it's of particularly any historical importance—though it has plenty of history—but mostly it's because it's the halfway point between Portland and Seattle and a convenient place to stop for gas or to grab some fast food.

In 1977 Centralia was a town of only 10,000 residents and neighboring Chehalis had only about 5,000. Together they were known as the Twin Cities. It was a beautiful rural area surrounded by miles and miles of dense forest in every direction.

The story of the murder of thirteen-year-old Bruce Kim is almost entirely absent on the internet. I only know of the story because I lived only a few blocks from Bruce and he was just a few years older than me. Though we lived close to each other, I barely knew the boy; Bruce had an entirely separate circle of friends. Though only thirteen, like many other kids in the seventies, Bruce got involved with the wrong crowd.

On the evening of New Year's Day in 1977 Bruce Kim attended a house party at number 7 in the Lemac Apartments, an old, run-down apartment building near the railroad tracks at the north end of town. The resident of apartment number 7 was an older man who was known to have parties to which anyone could come, drink, party, or buy some weed or LSD—regardless of age.

On New Year's Day, friends had seen Bruce riding his bicycle on the streets of Centralia, but that evening he didn't return home after the party. The next morning Bruce's mother, Joan, called the Centralia police,

 "He has never stayed out overnight without calling me. He wouldn't have gone away willingly."

Bruce's bicycle was in front of their house at 1002 L Street, but he was nowhere to be found. Bruce was small for his age and had long reddish-brown hair. The last anyone had seen him he was wearing blue jeans, a jean jacket, and a printed t-shirt. There were no clothes missing from his closet and he had very little money to his name, so police ruled out the chance that he had simply run away from home.

Local detectives immediately contacted Bruce's closest friends to try to backtrack his last known events. That's when they found out that he had attended the party in the Lemac Apartments.

Detectives spoke to the resident of the apartment who gave police a list of attendees of the party as best he could remember. They then spent the next few days tracking down the attendees and questioning them one by one. Unfortunately, the apartment was a known drug den and most of the party-goers that attended weren't too excited to speak to police. The interviews uncovered no new clues in tracking down the boy.

Just before midnight on January 6, a man ran to the Centralia fire department and pounded on the locked doors. It was late, and nobody was answering. He had just run six blocks from the Lemac Apartments, which was engulfed in flames. Frustrated, he ran another three blocks to the police department who then alerted the fire department. By the time firetrucks arrived at the Lemac Apartments, it was too late.

By morning the building was nothing but charred black sticks and rubble.

When the fire marshal assessed the damage, at first glance it seemed clean. There was no evidence of accelerants. The building was very old and had archaic wiring so the chance of the cause of the fire being faulty wiring was high, but intuition told him it was more than that. He suspected an experienced arsonist. When the fire marshal heard that the building was the last place Bruce Kim was seen alive, it only solidified his suspicions. The cause of fire was initially determined to be inconclusive.

Centralia detectives told reporters,

> "If Bruce Kim's body had been in the apartment, there would have been some evidence of his remains in the fire debris. Fragments of bone... something. It is extremely rare for a body to be completely destroyed in a fire, even a Holocaust as fully involved as that of the Lemac."

As the days passed police grew frustrated at the lack of clues, but on January 13 their luck turned. A woman named Susan Ragan called the county Sheriff and told him she had something to show him. The woman told him that Bruce Kim was most likely dead and showed him a pair of blue jeans that her brother had left with her. The cuffs of the jeans were stained with what appeared to be blood. She was holding the jeans for her brother, and she was clearly terrified.

> The lead investigator recalled, "She says Tommy brought her the jeans and told her he'd gotten the stains on the cuffs when he'd turned a body over with his foot."

Susan Regan was the sister of thirty-three-year-old Tommy Regan, a name that was well known to the Centralia Police and the Lewis County Sheriff. Tommy's conflicts with police dated back to his teenage years.

Even as a teenager Tommy Ragan was in trouble with the law. At fifteen years old Ragan had stolen a car and was confined to the Green Hill School, Washington's maximum security lockup for older juveniles. One night Ragan and another young inmate broke out of the school, stole a 1.5 ton vehicle, and went on a rampage. The two went the wrong way up the highway, crashing through a police barricade, ramming six other cars and almost running over a police officer. They led police on a forty-five mile high-speed pursuit before they were finally stopped.

Over the next seventeen years Ragan spent more time in prison than out with charges ranging from burglary, larceny, and car theft, to rape and kidnapping.

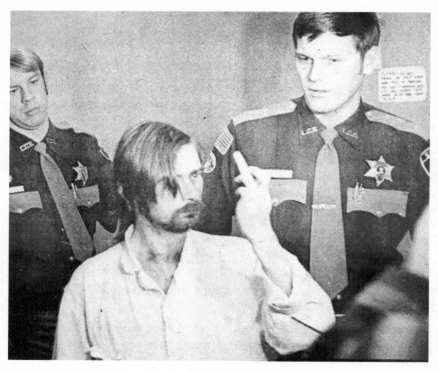

Tommy Ragan

The worst of his offenses was when he was twenty years old. Ragan was charged with kidnapping a fourteen-year-old boy named Bobby at knifepoint. Ragan approached two young boys after a baseball game in Fort Borst Park and asked for help to push his car. When they started pushing Ragan pulled a switch-blade knife on them. One boy ran away, but Ragan grabbed Bobby and dragged him into the forest, cutting him several times in the ribs with the knife. Once in the forest he sodomized the boy and dragged him across the Skookumchuck River. The boy that got away had alerted police and Bobby was able to get away when Ragan was distracted by police sirens.

At the time, Ragan was only charged with kidnapping, but years later the boy confided the entire story to police that he was orally and anally raped by Ragan at knifepoint. Coincidentally Bobby went on to be one of Centralia's few celebrities, playing Major League Baseball for five years.

At the time of Bruce Kim's disappearance, Tommy Ragan was out on parole. His address at the time was ninety miles away in Seattle, but he had been visiting family in Centralia. Ragan had also been an attendee at the party in the Lemac apartments, in fact police had questioned him in the days after. Detectives were very keen to question him further since they had the additional information about the bloody jeans.

Detectives needed to find Tommy Ragan. According to his parole officer in Seattle, he was living with someone named Christina Keithana Kempf. Christina's past was every bit as sordid as Ragan's. She was actually born Charles Wheeler. At an early age he realized that he had a boy's body but identified as a girl.

 "All I knew was I wanted to be a girl... and I wasn't."

In his teens Charles assumed he was just gay. He was married at sixteen but was divorced by twenty-one.

"The homosexual life was a disappointment, I wanted to talk love and marriage, pots and pans, and they wanted to talk sex."

After the divorce, Charles turned to alcohol and entered a traumatic depression that landed him in the Easter State Mental Hospital with a diagnosis of incipient schizophrenia. Upon release from the hospital, Charles decided to become Christine. She changed her name and started wearing women's clothes and makeup. She desperately wanted to make it official by getting a sex change, but she lacked the funds for the expensive procedure.

It wasn't long before Christina was arrested and sentenced to twenty years in prison for cashing stolen checks, but was released after only three years.

Within twenty days of her release, she was arrested again. This time for murder. According to Christina, she was accosted in the parking lot of a grocery store by a man that was trying to force her to have sex. During the altercation, she stabbed the man to death.

Christina was sentenced to life in prison in the Washington State Penitentiary in Walla Walla—a men's prison. Identifying as a woman, she was harassed in prison and ridiculed for being a cross-dresser. Prison psychologists criticized her, telling her that she was just homosexual.

Though she was sentenced to life in prison, she was released in 1973. Upon her release an anonymous donor had sent her $1,000 to start a fund to help her pay for a sex change. The anonymous donor ended up being an odd, flamboyant "church" in Seattle. The donation wasn't enough for a full sex change, so Christina got breast implants and started hormone therapy.

In the spring of 1973 Christina had married again. This time to a man named Andy. The wedding took place in a huge, opulent mansion on Lake Washington that was the headquarters of the church that gave her the donation. The preacher of the church and owner of the mansion was a large, eccentric man with 40D fake breasts who dressed in flowing silk robes. The church televised their wedding and paid for their honeymoon in Hawaii.

The marital bliss didn't last long. Both Christina and Andy were arrested on drug charges and sentenced to prison. They arrested Christina as Charles Wheeler, and she shared a cell with her husband Andy.

After only eighteen months Christina was out of prison again and moved into an apartment in Seattle with Tommy Ragan while Andy still sat in jail.

On January 14, Centralia detectives were still searching for Tommy Ragan. They had pulled him over in his 1960 green Corvair on January 12 for a traffic violation, but that was before he was wanted for questioning and nobody had seen him since. In addition to the Corvair, Ragan often drove a brown 1965 Barracuda which belonged to Christina Kempf. Police were on the lookout for both vehicles, but were cautious knowing that he may be armed. It was rumored that Ragan often carried a sawed-off .22 caliber rifle.

The Seattle police were looking for Ragan too. Neither Christina nor Ragan were at their Seattle apartment.

That same day Centralia detectives went back to Ragan's sister's house to see if they could get any more information out of her and they were in luck. His sister was nothing like her brother. She didn't want any part of him if he had murdered a fourteen-year-old boy and told police exactly what Tommy had told her. She told police that Ragan admitted to her he had killed Bruce Kim. She said that Tommy told her he had buried the body somewhere near Yelm, Washington, a tiny town about thirty miles northeast of Centralia.

The problem was, Centralia was surrounded by dense forest, and Yelm was even more so. It would take a miracle to find a grave in such a vast wilderness without more specific information.

Centralia police contacted the Yelm police for help. Ragan had some prison buddies in the area that they thought he might stay with, but they hadn't heard from him.

When police checked on the status of the 1960 Corvair they saw that Ragan had just sold it the day before, January 13—the day after he had been pulled over for a traffic violation. Detectives contacted the new owners of the Corvair and impounded the vehicle. The new owners quickly stopped payment on the check that they wrote to Ragan before he could cash it.

Inside the car they found what looked like bloodstains on the seats and tiny bits of dirt. On the bottom side of the car they saw that the under-carriage had recently scraped something. Their assumption was that Ragan had bottomed out the car somewhere on an old logging trail in Yelm when he was disposing of the body.

That same evening, January 14, Seattle police found Ragan and took him into custody for breaking parole. On the ninety mile drive in the back of a patrol car back down to Centralia, he kept his mouth shut.

Ragan's sister was desperately trying to distance herself from her brother. She had very little doubt that her brother had killed the boy and she called police one more time. When detectives came to her house, she gave them two items that Tommy had left with her: A shovel still covered with dirt and a pocketknife.

She also had a little more information than she let on the first time. She told detectives that she didn't know the exact location that he had buried him, but said,

 "It's supposed to be near the Cougar Mountain area of Yelm. There's an old logging road, a mud hole where you have to turn and go through a fence—a kind of rise in the land as the road bends around. There're trees. Just small fir trees..."

Police hypothesized that the "rise in the land" was where Ragan may have bottomed out the Corvair. On the morning of January 16, a search

team of officers scoured the area near Cougar Mountain. The January weather in southwest Washington was notoriously miserable, rainy, and wet making old logging roads muddy.

The terrain in the Yelm forest was filled with thick blackberry bushes, vines, and fir trees. Searching a forest so thick and overgrown was almost pointless, and the first day of the search was a failure.

The next day the crew searched again. This time they were armed with aerial maps of the area and plaster impressions they had taken from the Corvair tires. At a fork in an old logging road, they came across their first clue. A match in the mud to the Corvair tires.

They followed the Corvair tracks and further up the old road found a hump that could have caused the scratch marks on the bottom of the car. Detectives took dirt samples from the road, hoping they could later match it to the dirt found on the underside of the Corvair.

Where the tracks seemed to end, police spread out to search the dense forest. Most of the police in the area were also regular deer hunters and had a lot of experience rummaging through the thick woods.

About 100 feet into the forest from the logging road, one detective noticed a fallen tree that had recently been burned. He thought he may be onto something. There were also what seemed to be drag marks in the mud near the log.

Not far from the log he noticed a patch of buffalo grass. The grass wasn't planted in the ground though. It seemed as if it had been torn away and was lying on the ground. It was obvious that someone had intended to hide something beneath.

The team was called to the site, and they dug very lightly, using only their hands. The dirt was fresh and not packed down. Just six inches below the surface they reached flesh. As they pushed the dirt aside, they could tell it was the back and hip of a small person. Face down.

There were what appeared to be slashes and scratches across the back. As they cleared the dirt away from the rest of the body and reached the neck, they realized there was a massive gash, but nothing could prepare them for what they saw next. As they continued to dig they realized that it wasn't a gash at all. The head had been completely severed. There was no head at all in the grave.

When the decapitated body was pulled out of the shallow grave and laid on the ground, it was clear that someone had tried to dissect the limbs, but failed. Other joints were cut but not all the way through. Possibly the killer was unaware just how hard it is to dismember a body. When they rolled the body over onto its back they were in for another shock. They could tell that the body was male, but the genitals had been severed completely. Additionally, there was a massive gash from the pubic bone up to the chest.

As the day progressed, investigators painstakingly processed the crime scene, scouring the area for anything the killer may have left behind. All they found were some scraps of toilet paper with a distinctive brown floral print on them.

The body was taken back to Centralia, and they brought a forensic pathologist up from Portland, Oregon for the postmortem examination. Although investigators knew this had to be the body of Bruce Kim, they would still need some confirmation of identity. The cold January weather was helpful as it had minimized decomposition.

Bruce had never been fingerprinted and since they didn't find a head buried with the body, they couldn't identify him by dental records. Just a year earlier, however, Bruce had suffered a severe leg break. When the body was X-rayed it showed the break. The break matched with the X-rays on file with Centralia General Hospital. It was indeed the body of Bruce Kim.

During the autopsy Bruce's blood alcohol level was read at .21, an impossibly high level for anyone, let alone a thirteen-year-old boy. Decomposition and the extreme blood loss can alter the reading though, so the pathologist wasn't sure that it was accurate.

Tommy Ragan was in lockup for parole violation, and he wasn't talking. Investigators then retraced all of his movements since the first of the year. They already knew that he was at the party at the Lemac

Apartments. They also learned that he borrowed a shovel from a prison friend of his at 1:30 p.m. on January 3, returning it later that evening. They also learned that he had slept in Christina Kempf's Barracuda one block from the Lemac Apartments on the night of the fire. He had also been seen in the Yelm area near where the body was found on January 12.

Though they had found what they thought to be bloodstains and mud in the Corvair, none of that evidence was useable.

Christina Kempf was still nowhere to be found, and police desperately wanted to speak to her. They were unsure if Ragan may have had help with the murder.

On January 20, police got a warrant to search Ragan and Christina's apartment in Seattle and her Barracuda. Inside the apartment detectives found work gloves caked with dirt and maps of the Yelm area along with miscellaneous paperwork that belonged to Tommy. In the paperwork were several handwritten pages penned by Ragan. It was a story of a homosexual killing involving two killers and one victim.

They also found rolls of toilet paper with a brown floral print - exactly the same as the shreds they found near the gravesite.

The search warrant, however, was very specific and one detective spotted something that could be useful, but legally wasn't included in the warrant. They needed the signature from a Superior Court judge to get an additional warrant, but it was late at night. That night they found a judge to sign for a second warrant and went back to the apartment again.

The item they wanted was a photo they'd seen in a photo album. One picture in particular showed Ragan staring wide-eyed into the camera framing his face. On both cheeks were smears of red liquid that looked like blood in the shape of a pentagram - a five-pointed star pointed downward, often associated with the occult or devil worship. Investigators now questioned whether Bruce Kim had been murdered as part of some sort of cult ritual.

Detectives later questioned every tenant of the Seattle Apartment building. In that questioning they found that Christina owned a third car, a Toyota that was still sitting in the parking lot. With another warrant police searched the car and found pick axes, dirt, ropes, and an army shovel.

Another tenant told detectives that Christina had confided in them that Ragan had told her he accidentally hit a young boy with his car, breaking his neck. According to Christina, Ragan panicked and buried the boy. Police knew there was no truth in this story. Bruce's body had no broken bones and no bruising to indicate being hit by a car.

Detectives still needed to talk to Christina, but she was nowhere to be found. The next obvious person to talk to was the church minister who had conducted her wedding and paid for her breast implants and honeymoon to Hawaii.

When police arrived at the church minister's opulent mansion, it was clear they had stumbled onto a cult of sorts. It seemed that many people lived at the mansion with dramatic artwork, two-inch thick shag carpet and a view overlooking Lake Washington. Another thing they noticed right away was that the room they were in was the background in Ragan's pentagram photo. The picture had been taken there.

One of the women at the mansion remembered Ragan and said she was the person that took the photo of him. She claimed it was all just a joke, and she painted the pentagrams on his face. Ultimately, the residents barely remembered Ragan; they said they hadn't seen Christina in quite some time and had no idea where she might be.

In a strange coincidence, there was an article in the Sunday, January 30 edition of the Seattle newspaper about Christina. The article wasn't about the police search for her, but rather a sympathetic piece about the struggles with homosexual and transgender life featuring a photo of her lounging in silk pajamas showing her artificial cleavage. The newspaper had no idea about the search for her and her possible involvement in a horribly sadistic murder.

Christina Kempf

On February 8, Christina gave up hiding from police and walked into the police station with an attorney. She insisted she had nothing to do with the murder and had no knowledge of it at all and therefore could give no testimony. But when prosecutors offered her immunity to testify against Ragan, she quickly took it.

Tommy Ragan was initially charged with aggravated murder, meaning that a murder was committed in the course of or in furtherance of the crime of rape or kidnapping. It was the only crime in Washington state punishable with a mandatory death sentence. Prosecutors believed that Bruce had been sexually assaulted before he was killed and the death was an attempt to cover up the crime of rape.

Once Ragan was behind bars, detectives revisited Bobby, the young boy that had been kidnapped by Ragan thirteen years earlier. It was then that Bobby broke down and told police of the rape. He told detectives he was severely traumatized and thought of himself as lucky to be alive. He told detectives that Ragan took him into the woods, tied him up, put the switchblade to his throat and told him he would cut off his genitals if he wasn't cooperative. Even with Bobby's testimony, prosecutors knew that trying to prove aggravated murder would be a stretch.

When word got to the public that Ragan had been charged, another witness came forward. A man that was at the Lemac party in the early hours of January 2 told police that he saw Ragan having sex with Bruce Kim. Though this information didn't suggest the sex was forced and showed nothing to prove that Ragan murdered him, it still helped solidify the case.

The trial was set for late April, but just before the start date of the trial Ragan's attorney told police that he wanted to talk. Ragan and his attorney asked for a deal. Ragan offered to plead guilty to a lesser charge of second degree murder. To sweeten the deal, Ragan told detectives he would show them where he buried Bruce Kim's head.

Ragan had already been convicted of three felonies, making him a likely candidate to be "bitched," a slang term used to describe a habitual criminal. If prosecutors could get Ragan convicted as a habitual criminal he would be sentenced to life and would likely never be released.

On April 18, Ragan pleaded guilty to second degree murder and led detectives to the head of Bruce Kim. Investigators considered themselves lucky to find the body, but it would have taken a miracle to find the head on their own. The lead detective said it was,

 "Buried in brush so thick a coyote wouldn't crawl through it."

The head was located in dense blackberry bushes about 300 yards from the gravesite. Using dental records, the identity was confirmed to be that of Bruce Kim. Ragan told police that he had thrown Bruce's clothes from the car as he was driving along the logging road. Backtracking the road, police found several pieces of his clothes.

Ragan then explained the details of the killing to detectives. He claimed that they both left the party at the Lemac Apartments and went to Bruce's house. They were both extremely drunk and Bruce swore at Ragan, which threw him into a rage. Ragan said he wrapped his hands around his neck and started to strangle the boy. Bruce was much smaller and younger than Ragan.

> "I didn't realize I had killed him. I thought he was breathing."

When Ragan finally released his grip, it was too late. Bruce was dead. He said he then put Bruce's body into the trunk of the Corvair and drove to Seattle. Later he drove back down to Yelm and buried it. He told police he cut off his head at the gravesite to avoid identification.

When asked why he cut off Bruce's genitals and where they were, he had no recollection of it. He claimed to not remember anything about any additional mutilations, the slash marks, or the attempted dismemberments. Ragan insinuated that he must have blacked that out.

Because of the media attention in the Centralia area, Ragan's trial was moved from Lewis County to Pacific County. One evening when driving back to the Lewis County jail with the Centralia Chief of police, they passed a familiar hamburger stand. Ragan lamented that he would probably never taste another milkshake for the rest of his life. Chief Jones was a firm believer that all men deserved some sense of dignity, regardless of what they may have done in their lives. He stopped by the drive-in and bought Ragan what was most likely his last milkshake.

Jones' kindness eventually paid off. A few days later Ragan asked to speak to Chief Jones,

> Ragan said, "It came down just like you had it put together. I trust you. I won't talk to anyone but you. There are some things I could clear up if I knew I wouldn't get prosecuted for it. I could clear the board some."

In an extremely controversial move, Chief Jones spoke to prosecutors and asked to grant immunity for Ragan from any prosecution for crimes other than homicide or crimes out of his jurisdiction. The prosecution agreed.

Ragan then admitted to setting the Lemac Apartments on fire. On the evening of January 5, just before midnight, Ragan was parked near the building.

 "It was so ugly. I just went back to burn it down because it was ugly."

He told police that he was drunk and simply wedged newspaper into the frame of the building and lit it ablaze. He also admitted to setting several other fires in the area including forest fires, buildings and bridges—with no regard for human life. He said he always just used newspapers and a match.

He then confessed to several other burglaries, larcenies, assaults and another rape of a young boy.

Ragan was found guilty of second degree murder, being a habitual criminal, second degree assault with a deadly weapon in the first degree, and two counts of sodomy.

In an unprecedented move the prosecutor tried him for a second habitual criminal charge strictly to solidify the chance that he would never be released.

 "Under our present system of perpetual appeals and post-conviction writs, no condition is 100 percent solid."

Tommy Ragan was convicted of a total of seven felonies in Washington and another burglary conviction in Alaska. As of this writing, seventy-seven-year-old Ragan is still held in the Monroe Correctional Complex in Monroe, Washington. His listed possible release date is July 17, 2022.

CHAPTER 3
THE BODY IN THE BAG

A s a young child in suburban Sydney, Australia, Will Matheson seemed to be a normal kid by all accounts. But life at home was far from normal. Will was born in 1982 to two talented and highly intelligent parents, but their eccentricities were beyond extreme.

His mother was a professional violinist and his father was a former teacher and musician who collected junk for a hobby. As a young boy Will and his father would walk the streets late at night rummaging through garbage cans and dumpsters looking for anything his father might find interesting.

The Matheson family were extreme hoarders. Their home was in constant disarray, filled to the ceiling with a chaotic mess of junk, leaving only a small path to walk between rooms. Will's parents didn't have a bedroom, instead they pulled out a small mattress and laid it on the kitchen floor every night.

Both his mother and father suffered from psychiatric problems and his older brother, Edward, had been diagnosed with schizophrenia.

Will was just nine years old when his seventeen-year-old brother was admitted to a mental hospital. During a visit by Will, he and Edward walked the grounds of the institution. Edward led Will to the roof of the building where he jumped to his death while Will watched in horror.

At such a young age, Will was unable to properly process what had happened and his eccentric parents weren't best suited to help him. Will retreated into his mind and his own eccentricities. By his teenage years Will had developed a deep fixation with death. He listened to music called Horrorcore, a subgenre of Rap music, but with psychotic, supernatural, and violent themes.

Though Will didn't have many friends, he became known throughout the school as "PK", an acronym for "Porn King", because he would duplicate porn tapes and sell them to the boys in his school.

Like his family members, Will excelled musically. He played several instruments, but was a particularly talented cellist, playing in a quartet that would often play gigs at various events.

Will Matheson with cello

When he finished high school in 2000, Will had no close friends to speak of apart from the friends in his quartet. Like his father, he scavenged things from the streets of Sydney and developed a fascination with dead animals. His bedroom was decorated with his collection of bones, skulls, and dead animal skins he had collected.

Will made a living breeding rats. His bedroom and bathroom were filled with as many as 300 rats, some in cages, some running loose.

After graduation from high school, Will remained in his quartet and occasionally played paid gigs. It was at one of these gigs in April 2001, a wedding, that he met Lyndsay Van Blanken.

Eighteen-year-old Will Matheson was a last-minute replacement for the regular cellist in the quartet, and fifteen-year-old Lyndsay was a bridesmaid at her mother's wedding. Lyndsay's best friend noticed Matheson and by the end of the evening gave him both her own number and Lyndsay's.

Lyndsay Van Blanken was like any other young Australian girl. She was shy, loved to play online video games, and had a passion for drawing. She dreamed of working in animation someday.

Lyndsay Van Blanken

Not long after the wedding, Lyndsay and Will began dating, but it was an odd relationship. Will was aloof and non-committal, always keeping her at arm's length. Perhaps this intrigued her, or perhaps she was fascinated by his dark side.

Over time, the two developed a relationship, and Lyndsay started to change. She became fascinated by the same macabre things as Will. She began to dress in dark drab clothes like him, talk like him, and would walk the streets at night with him, often through cemeteries. Though the two grew close, Will remained reserved and distant. He was Lyndsay's first boyfriend and his indifference only intrigued her more.

Eventually Will confided to her that his brother had committed suicide in front of him and he told her of his own suicidal thoughts. One evening when they were chatting on the computer he told her he was going to kill himself. Terrified, Lyndsay had her parents rush her to his house, but when she arrived in tears, he was laughing at her. He had been toying with her the whole time.

On Valentine's day she bought a small teddy bear and a single rose and placed it on the front steps of Will's home. When Lyndsay's mother later asked her how he liked the present, she told her mother that he gave it back to her. He told Lyndsay that he wasn't the sort of person that wanted presents. Their relationship was an unconventional one.

Lyndsay was a talented artist, having drawn since a very young age. The longer she dated Will, the more her drawings and paintings became sinister and eerie. By the time she turned sixteen, her parents began to worry about her new persona, and with good reason. Lyndsay had always been an excellent student, but uncharacteristically she became depressed and dropped out of school during her senior year.

Lyndsay Van Blanken

After more than two years of dating, Lyndsay knew her relationship with Will was affecting her life negatively. She wanted to end it, but had no idea how to break it off.

Lyndsay loved to play online video games and used the nickname demon_nurse. One of her regular opponents in the online game was a twenty-year-old from Seattle named Brandon Leonard. After several months of playing online with Brandon, they began chatting and sending photos to each other. Though they hadn't met in person, it wasn't long before the exchange formed into an online romance.

Though Lyndsay was now committed to her online boyfriend Brandon, she still hadn't broken it off with Will. As with many eighteen-year-old girls, she just didn't know how to do it and kept putting it off.

During the same time, Lyndsay had heard that Disney Animation Studios had opened an office in Sydney and they were looking for trainee animation artists. It was her dream job. Lyndsay submitted her illustrations, as did over 300 other applicants. To her delight, Lyndsay was the most talented of the applicants and started her exciting new career with Disney.

Lyndsay's parents were elated. Her attitude toward everything began to change back to the old Lyndsay. She started dressing in more presentable clothes, went back to her cheerful attitude and saw Will less and less.

Brandon was happy for her as well and the two of them were now madly in love. That's when Brandon proposed to her over the internet and she joyfully accepted.

On September 8, 2003, Lyndsay knew it was time to break it off with Will. Brandon was flying to Sydney the next day, and she knew it had to be done. When she told Will it was over, he was heartbroken and angry. He cried, pled with her, and told her he would kill himself, but she was steadfast and ended their relationship. However, she didn't tell him about Brandon, or that they were planning to get married.

When Brandon arrived in Sydney the two of them were a happy couple planning the rest of their lives together, but Will had no intention of letting her go. He began stalking her on her way to work at her new job.

When Will inevitably saw Lyndsay with Brandon, he exploded in anger. Knowing he could never get Lyndsay back, he confronted Brandon at the apartment where he was staying.

Will told the few friends he had that he was considering suicide. He was still deeply in love with Lyndsay, but he hated her at the same time. His anger consumed him.

Lyndsay was terrified. Will spent almost every day following her to and from work. He would be waiting at bus stops knowing the times she was due to show up. He would even stand across the street in the middle of the night, staring up at her bedroom window. This went on for two months. He wanted her to know he would be a part of her life whether she liked it or not.

Brandon wanted Lyndsay to meet his parents and the two of them made plans to travel back to Seattle for Christmas. On November 22, Lyndsay got a text from Matheson. "I see you," was all it said. Terrified, she broke down crying. Her parents reassured her and told her not to worry, she would leave for Seattle soon and it would all be over.

On November 24, one of Lyndsay's coworkers at Disney noticed her arguing with a young man outside of the office during the lunch break. He could see it was a heated argument, but didn't want to interfere. That same evening Lyndsay took the train back to her home in Queen's Park. She got off the train at the Bondi Junction railway station where she was seen on security cameras at 5:58 p.m. leaving the station. That would be the last time she was seen alive.

That evening when Lyndsay didn't arrive at home at her normal time, Brandon and her parents became worried. Though they tried all night long, there was no answer from her phone and no text messages. Early the next morning Brandon called the police and reported his fiancé missing.

Her parents explained to the police that it was completely out of character for Lyndsay to disappear on her own. They also informed the police that she was being stalked by her ex-boyfriend, Will Matheson.

The family suspected Will had something to do with her disappearance, and Lyndsay's older sister Louise called Will to see what he had to say. Will claimed he had seen Lyndsay that evening as she got off the train at Bondi Junction. He told Louise that he had walked with her toward her home for about ten or fifteen minutes, then left her. He said that the last time he saw her was in an alley behind the Charing Cross Pub. Louise thought it was odd that Lyndsay would be in an alley behind a pub. Walking through an alley was not something that Lyndsay would normally do.

Adding more confusion to the call, Will's eccentric father burst in on the line during their conversation and said,

 "Well, I didn't see any blood on his hands."

This startled Louise, and she later informed police about the strange conversation.

Two days after she had gone missing, the police pulled Matheson into the station for an interview. He was calm and morose, speaking in a monotone. His demeanor alone raised the police's suspicion. Again, Matheson stuck to his story and said that he had walked with her after she had got off of the train, then left her.

Investigators asked for a DNA swab, fingerprints, and photographs, and Matheson agreed. But when he pulled off his shirt for the photographs, it raised hairs on the back of investigator's necks. He had several cuts and scrapes on his chest, hands, and arms. He also had scrapes on his knees. Will explained that the cuts and scrapes were from his rats and cats, and he claimed the scrapes on his knees were from a skateboarding fall.

Matheson told the police that when he heard Lyndsay was missing, he called her family and her friends. But the police noticed something he had omitted. He didn't mention that he had actually tried to call Lyndsay. If he believed she was still alive, he would have tried to call her. This was yet another aspect of the interview that raised the police's suspicion; they were sure he was involved. But with no definitive evidence, they had to let him go.

Detectives retraced her last steps, and an extensive search of the area began. Police searched parks and streets in the area and divers searched the lakes in Centennial Park near her home, but their efforts garnered no clues.

Police then showed Lyndsay's coworker a line-up of mugshots to see if he recognized the person that was arguing with Lyndsay outside of her office that day. He easily pointed out Will Matheson.

Two weeks after Lyndsay's disappearance, police received a phone call at 1:30 a.m. from a member of the public reporting what they thought was a prowler. When the police arrived, they found Will Matheson walking the streets and alleys carrying a backpack. Inside that backpack was another backpack containing several suspicious items: A pair of metal scissors, a box cutter, and a hatchet. They also found three pairs of latex surgical gloves, hospital grade disinfectant, two flashlights, candles and candleholders, black plastic garbage bags, several newspapers, moisturizer, and a small bottle of water. Matheson told police it was "holy water."

Police brought Matheson in for questioning, and again his demeanor was subdued. He claimed the items were for "a picnic."

 Investigator: "What can you tell me about those items?"

Matheson: "I was going to um... go up to the park and have a... picnic."

Investigator: "At 1:30 in the morning?"

Matheson: "Yeah."

Police suspected Lyndsay was already dead and his plans were to dismember and dispose of her body. Again, they had no definitive evidence that they could use to hold him. Matheson was free to go, but police started twenty-four-hour surveillance on him.

Will Matheson

On January 10, 2004, the residents of a small apartment building in Queen's Park complained to their building maintenance man of a horrible stench coming from the storage room below the apartments.

The maintenance man went into the storage room and noticed a mattress covering an interior doorway. When he pulled the mattress away and pushed the door open a horrid smell knocked him back. The small room was filled with junk, boxes, and furniture. As he pushed aside items and made his way to the back of the room, he noticed an oversized sports bag. It was a huge bag used to carry cricket bats and equipment. He tried to pick it up, but couldn't. It was too heavy. Barely able to handle the foul smell, he dragged the bag out of the room into the open air. He then used a pocketknife to cut it open and a small human hand fell out.

Cricket Sports Bag

When detectives arrived, they had a sinking feeling it was the body of Lyndsay Van Blanken. Before they had a chance to identify her, the media got word of the body being found and broadcast it on the news. Lyndsay's grandmother saw the news and called her granddaughter Louise and asked if it might be Lyndsay. Louise assured her grandmother that if it was Lyndsay, the police would surely have alerted the family before they would let the media know.

Louise's curiosity overwhelmed her and she called the lead investigator. Sadly, the investigator told her that it might be the body of Lyndsay. Using the clothes she was wearing and the engagement ring on her finger, they positively identified her as Lyndsay Van Blanken.

She had been strangled using cable ties. Two cable ties had been put together to make a loop large enough to slip over her head and a quick pull would have ratcheted down on her throat. The loop had been tightened down to only ten inches, closing off her ability to breathe. Her fingernails were almost ripped off, most likely from scratching her attacker. Her body had then been folded and stuffed into the bag, then tucked in the corner of the storage room for eight weeks.

The day after Lyndsay's body was found Will Matheson was having a mental breakdown. He told his father he was hearing voices in his head. Will sat his father down in front of the television and showed him the nightly news he had recorded of Lyndsay's body being found. His parents called the hospital and mental health workers admitted him into a psychiatric hospital where he remained for the next eight weeks.

> Will's father said, "So he came inside and looked at the midnight news. And when he finished looking at it he just sat down and cried. He said 'I think I've done that.' And he pulled his legs into his chest in the fetal position and just cried and cried."

Because Will had been admitted to a mental hospital, police were not able to question him, but they were allowed to search the family home.

Inside Will's bedroom was a stench almost as bad as a rotting corpse, but the smell came from his rats and rat excrement. There were rats everywhere, and the ceiling was covered with flies. Will had collected clippings from all the newspapers with any stories pertaining to Lyndsay. The room was full of keepsakes of Lyndsay such as notes, letters, and videotapes. Also in his room was Lyndsay's diary of notes and drawings. It was a very personal and precious diary to her that she would never have given to Will or anyone else. The most incriminating evidence was found in the top drawer of his dresser. They found a small Dictaphone and two tapes.

When police played the tapes, they found what they considered to be a confession. One tape had a song he had recorded in a muted, tragic voice. The lyrics were:

> "Just the other day I watched you pass away. You said I love you. Please let me stay. Help is not here for you or me. Close your eyes. When you go is where I'll be. I'll meet you in eternity."

He also spoke in a whispering voice into the Dictaphone,

"It's all because of him. He didn't want you to hurt me as a friend. I hope you understand that. I didn't want to let you go. I told you I didn't want to let you go."

In many of the additional musings on the tapes he spoke of Lyndsay in the past-tense.

When detectives questioned his parents, Will's father admitted that he had been shopping with his son in Bondi Junction two days before Lyndsay went missing. He told police that when Will returned to the car, he was carrying a large sports bag.

The bag that Lyndsay's body was found in was a very specific type of cricket bag. Using the brand and model of the bag, police were able to find that there was only one store in the area which carried that specific bag, and they had only sold one of them. It was sold two days before Lyndsay went missing at 1:30 p.m. for $120 and was paid for in cash.

Investigators then searched through security cameras in the Bondi Junction shopping area during the time that Will's father said the two of them were there. They found footage of Will walking near Rebel Sports just before 1:30 p.m.

In March 2004 Will Matheson was discharged from the psychiatric hospital and police immediately brought him back in for additional questioning.

Despite his admission to his father and to hospital staff, during his interrogation he continued to deny any involvement in Lyndsay's death. Even when shown the video evidence, Matheson still denied purchasing the sports bag.

Detectives then took Matheson on a walk around Bondi Junction and ended up at the storage room where her body was found. He admitted he and Lyndsay had been in the storage room months before, but claimed he had never been into the interior room. When they asked him to walk into the interior room and told him that was where her body was found he broke down and asked to leave,

"Can we go somewhere else. Can we just go somewhere else."

Again, without sufficient grounds, the police let him go while they gathered more evidence. Surprisingly, just a few days later, Matheson requested another interview with the police. He had something to tell them.

In the subsequent interview Matheson confided that he had been hearing voices,

Matheson: "I've been under distress of mental problems, hearing voices and the such."

Police: "What are these voices saying to you?"

Matheson: "Just... to cause destruction. To kill people. To cause harm to myself."

Despite having no previous diagnosis, Matheson and his parents claimed he was mentally ill.

On May 19, 2004, police arrested Will Matheson for the murder of Lyndsay Van Blanken.

The prosecution spent the next year and a half preparing for the trial. During the trial Matheson was as emotionless as ever and had trouble maintaining eye contact with anyone in the courtroom.

Despite his claims of mental illness, the prosecution showed that the murder was premeditated. He had purchased the cricket bag just two days prior to killing her; he had tied two cable-ties together and trimmed off the edges making it easier to slip over her head. He had lured her to the storeroom and had the bag there waiting for her. All the evidence showed that he had clearly planned the murder ahead of time. The judge found that whatever psychiatric condition he had been suffering from had little to do with his premeditation.

In 2006 Will Matheson was sentenced to a minimum of eighteen years in prison without the chance of parole, and a maximum of twenty-seven years. In 2015, however, the court ruled that a legal error had been made during his trial and his maximum sentence was reduced, making him eligible for parole in 2022. Though he had originally denied his involvement in her murder, once in prison he finally admitted that he had killed Lyndsay.

In 2016 a backpack was found when a construction crew was clearing a building site in the Sydney suburb of Randwick. The backpack was determined to belong to Lyndsay Van Blanken, and inside they found over forty bone fragments. Twelve of the bones were human, and the remainder were from animals. Of the human bones, one was a leg bone, and another was a skull fragment with a nail driven through it. The bones belonged to as many as eleven different humans.

Forensic pathologists, however, determined that the bones were most likely just random bones from medical cadavers that Matheson had collected for his collection and were not connected to a murder.

CHAPTER 4
MR. MOM KILLER

I n 2007, Washington International Group was a successful multi-billion dollar company that provided engineering and construction services in more than thirty countries around the world. Tara Grant was a successful, well-educated, and well-paid executive in the company. Though she was a systems manager based in the Detroit, Michigan office, she commuted Monday through Friday all over the world. Every Friday evening she would hop back on a plane so she could spend the weekends with her two young children and husband, Stephen Grant.

On Valentine's Day 2007 Stephen walked into the Macomb County Sheriff's office to report his wife missing.

Tara Destrampe grew up in a tiny town called Perkins with a population of less than 100 located in the upper peninsula of Michigan. Though the rest of her family was perfectly happy with small-town life, Tara was destined for more. Even from a young age she wanted to excel in her life and longed for the big city life. She was determined to go out into the world and create her fortune.

In her teenage years Tara grew into a brash, outspoken young woman, often berating and verbally attacking boyfriends who didn't seem strong enough in her eyes. She was known for her controlling nature and her explosive anger.

After graduating third in her high school class, Tara attended Michigan State University in Lansing. It was there that she first met Stephen Grant.

During the Summer of 1994, Tara was just finishing up her degree. Stephen was in her immediate group of friends and had pursued Tara for several months before she finally gave in and accepted his invitation for a date.

Stephen was obnoxious and a bit awkward, but he wasn't submissive like other boys that Tara had dated. She saw potential in him. Though he had dropped out of college, he worked in the office of a Michigan State Senator and that impressed her. Steven often bragged of his aspirations to pursue a law degree and she envisioned him having a career in politics.

Stephen knew that Tara had grown up in a tiny town and longed for the big city life. On their first date he gave her a tour of Detroit, driving her through the mansions of Gross Pointe, the Detroit Institute of Arts, and taking her for a meal in Greek Town. Tara was impressed, but what really sealed the deal for her was when her grandmother died, Stephen showed up unannounced to the funeral to console her and charmed her family. Tara was in love.

Stephen & Tara (Tara inset)

That December Tara graduated from university and moved in with Steven. It wasn't long after that before he proposed, and she cheerfully accepted.

Eventually Stephen's job with the senator ended, and he was perpetually having trouble finding work. In early 1995 Steven's father offered him a job at the family tool and die shop in Mount Clemens, just north of Detroit. The pay wasn't that great, but it was enough to survive and Tara liked that it was closer to a big city.

In September 1996 Tara and Stephen were married and Tara got a temporary job at a company called Morrison Knudsen which would later be acquired by Washington International Group. She was a perfect fit for the company and was very focused on her new career. It wasn't long before her determination paid off and she was quickly offered a permanent position.

Though money was still tight, the couple had their first child, a daughter, in 2000. Two years later they had a son. Even through the pregnancies, Tara continued climbing the corporate ladder, eventually landing a high-paying executive job. By 2003 her job duties required her to travel to sites where the company had construction jobs all over the globe, which left Stephen to deal with the children.

Stephen, still working at the tool and die shop, couldn't work and take care of the kids, so the couple hired an au pair. Through the years the Grants went through seven different au pairs, eventually settling on a beautiful nineteen-year-old from Germany, Verena Dierke.

Verena Dierke

Stephen spent as much time as he could with the kids, but because of her job, Tara was only able to squeeze in the weekends. Though the income she brought in was good, Stephen resented his wife for leading a jet-setter lifestyle while he stayed at home.

By 2006 Tara was making $168,000 a year. Even her year-end bonus of $28,000 was more than the measly $19,000 he was bringing home from his father's machine shop.

As an executive, Tara was on a regular schedule of flying Monday through Friday 2,000 miles away to San Juan, Puerto Rico. The flight was five hours each way, but she came home to be with the family every weekend.

Over time, Steven's resentment of Tara continued to build. But when Tara decided to start taking golf lessons on the weekend, it didn't sit well with Stephen. Tara, always wanting to enhance her career, knew that lots of business took place on the golf course.

Frustrated and angry with the lack of attention from his wife, Stephen developed a relationship with their young au pair, Verena. It started out as harmless flirting, but in early February 2007 it became physical. It started with kissing and continued with him requesting sex. On Thursday, February 8, before Tara returned home from Puerto Rico, he gave her oral sex for the first time.

While Tara was in San Juan that week she wrote a lengthy letter to Stephen. In the letter she apologized to him for pushing him away and making him feel inadequate. She thought it would be a good idea for them to renew their wedding vows. Tara possibly intended to give him the letter on Valentine's Day the following week, but she never got the chance. By Valentine's Day Stephen had walked into the Macomb County sheriff's department and reported his wife missing.

As Stephen talked to detectives, he gave a long and rambling description of what had happened five days prior; the night she went missing. He said that he and Tara argued that Friday night over the phone as she drove home from the airport. She had been delayed by a snowstorm and informed him she would need to go right back to San Juan the next day.

When she got home, they argued for twenty minutes more before she made a phone call and told someone to come pick her up. He assumed she had called the car service she normally used to take her to the airport. Stephen told detectives the last thing she said to him was to make sure to bring the car to the dealership on Monday to get a dent fixed. Then a black car came to the front of the house, she got into the back, and it drove away. Ten minutes later their au pair, Verena, came home.

When detectives asked why Stephen had waited so long to report his wife missing, he told them it was the suggestion of her boss. Stephen had called her work just after she went missing and her boss told him he knew nothing about Tara needing to go back to San Juan early, but advised him to wait before reporting her missing and he would talk to public relations first. Stephen had also called Tara's sister and mother, but neither of them had heard from her. He told them he'd be happy to know she was just in a hotel with a lover. He just wanted to make sure she was ok.

Stephen told the police he didn't trust Tara's mother or her boss and suspected they were both lying to him—possibly trying to cover up an affair she was having with her boss. Stephen then confided to the police that he and Tara had been to marriage counseling and he was considering hiring a divorce lawyer. To detectives, this was an immediate red flag.

Stephen then rambled on about the company that she worked for. He explained that Washington International Group was involved in the manufacture of chemical weapons and suggested possibly that she had been exposed to nerve gas or kidnapped by terrorists. Again, detectives thought these were extremely odd details to add to the story.

During the questioning, in an attempt to show detectives he was honest, Stephen also admitted that he had a warrant out for his arrest for unpaid traffic tickets. Detectives weren't interested in that and let him go and started their investigation.

When asked about their au pair, Verena, and if he was having a relationship with her, Stephen jokingly replied, "she'll never tell," and left it at that. What he didn't tell the police was that he and Verena had had sex for the first time just minutes after he claimed Tara disappeared in the black car.

The interviewing officer also took note of a scratch on Stephen's nose and asked if he had got into a fight with Tara on the night she left. Stephen said he hadn't, but he said that he told her if she went back to Puerto Rico the kids wouldn't even miss her because he was the one that took them to soccer every day.

Then he told the detective he wasn't even sure if he wanted Tara to come back, and that his family all thought she was having an affair with her boss.

The first thing detectives did after Stephen left was to call Tara's work. Her boss confirmed that she hadn't shown up for work that week and had never missed a day of work in her ten years with the company. Tara also used a company cell phone and credit card. Her employer verified that neither had been used since she had arrived home the evening of February 9.

The police also contacted Tara's family. Her sister told them that she had spoken to Tara for forty minutes during her layover in Newark on February 9 and she hadn't mentioned anything about going back to Puerto Rico early that weekend.

Police were instantly suspicious of Stephen and assigned someone to watch his house, but Stephen wasn't stupid and noticed right away. When he called the lead investigator to complain, the investigator explained that they couldn't be too careful and asked if he could come over to Stephen's and ask him a few more questions.

When Detective Sergeant Brian Kozlowski arrived at the Grant house, he brought Detective Sgt. Pamela McLean with him. Kozlowski took Stephen into the kitchen to question him more while McLean questioned Verena.

Verena told Detective McLean that she was out with some friends on the Friday evening and when she arrived home that night Tara had already gone and the kids were asleep. She told the detective that she thought it was odd that Tara had left and that she had called a car service to take her to the airport. She told police that Tara normally drove herself to the airport each week. This contradicted what

Stephen had told the police. He told them Tara had always used a car service.

In the kitchen, Detective Kozlowski asked Stephen about the scratch on his nose. Stephen claimed he had received the scratch while working at the machine shop. He said that some metal shavings had got under his safety goggles, and then showed Kozlowski scratches and bruises on his hands and legs, claiming they were all from his work.

Kozlowski then asked if Stephen had been having an affair. He denied it; he said that Tara had had an affair in the past, but it was now over.

The detectives then asked if they could search the house and Stephen agreed. Inside they found a handgun with two loaded magazines and some duct tape in the master bedroom. Stephen told them he had just forgotten to put away the gun.

On the master bedroom nightstand they found a red photo journal that belonged to Verena. This struck detectives as odd because the journal was in the master bedroom and not in Verena's own bedroom.

When detectives checked the walk-in closet, they noticed there were no empty spaces where Tara kept all of her business suits. Her suitcase was still in the closet, but Stephen explained that she had packed a second suitcase for the trip.

The following day Stephen was pulled over and arrested for driving on a suspended license. Stephen complained that the police were just using that as an excuse to detain him. After the arrest police searched his car and found two envelopes of cash totaling $3,000.

Stephen immediately hired the most expensive attorney in town and was released on bail within six hours. From that point forward Stephen was much more cautious. He refused to answer any questions without his attorney present, and only in writing.

Stephen had no problem talking to the media though. He loved to cry in front of the cameras, pleading for the safe return of his wife. He naturally had strange facial expressions and bulging eyes, which only made his crying seem more awkward and forced. Initially, his appearances were filled with tears, but over time the tears dried up and he began complaining about her excessive business travel and the possibility that she was having an affair.

"I get that she has to travel for business, but too much is too much, and that was too much."

"A couple of years ago, Tara and I did have a problem in our marriage with the... I don't want to call it an infidelity, but pretty close to an infidelity."

The denigration of his wife didn't play well with the local TV viewers who began to question his sincerity.

The police asked Stephen to take a polygraph, but he denied their request. Instead he and his attorney opted to have him take a polygraph privately, but police assumed he must have failed the test as Stephen kept the results to himself.

Having seen Stephen on the nightly news, a former girlfriend of his came forward and told police she had recently received emails from him which read,

"I am still in need of some excitement in my day ... Wink wink! I just think of marriage vows like speed limits. Sometimes you have to break them."

As police looked further into Stephen's explanation of Tara's disappearance they came across more and more holes in the story. Airline records showed no flights with Tara on them and her normal flight booking for the following Monday had gone unused.

Her cell phone records also didn't show a call at the time that Stephen said she called a car service. The last call on her phone was to Stephen eighteen minutes before she had arrived home that night.

Despite Stephen claiming she always used a car service, she had actually only used a car service once in the past year. Police verified that she almost always drove herself to the airport and parked her car in the airport parking lot during the week. Additionally, nothing had been charged to her credit cards since she had paid for the airport parking at the lot that night on her way home.

Stephen's cell phone records, however, were much busier. That evening he had called Verena four times. In the days following her disappearance Stephen had called Tara's phone six times pleading for her to come home.

 "Hey, I get that you're pissed at me. I just left the house; I have to go to the bank for my dad. Verena's at the house with the kids. Please, at least call your kids. It's ridiculous Tara. It's not right. Just call please so I can talk to you. They didn't get to see you last night."

"It's me. Call us. Just let us know what's going on. The kids and I would like to talk to you. Please. I just don't know what the deal is so call me. We're here. I'm just ordering pizza for dinner so we'll be here. I'm just gonna have it delivered I think, so call us. Bye."

In other messages he showed his anger,

 "Tara, next time I call you, pick up your phone. It's absolute bullshit that you can't call me or your kids. I know you're mad. I'm mad too. You traveling this much is not right."

During the initial interview Stephen had mentioned several times that he and Tara spent quite a bit of time exercising in nearby Stoney Creek Park. The police now suspected that Stephen had killed his wife and possibly dumped her body in the park. Eight days after her disappearance, police began an extensive search of the area.

Stoney Creek Park was over 4,000 acres of thick woods and swamps. The media carried the story of the search and Stephen spoke to the cameras several times, playing the role of grieving husband,

"Please call anybody. Call the police, call me, call my in-laws, call someone."

On the afternoon of February 28, a woman was walking along Mt. Vernon Road on the edge of Stoney Creek Park, not far from the Grants' home. Just a few yards from the roadway she noticed something plastic crammed between the branches of a fallen tree. When she got closer, she could see that it was a large, one-gallon ziplock bag with something red inside. The red color stood out in stark contrast to the snowy surroundings. When she picked up the bag she could see that the red was from blood pooling in the bottom of the bag.

Inside the bag, police found four clear plastic garbage bags, one pair of latex gloves, metal shavings, a 7-11 bag and another ziplock bag. All the items were covered in human blood.

Using the newly found evidence, detectives were able to get two search warrants: One for Stephen Grant's home and another for his father's tool and die shop.

When police broke the door down at the tool and die shop, they found a dark and messy metal shop. Metal lathes, presses and other work equipment were covered with thick metal dust. What stood out to investigators was a large, clean, square-shaped area on the floor. It looked as if someone had laid a tarp there. On the floor directly under the door handle they found what seemed to be a few tiny drops of blood.

Simultaneously, another group of police showed up at the Grants' house. Though Stephen wasn't home, live news cameras filmed as officers entered the house. When Stephen arrived home shortly after the police had entered, they stopped his car as he drove up the street. Police requested him not to disturb the search and he was calm and cooperative, but asked officers if he could take his dog for a walk. Police agreed and Stephen put a leash on his dog and walked down the snowy streets while television cameras watched him leave.

As investigators searched the house, they noticed a green Rubbermaid tub with a blue lid in the garage next to a little red wagon full of children's toys.

Detective Kozlowski pulled off the lid to the tub and found a pile of black plastic bags stacked near the top. He touched the top one and noticed it was soft and mushy. As he tugged at the black bags, it tore and showed another bag and another bag. As he got deeper, he came to a clear plastic bag smeared with blood.

Using a flashlight, Kozlowski initially thought possibly Stephen was storing some deer meat in the freezing cold garage, but as he dug deeper, he found a woman's bra. It was clear this was the body of Tara Grant.

The tub was filled with Tara's frozen torso. The arms were severed at the shoulders, and the legs were severed at the tops of the thighs. Her head, arms, and legs were all missing. The torso still wore the gray Ann Taylor blouse that Stephen had told police she was wearing when she disappeared.

Investigators now realized that Stephen had been walking the dog for more than an hour and hadn't returned to the house. He was on the run, and the manhunt began.

Stephen, of course, knew exactly what the police would find. When he left the house with his dog, he phoned his friend Mike Zanlungo, a neighbor in the same subdivision. Stephen told Mike that he needed to borrow his truck for a bit so he could go visit his children at his sister's house. Mike later said that trusting him was the biggest mistake of his life.

Stephen took Mike's truck and headed towards his sister Kelly's house. He called his sister as he drove; she told him they weren't at home, but were at their church having a fish fry.

Stephen drove to the church and met his sister in the hallway. She immediately noticed he was extremely agitated and disoriented. He told Kelly,

"I'm going to get arrested. They told me if they find a drop of blood in my house I'm going to prison."

Stephen then kissed his kids goodbye and drove to his sister's house to drop off the dog. When he got to the house, he looked for her .38 handgun, but couldn't find it. Instead, he grabbed a full bottle of Vicodin that he found in the medicine cabinet and got back in the truck.

He drove toward Lansing, Michigan drinking whiskey and taking Vicodin the whole way. Along the route he stopped to buy razor blades, a pre-paid burner phone, a notebook, Tylenol PM, a black Sharpie pen and a plastic toy gun. He was intent on killing himself, but was worried that he wouldn't have the nerve to do it himself. He took the Sharpie pen and marked over the red end-cap of the toy gun. He hoped that if the police found him, he could pull the gun on them and they would shoot and kill him.

As he drove Stephen avoided highways and took the back roads. He stopped again to get $500 out of an ATM and bought more whiskey and some Baileys Irish Cream.

Highly intoxicated and crying, Stephen called his sister one last time and called Verena, who was now in Germany. At 1:30 a.m. he made one last call to his attorney who encouraged him not to kill himself and to come back home, telling him that his kids needed him.

Stephen cried,

 "She treated us like shit. It's her fault this happened. Everyone hates me, but it's her fault. She cheated on me, she left us alone, we meant nothing to her. Tell my kids I love them. I tried to be a good dad. I did. I love them so damn much."

At 3:30 a.m. Stephen called his attorney again, telling him it was all an accident and the only way out of it was if he ended his own life.

Barely able to speak from the drugs and alcohol, Stephen again called Verena and then called his sister Kelly one last time. He told Kelly he was in the Wilderness State Park and was planning on killing himself. Police were already waiting outside her home. After the call she walked outside and told officers where to find him.

Detective Kozlowski's phone rang and when he saw that it was an international number he knew it was Verena Dierkes calling from Germany. Verena was crying and had just gotten off the phone with Stephen,

> "Everything he said was a lie. Everything. And I believed everything."

> "He told me it was an accident. He said, 'She smacked me and she yelled at me and I pushed her back and she banged her head and was dead.' "

Initially Verena denied having an affair with Stephen, but eventually admitted that it was true,

> "We liked each other. We liked each other more than we should. And it started about four weeks ago. It was just talking. I don't know what... maybe because Tara was always gone. And then... it just happened. But it was never physical. On that, I swear. We kissed, but that's all."

Detective Kozlowski questioned her more and got her to admit that Stephen had performed oral sex on her,

> "But it was just one time. And it was before that happened to Tara. It was before the... February the 9th."

Verena then told the detective that Stephen intended to kill himself.

Helicopters scoured the vast Wilderness State Park and quickly found his abandoned truck. Within a few hours searchers followed footsteps leading away from the truck and found his plastic gun, the notebook, and a half empty bottle of whiskey.

By 7:00 a.m. searchers found Stephen barely conscious in the snow beneath a tree. His body temperature was down to 78 degrees Fahrenheit. Suffering from severe hypothermia and frostbite, Stephen was airlifted to the nearest hospital.

That morning police searched Stoney Creek Park again. This time they found one of Tara's hands, her feet, a leg, and chunks of her flesh. Still in intensive care, Stephen was charged with murder and handcuffed to his hospital bed.

Stephen Grant mugshot / Stephen & Tara

Though still suffering from hypothermia, Stephen just couldn't keep his mouth shut. His attorney had dropped him as a client; Stephen called Detective Kozlowski and told him he wanted to talk. When confronted with the evidence against him, he rambled on for almost four hours in a long detailed confession from his hospital bed.

He explained that Tara had come home that night, and they continued the argument that had started on the phone. He said that during their eleven-year marriage, Tara had constantly belittled him and he had had enough of it. When she slapped him in their bedroom, his anger grew out of control. He said he had told Verena that when he hit her, she fell and hit her head, but that was a lie. He had actually strangled her to death on the bedroom floor.

Grant: "I was ready to go to bed, and it just kept getting worse and worse. And when she smacked me, I lost it. ... Tara had, as long as I can remember, she belittled me and - and her one way - she knew if she hit me I'd hit her back."

Grant: "She said, 'I got to do what I have to do in my job and it's none of your business.' So she started to turn around, and I grabbed her wrist ... 'Just stop,' I said, 'you're not going anywhere.' And I said, 'We're going to finish this conversation' and she slapped me ... and after that I don't really remember what happened ... she fell. I know that she banged the back of her head on the floor, and then she said something like, 'That's it. I'm going to take the kids. You're going to be fucking homeless. You're a piece of shit.' And I choked her on the carpet. She had started to get back up when I put my hand on her neck. I grabbed her neck and choked her."

Detective McLean: "Were you looking at her face?"

Grant: "No, I covered her face up."

Detective McLean: "What'd you cover her face up with?"

Grant: "Gray underwear or a gray t-shirt."

Detective Kozlowski: "How did you know that she had died?"

Grant: "When she stopped moving. And I was worried. I was really worried."

The Grants' children were asleep in their rooms down the hall while Stephen murdered their mother. Immediately after strangling his wife, Stephen sent a text to Verena, "You owe me a kiss." He left a note saying the same thing on her pillow, then returned to his dead wife on the bedroom floor.

Grant tied one of his belts around her neck and dragged her down the stairs and into the garage. He put her body in the back of her Isuzu Trooper SUV.

 "And I dropped her. She was too hard to pick up, and the belt broke, and she fell. It was the most disgusting noise. It just sounded like dropping a watermelon on the cement."

Moments later Verena returned home,

 "And I kept thinking we've got a body in this garage. What the hell do I do with the body? And thinking I killed my wife. I was thinking my life was over."

Stephen explained to detectives that he let the body sit in the back of the SUV all of that Saturday. On Sunday he drove her body to his father's tool and die shop, where he used the tools there to dismember her.

 "So I looked around the shop ... I was looking for something. I was looking for a hacksaw or something."

"At some point I threw up. And I threw up again. And then I drank some more whiskey. And then I just told myself, 'look if you don't do this you're going to prison for the rest of your life.' ... and I kept cutting her up."

Worried that the body would smell, he put the body parts back into the SUV and came home to spend the rest of the day with Verena and the kids.

 "I tried to make things as normal as possible for everybody. And I continuously flirted with Verena because I thought that was the only way I was going to be able to get through this."

That Sunday evening Stephen put the kids' red sled in the back of the SUV and at 3:00 a.m. he snuck out of the house and drove to Stony Creek Park to dispose of the body parts.

At the park he piled the body parts onto the sled and dragged it up a hill, but things went wrong,

> "And as soon as I started going it was like Keystone Cops. The sled took off and now I'm chasing after this sled that has my wife's cut-up body in it down a hill... finally got it stopped when it fell over and it broke. So now all these pieces are now fallen all over the place."
>
> "So Tara's torso I took, and I buried in the snow. And then the pieces I put on the sled and I buried that in the snow."
>
> "I'd done a very, very bad job of hiding anything. It's right there in the open."

By Tuesday evening he was worried that he had done a poor job of hiding the body parts and returned to the park. He cut open the clear plastic bags that he had wrapped the pieces in and distributed the parts randomly throughout the park, leaving one ziplock bag near the road that was later found.

The following week when Stephen heard that the police were going to search the park, he went back to gather the pieces.

> "I thought, I'm screwed. They're going to find that, because that torso at this point is still buried in the snow. I had to dig it out. It was frozen in the ground. I threw it over my shoulder and carried it."

Confused and worried that he would get caught, Stephen moved the body parts back and forth several times, eventually storing the torso in his garage.

And I kept thinking, 'I got away with this. I can't believe I got away with this.'

Search teams found other parts of Tara in the area where the first ziplock bag was discovered. Stephen had cut her body into fourteen different pieces, but some parts were never recovered. It was assumed that animals may have made off with the missing parts.

Despite his recorded confession, which Stephen also wrote and signed, he pleaded not guilty.

Verena, who had returned to Germany, came back for the trial to testify against Stephen. She told the jury how her employer constantly tried to kiss her, exposed himself to her, and eventually, just moments after he killed his wife, had sex with her.

On Friday, December 21, 2007, the jury found Stephen Grant guilty of second degree murder and sentenced him to fifty years in prison. Stephen tried to appeal the decision, but was denied and will likely spend fifty to eighty years behind bars.

Tara's sister was given control of the estate, and custody of their two children, but their grandfather, Stephen's father, was denied visitation rights. Stephen's father tried desperately to regain visitation rights, but eventually lost hope and committed suicide in June 2008.

Tara's children now participate in a yearly walk called "Tara's Walk". The walk has raised tens of thousands of dollars to help the victims of domestic violence.

(The complete text of Stephen Grant's confession is available in the online appendix at the end of this book.)

CHAPTER 5
THE INCEST KILLER

Alyssa Garcia met twenty-year-old Steven Pladl in 1995 in an online chatroom when she was just fifteen years old. Alyssa lived in San Antonio, Texas, and Steven lived 2,000 miles away in New York. Alyssa would later recall that Steven was "grooming" her.

Within a year Alyssa had run away from home to be with Steven, married, and pregnant. By the age of just seventeen, she and Steven had a baby girl and named her Denise.

Shortly after the birth, Alyssa realized that Steven wasn't prepared for fatherhood. Beside the fact that they were poor and could barely afford to feed themselves, Steven had no patience with the child. When the baby cried he would put her in an empty ice chest and close the lid. When Alyssa saw Steven pinch Denise's arm just to see if he could make it turn black and blue, she knew what she needed to do.

Alyssa put baby Denise up for adoption. Eight-month-old Denise was adopted by a happy, loving family in Dover, New York and spent the rest of her life with a new name; Katie Fusco.

 Alyssa later recalled, "It was so hard to give her up, but I had to because I wanted her to live and be happy."

Despite the trauma of giving up her baby and having Steven's abuse directed at herself, Alyssa still stayed with him through the years. Though it was common for Steven to throw things around the house and punch holes in the drywall, she believed they were both "more grown up and ready." In 2007 they had another baby girl.

Steven's temper never ceased, but Alyssa still stayed in the relationship and in 2012 they had yet another baby girl. All the while, Alyssa was the subject of Steven's emotional and verbal abuse. By 2016 Steven and Alyssa were sleeping in separate rooms of the house and had decided they would separate later that year.

 "I was always on eggshells, whatever his mood was, everybody knew, and that mood was often not happy, a lot of yelling, a lot of things smashed in the house, in front of our kids."

In January 2016 Tony and Kelly Fusco finally told their adopted daughter Katie that they were not her biological parents. Katie had just turned eighteen and like any adopted child, she grew curious about her biological parents.

In the years since Alyssa had given her up for adoption, Katie had led a normal American life. She had a brother and a sister, she was a vegetarian, loved animals and had the nickname "Pac-Man," because she was always eating.

Katie attended Dover High School, about eighty miles north of New York City, and loved to draw. She had plans to study digital advertising at the State University of New York, starting in August 2016.

 She wrote in a blog post, "A pen and something to draw on became a safe place for me. Ink became my weapon against rules and regulations. ... To be short; for me, a life without art is no life at all."

Katie's curiosity about her biological parents grew. It didn't take much to find Alyssa, now thirty-seven, and Steven Pladl, now forty-two, on social media and she messaged them. The couple, though on the verge of separation, happily invited her down to visit them in Henrico County, Virginia.

Katie meets with her biological family for the first time

Katie's adoptive parents weren't happy about Katie visiting her biological parents, but believed she was eighteen and old enough to make her own decisions. Their apprehensions were confirmed, though, when Katie informed them that August that she had decided not to go to college and would move in with Alyssa and Steven instead.

Alyssa was also apprehensive. She was already on her way out of Steven's life when Katie moved in and privately informed Katie that the reason she gave her up for adoption was for her own safety. She told her of the abuse she had been subjected to when she was a baby, but Katie didn't seem to be concerned.

When Katie moved in with her biological parents, Steven's behavior changed. Suddenly he was wearing tight-fitting shirts, skinny jeans, shaved his beard and let his dark brown hair grow long.

Katie had been living with them less than two months when Steven spent the night on the floor in Katie's bedroom. When Steven did it again the following night Alyssa confronted him. He screamed at her, "It's none of your business!" then took Katie and left the house in a rage.

Steven's actions were more than Alyssa could take, and that November she separated from Steven, moved out of their house, and shared custody of their two other daughters. Katie remained living with Steven. Though she had no proof of it, Alyssa believed the relationship between Steven and Katie had gone too far.

In May 2017, Alyssa peeked inside her 11-year-old daughter's diary and saw what she had written about Katie. She was in for the shock of her life when she read,

> "… but now she is pregnant and gained weight and my dad calls her baby 'his' baby. Did he make her pregnant? My dad even says she's my 'stepmom.' WTF! He doesn't even want me to call her sister anymore. Katie is my sister. She's probably his wife now, but in nature she's only my sister. Does she see me as a daughter or a sister? Katie now tells me sometimes to 'get the fuck up!'"

Alyssa immediately called Steven,

> "I started to become hysterical, and I called him. I said, 'Is Katie pregnant with your baby?' He just said, 'I thought you knew. We're in love.' I started screaming. I was just cursing him out: 'How could you? You're sick. She's a child.'"

Katie is my big sir.
I REAAAALY
f██████ loved him.
I ter praised when I
wont up, she came go ph with,
and as she walked down
the hallways 'tairs, or
before she did, she
said "Hey, sam".

me in my head:
OH MY GOD SHE
SAID MY NAME!!!

I would get very
depresied every time she
would have to ride the
train back to NY,
I also loved how
she was kinda skinny
in

areas, and has smaller
breasts. But now,
She is pregnat and
gained weight and
my dad calls her baby
also "his" baby. Did
he make her pregnat?
My dad even says
shes my "step mom"! Wtf!
He doesn't even
want me to say, or
call her sister anymore!
Katie is my sister.
Shes probably his wife
now, but in natures
she's only my sister.
Does she see me
as a daughter, or
a sister? Katie now
tells me sometimes to
"get the f___ up!"

Alyssa called the police, and an investigation began. Steven and Katie were interviewed by Henrico County police, as were the two other children, but no arrests were made. Steven and Alyssa's divorce was finalized days later.

Katie wore a short black dress and Steven wore a black shirt and black trousers at their July wedding in Maryland. Despite the investigation into their incestuous relationship, they lied on their marriage application and said they were not related. Steven's mother, Grace, was in attendance as were Katie's adoptive parents. Tony and Kelly Fusco believed that there was nothing they could do but show support for their daughter.

Katie Fusco & Steven Pladl wedding day

The couple had moved to Knightdale, North Carolina that summer and on September 1, 2017 Katie gave birth to a baby boy they named Bennett, but their family bliss wasn't destined to last long. In late November Henrico County police issued arrest warrants for both Steven and Katie Pladl.

In late January 2018 Steven and Katie were arrested in their Knightdale home and charged with incest and adultery, which was still a misdemeanor criminal offense in Virginia. Both were released on bond but ordered by the court to have no contact with one another.

Steven Pladl & Katie Fusco mugshots

Katie moved back to New York with her adoptive parents and custody of their four-month-old son Bennett was given to Steven's mother, Grace Pladl.

Steven's lawyer told the media that there was no accusation that Steven pressured Katie into the relationship, they were simply in love,

 "This case is an eighteen-year-old girl who shows up at the doorstep of a forty-two-year-old man who's going through difficult times with his wife. They have a bond because they're biologically related, but they never knew each other before they had a sexual relationship. He was head over heels in love with her, so much so that that outweighed the issue of them being biologically related."

After spending the following two months with her adoptive parents in New York, Katie finally realized that her relationship with her biological father was wrong. Violating the no-contact order, Katie called Steven and gave him the news. Their relationship was over. Forever.

The news was more than Steven could handle. On April 11, 2018, Steven drove to his mother's house to pick up their baby boy. He took the seven-month-old Bennett back to his house, where he laid the boy on the floor and put a pillow over his face. Police later found the baby, suffocated and stuffed in a closet.

Immediately after killing their son, Steven drove nine hours through the night from North Carolina, north toward Katie.

Every Tuesday and Thursday Katie visited her adoptive grandmother in Waterbury, Connecticut. That morning Katie and her father Tony left their home in Dover for their trip to Waterbury while Steven watched from his minivan parked nearby.

Steven followed Katie and her father for fifteen miles before forcing them to the side of the road near New Milford, Connecticut. Steven jumped out of his van and pointed his AR-15 semi-automatic rifle at their truck and opened fire. Twenty-year-old Katie and her fifty-six-year-old father Tony Fusco were both dead. Steven got back in his minivan and sped off.

An off-duty firefighter heard the shots and rushed to the scene just seconds after Steven had fled the scene. He called 911:

 "This is on Route 7 and 55. Someone just went by and shot this guy in the truck. I'm a firefighter out of New York. The car pulled up, went round and shot him. A whole clip full into his head. He's deceased, boss. The truck is in the middle of the road. He's dead. We need the police, we need everybody. There's two people in the car."

Steven called his mother as he drove toward Dover, New York. He told his mother that he had just killed Katie, her father, and their baby. Frantic, she hung up and called 911.

 "He left the baby dead. Oh God. He told me to call the police… I shouldn't go over there. The house is empty.

He said he put a key under the front mat.

His wife broke up with him yesterday over the phone. She's in New York and he told me he was on his way and after bringing the baby to her and then he was coming back. He killed his wife; he killed her father. I can't even believe this is happening."

Steven only drove nine miles back to Dover before he pulled over to the side of the road and killed himself with the same AR-15 rifle.

The case of Steven and Katie Pladl highlights a concept known as genetic sexual attraction. The term is used to describe a strong sexual attraction that develops between close relatives who meet for the first time as adults.

The concept is frequently reported as an unreliable anecdote and is often referred to as pseudoscience among psychology professionals since there have been no studies showing that people are attracted to people genetically similar to themselves.

CHAPTER 6
THE COPPER GULCH KILLER

I don't usually cover unsolved cases in the True Crime Case Histories series, but when I came across the story of the murder of Candace Hiltz it was just too engrossing to pass up. Though it's officially unsolved, there's plenty of suspicion and speculation.

Candace Hiltz was raised in the remote area of Copper Gulch, Colorado, an extremely rural area a few hours south of Denver. Though she was a small-town girl in every sense, she was exceedingly intelligent. By the age of eleven she was performing calculus, and by seventeen, when most of her friends were in high school, Candace was already in her third year of an online degree at Brigham Young University.

Candace dreamed of being a lawyer and was awarded a scholarship to Stanford Law School, but when she found herself pregnant at sixteen, she began to rethink the idea of going away to school. To make matters worse her baby, Paige, was born with hydrocephalus, a disorder that causes an abnormal buildup of fluid in the brain. Because Paige's life expectancy wasn't long, Candace knew her time with her daughter would be limited. Stanford would have to wait.

Candace was an outspoken young girl with a firm sense of right and wrong, which is probably why she wanted to be a lawyer. She could be very confrontational and if she witnessed bullies or someone breaking the law, she had no problem speaking her mind.

Candace Hiltz

Candace's brother Jimmy was nothing like her. He was a somber and quiet young man, and when their father died he struggled to cope with the loss. Jimmy fell into a world of drugs, alcohol, and suffered with very deep depression. He sank so low that he couldn't hold a conversation of more than a few sentences. Over time Jimmy withdrew from the family, unable to communicate with anyone at all. He packed a backpack and a tent and lived in the enormous wooded area of Colorado on his own.

In the summer of 2006, Candace and her mother Delores were driving toward their home on Copper Gulch Road when they passed two vehicles parked on the side of the rural road. Candace recognized both vehicles: One was a local Sheriff vehicle of an officer who was rumored to be corrupt. The other was a well-known meth cook (producer of methamphetamine drugs) in the area. As they passed the vehicles, Candace and her mother both witnessed the drug cook handing the

Sheriff's deputy a thick envelope. In Candace's opinion, it was clear that a payoff or some sort of bribe was taking place. Candace was livid when she saw this, but with no proof there was nothing she could do.

A few days later in early August there was a knock at the door of the Hiltz home. Delores answered the door: It was the same Sheriff's deputy and he was looking for Jimmy. The deputy told her they believed Jimmy had been breaking in and burglarizing homes in the area.

The accusation upset Delores. She explained that Jimmy lived in the hills behind their home, had severe mental problems, and could never break into other people's homes because of his condition. Jimmy had been in and out of Colorado Mental Health Institute for severe social phobia and anxiety. She told the officer that Jimmy could barely speak to people and could never deal with that kind of confrontation. It was impossible that he could have been breaking into homes.

When the deputy called Delores a "damned liar" Candace overheard and ran to the door in a rage. She screamed at the deputy who told her that if she didn't calm down, he would arrest her. Candace reacted by holding out her wrists in front of her and yelled,

 "Go ahead! I will scream at the top of my lungs, 'what the hell are you doing taking envelopes from the drug cooks up here?'"

The deputy was furious, but speechless. He angrily turned and stormed back to his vehicle and drove away.

Later that week the family dog, Jackson, went missing. Jackson was a house dog, and it was rare that he got outside unattended. On the occasions that he did get out, he wouldn't venture far from the house. Candace and her mother called and searched for the dog all day, but Jackson was nowhere to be found. When several days had passed and Jackson hadn't returned, they assumed that a mountain lion, which were common in the area, had possibly attacked him.

Five days after Jackson had gone missing, Delores drove into town to run some errands and left Candace alone in the house to look after Paige. That afternoon around 3:20 p.m. Delores arrived home to find that someone had broken the back door open and she could hear Paige crying in one of the bedrooms. As she walked into the hallway, she knew something was dreadfully wrong. There was blood all over the hallway.

As she entered the first bedroom she saw that Paige was in her crib, crying, but at least safe. Delores then ran further down the hallway into Candace's room. There was blood pooling on the floor, but initially she didn't see any sign of Candace. It was then that she noticed that the bed was slightly angled and raised at one end.

Underneath the bed it looked as if someone had shoved a large green quilt under the bed, causing the inclination of the bed. But when she tugged at the quilt, she soon realized the disturbing truth. Candace had been shot point-blank in the face, head and chest, rolled into the quilt and callously stuffed beneath the bed. A shotgun shell was found in front of the fireplace in the living room.

Just days after accusing a Fremont County Sheriff's deputy of taking bribes, the Fremont County Sheriff's Office was now in charge of investigating Candace's murder. Two detectives were assigned to the case: Detective Harry Sharp and Lead Detective Robert Dodd.

Jimmy Hiltz / Detective Robert Dodd

Delores was questioned only briefly, and it seemed to her that Dodd really didn't have an interest in what she had to say. It was evident that he already had a suspect for the murder: Her son, Jimmy Hiltz.

Police quickly developed their theory. They believed that Jimmy had broken down the back door of the house intending to kill his sister. One of houses that they suspected Jimmy of breaking into previously was missing a shotgun. They believed he had shot Candace with that gun and then stuffed her beneath the bed and fled.

Delores knew their assumptions were absurd. Jimmy was just not the type to go on a rampage like that. He loved his sister and had no reason to kill her. In any case, Jimmy wouldn't have needed to break down the door. He had his own key and could come and go anytime he liked.

Despite her contention, police started a multi-agency search for Jimmy Hiltz for the murder of his sister Candace.

Search teams canvassed the endless acres around the home. After five days of searching, police found the family dog, Jackson, dead with the leash still attached to his collar; he had been missing for over a week. From the amount of decomposition, it was clear someone had killed Jackson not long after he had gone missing.

Detectives assumed that someone had removed the dog from the house so that the killer could more easily get into the house to kill Candace. This made the murder premeditated. To Delores, it assured her even further that this was not the work of Jimmy. Jimmy loved the dog and would have no reason to have killed him.

Three days after they found the dog, police found Jimmy Hiltz camping in the woods. He was unarmed and had no idea police had been looking for him. Detectives spent days interrogating Jimmy, but he refused to confess to the murder or the string of burglaries they had accused him of.

Detectives Dodd and Sharp had no physical evidence against Jimmy. Without DNA, ballistics, or blood evidence, they had no reason other than their own hunch to charge him.

Jimmy was charged with burglary, but was eventually deemed insane and unable to defend himself. He was admitted back to the Colorado Mental Health Institute for an indeterminate amount of time until he was mentally stable enough to stand trial.

The fact that he was mentally ill only furthered the detective's belief that he was the killer. Delores, however, knew that wasn't true and was worried that his mental illness and the pressure of the accusations would drive him to consider suicide.

Years passed by and no other suspects emerged. The case remained open, but no additional investigation was ever done on the case. Seven years after Candace's murder, Paige died from complications of her disease.

When a person rents a storage unit and fails to pay the rent, the contents of the unit go up for auction. Without knowing what's inside, anyone who's interested can bid on the contents, hoping that whatever is inside is worth more than they paid for it.

Ten years after the murder, Rick Ratzliff attended an auction for an abandoned storage unit in Cañon City, Colorado. With a bid of only $80, Rick won the auction and clipped the lock off of the unit.

As Rick rummaged through the contents of the storage unit he was puzzled to find an envelope marked "Evidence". When he picked up the paper envelope a small axe dropped through the bottom of the deteriorating bag. Another bag marked "Evidence" contained a rope. Both the rope and axe were still covered in blood.

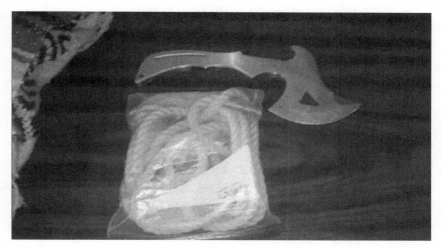

Axe & Rope

Inside the storage unit, Rick also found a box full of old police uniforms. When he held up one of the uniforms he noticed the name sewn into it read "Dodd." Rick knew the name and realized he had purchased Detective Robert Dodd's abandoned unit. He had remembered his name from hearing the news reports of Candace's murder ten years prior.

Astonished as to why the highest ranking detective in the Fremont County Sheriff's Office would have crime scene evidence in a personal storage locker, Rick handed the evidence over to the Colorado Bureau of Investigation.

The CBI verified that the items were indeed evidence from the Candace Hiltz murder investigation. Detective Dodd claimed he stored the items intending to take additional photos of them, but it slipped his mind.

When the story of the recovered evidence hit the local news, public pressure on the Sheriff's Office mounted and in January 2017 Robert Dodd was put on paid administrative leave.

The public also demanded more answers as to why there had never been charges brought against anyone for the murder. Because of the media pressure, police finally released the pathology report on Candace's murder.

The general assumption of the media and public had been what the police had told them: That Jimmy Hiltz had murdered his sister, but still could not stand trial due to his mental illness. But when the autopsy findings were released, public opinion quickly turned away from that assumption.

The autopsy showed that Candace had been killed with three separate weapons. She had been shot point-blank in the face with a shotgun. Then she was shot five times in the back of the head with a .22 caliber rifle. Lastly, she was shot in the chest, directly through the heart, with a medium caliber handgun.

Astonishingly, the Fremont County Sheriff's Office stuck by their theory that the murder was pulled off by Jimmy alone, despite any physical evidence pointing toward him.

Robert Dodd succumbed to the pressure of the media and public accusations and decided to move to Texas. When he was packing to move he had asked for a small dumpster to be parked in the driveway in front of his home so he could throw away the things he didn't want to move. After he had filled the dumpster he called Penrose Landfill to come pick it up and take it away.

Rob Orton was an employee for Penrose Landfill and was charged with picking up the dumpster from Dodd's property. Knowing Dodd's notoriety, Rob was curious of the contents of the dumpster. When he got it to the landfill and dumped it he noticed some strange items in amongst the garbage.

Not only did Dodd not go through the proper chain of evidence when he put the items in his personal storage locker, but he had also brought items home and later dumped them in his garbage.

Rob called a local reporter who had been covering the story and invited her to the landfill to go through the evidence before they called the Colorado Bureau of Investigation.

Together Rob and the reporter took photos of the items that Dodd had thrown away. They found a toolbox marked "Forensic Light Kit - FSCO Crime Scene Unit," assorted evidence DVDs, an FSCO laptop computer and more than twenty VHS video tapes labeled "Sexual Assault Evidence."

There were also envelopes full of sexual assault statements taken from victims. Many of the statements were from children who had drawn pictures of their attackers in crayon. Dodd had determined that this was evidence that could just be thrown in the trash.

It surely seemed that Robert Dodd had something to hide. In May 2017 he was charged with Official Misconduct.

At Robert Dodd's trial it was revealed that just days after the Candace Hiltz murder evidence was found in the storage locker, Dodd had logged into the official computer archive report of the murder and edited it six times. He had deliberately altered the case file with false information.

It was also revealed at trial that some evidence from the storage locker pointed to an additional person of interest in Candace's murder. The person of interest, however, was never revealed. Even if the person of interest had been revealed, the evidence had never been tested for DNA and because of degradation, was now useless.

Dodd's defense claimed that the Sheriff's Office had no specific policies or procedures for the handling of evidence. In July 2019, Robert Dodd was found guilty of two counts of Official Misconduct and abuse of a public record. He was sentenced to a $1,000 fine and 15 days of incarceration, but never spent a day in jail.

Because of this case and several others, eleven additional officers within the Fremont County Sheriff's Office were placed on administrative leave.

Twelve years after her death, no one has ever been charged with Candace's murder and Jimmy Hiltz is still a patient at Colorado Mental Health Institute; he also works there as a counselor for other patients.

CHAPTER 7
TAKING A CHANCE

Anyone living in the Phoenix area in the late eighties or early nineties is sure to remember Rick Chance. Rick's commercials ran continuously on every channel for many years. His business, Empire Glass, replaced car windshields, but he did it with flair and a marketing gimmick that worked amazingly.

The desert landscapes of Arizona meant lots of small rocks. Tiny rocks fly on the endless Phoenix freeway system, resulting in chips and cracks in car windshields. Rick Chance saw a massive opportunity. In 1982, he made deals with insurance companies and local restaurants to create Empire Glass.

Rick was the spokesman in his own commercials. He advertised that he would replace your windshield when it cracked at little or no cost to you and give you twelve free dinners at a nice restaurant for the trouble. Who's going to turn that down? Nobody. It was a massive success —so much so that after two decades, what started as a one-man operation, had expanded into six states was raking in $25 million a year.

Rick Chance in an Empire Glass commercial

Rick grew up in Maricopa, Arizona, a tiny farming town just south of Phoenix, and always had an entrepreneurial spirit. As a young boy his father wanted him to follow in his footsteps and encouraged him to work their farm with the tractor, but Rick told his father,

 "Dad, I don't need to do this. I'm going to be a millionaire."

At an early age he lost an eye to childhood glaucoma and wore a glass eye, but that only seemed to empower him. Rick lettered in basketball, football, and track at Maricopa High School and edited the school newspaper.

Rick became enormously successful at business, but his love life was a train wreck. In January 1979, Rick married Norrie Ann Rose. Within three months she had filed for divorce. He talked her out of the divorce initially, but it was destined to end, and in 1981 they divorced just before he started Empire Glass.

A year later he married Christine Gay Pyland. His marriage to Christine lasted longer and spawned two children.

Rick Chance lived his life being pulled in two directions. He loved the millions that his business made for him and thrived on extravagance. He owned a multi-million dollar home in the affluent neighborhood of Paradise Valley, drove a top-of-the-line Mercedes, and despite the Arizona heat, occasionally wore a sable coat. He wore expensive jewelry and frequently went to strip clubs.

On the flip-side, Rick was deeply religious and could quote long bible verses verbatim. He donated vast sums of money to charities and regularly gave money to evangelical churches, as well as funding international ministries. He believed his success was directly related to his relationship with the Lord.

After ten years of what seemed to be a picture-perfect marriage, his relationship with Christine was in trouble. Rick met a nineteen-year-old prostitute at The Phoenician resort who drugged him and stole $71,000 worth of jewelry and his Mercedes. Christine filed for divorce, shared custody of the children and moved to Denver. In court documents she accused him of "wasteful and frivolous spending" and ignoring his family.

 "He is frequently out of town and spends sixty hours per week in work and work-related activities...Rick was in an extremely embarrassing legal situation involving a prostitute which, unfortunately became front-page news."

Christine was awarded control of the Denver operation of Empire Glass, half of their Paradise Valley home, a $20,000 fur coat, her 1991 Infiniti convertible, and Rick was to pay for their children's private religious school tuition.

Though viewing himself as deeply spiritual, being drugged and robbed, and going through a rough divorce, Rick continued to flash his wealth and showed his vulnerability. The second marriage, however, was nothing compared to the third.

In 1995 Rick met a stunning green-eyed blonde named Jill Scott. Jill was a beauty queen that had won the title of Mrs. America in 1990. Rick married Jill on Valentine's Day in a fairy tale wedding that was broadcast live from Las Vegas on Good Morning America.

Rich Chance and Jill Scott Wedding

Jill, however, had some secrets of her own. Shortly after winning the Mrs. America title she was sued by the pageant because she was actually separated from her first husband at the time, making her ineligible for the title of Mrs. America.

She also hid from Rick the fact that she had had several plastic surgery operations and had signed a contract to star in a pornographic movie called, "Mrs. XXX-America." He filed for an annulment after only four months of marriage.

The judge threw the annulment out, but he filed for another in 1998 where he described his wife as a "gold digger," whose goal was to, "divest him of his assets and leave."

But Jill had no shortage of accusations against Rick. She claimed that she thought she was marrying a good Christian man, but found herself with a "religious kook" who would chant incantations, and order her to read scripture for hours while bent over, face-down, holding her ankles in adoration of God.

"When I say chanting, I mean he would repeat a prayer over and over again, or a phrase of his own, over and over again."

She claimed that Rick once received a complaint letter from a customer and screamed, "This is from Satan," then ripped it up, threw it on the fire and started chanting.

She also spoke of unusual sexual demands that Rick would ask for, claiming she once walked in on him in their bedroom with another man, both naked with towels wrapped around their waists.

 She recalled, "He seemed to be battling his inner demons. His desires were strong and went against his spiritual life."

By the time divorce number three was over in 1998, Jill was awarded $250,000, jewelry, and $8,333 per month for four years.

Though Empire Glass was still making him millions, Rick was getting bored with the glass business. His real passion had become jewelry, and he was determined to make his next fortune as a jewelry dealer.

A tight group of dealers operated the "jewelry circuit" in the Phoenix area and Rick had some trouble jumping into an already established industry. He sold his expensive jewelry to local dealers and low-end jewelry he would sell through newspaper ads.

Rick would buy wholesale from dealers and middlemen, then turn them around, selling them as his own designs. But his favorite jewelry he couldn't design himself—Rolex watches and raw diamonds.

Despite three failed marriages and being robbed, Rick was still overly trusting of people and would often carry a briefcase full of jewelry with him to show to clients in public places. A friend, David Hans Schmidt, recalled their evening at the cigar bar of The Ritz-Carlton in Phoenix:

"We were drinking Chambord liqueur at $9.50 a pop until it was coming out of our ears. I got up to go to the bathroom and, I swear, I came back and there's Rick's briefcase open on the table. There's a half million dollars' worth of jewels sitting here and he's at the bar talking to some bimbo."

Rick was very trusting of everyone, and whenever friends warned him that showing off valuables in public like that can make him a target he would scoff, "… eh, it's all insured." But one friend recalled telling him, "Yes, but insurance isn't going to cover your ass."

Rick and Schmidt would frequent the strip clubs of Phoenix together and Rick would pay the $600 fee for the two of them to go to the VIP Champagne room with the girl of their choice. One of their favorite strip clubs was Christie's Cabaret on 32nd Street. Rick preferred Asian girls and Christie's was where Rick met Brandi Hungerford.

Brandi Hungerford was born in South Korea in 1977 and adopted by an American family when she was only a few weeks old. She grew up in a typical Midwest setting in Grand Rapids, Michigan with eight brothers and sisters.

In 1995 Brandi moved to Tempe, Arizona with the intention of attending Arizona State University, but before she got a chance to enroll she saw an ad in the newspaper that read, "Looking for Models." ASU was put on the back-burner when she realized she could make $1,200 a week as an escort.

Brandi's father had developed cancer and much of the money she made stripping and escorting went to help with his care. Her father's illness and what she was doing for a living began to change her emotionally, according to her friends. The girl that was once happy-go-lucky, now kept things bottled-up; she became moody and indifferent.

Brandi worked the full-range of adult establishments in the Phoenix area. Christie's Cabaret was a more "high-end" strip club, while Bourbon Street was a little darker and seedier. She also worked at a "bikini club" called Southwest Attractions, a two-story building in an industrial area near the airport with no windows. Inside, after being checked for weapons, customers choose a girl and are escorted to a private room for thirty minutes of "companionship." The company also offered an outcall service, where a girl would meet a client in a hotel room of their choosing, usually accompanied by a male body-guard waiting in the car outside.

Rob Lemke was a tall high-school dropout from Spanaway, Washington, just south of Tacoma. He was known for his hot temper and his passion for guns and Asian girls. His rap-sheet included felony assault, illegal weapons possession, and parole violation.

Lemke moved to Arizona in 1999 with his girlfriend to avoid sentencing for a weapons charge in Washington State. His girlfriend helped him buy an assault rifle since he couldn't buy one legally with his felony conviction. Once established in Arizona he became a male stripper and escort. He was 220 pounds of muscle and became quite popular at male strip clubs like the Hideaway.

As a male stripper, Lemke was known to cross the line legally. He wanted a fast-lane to wealth and was willing to get there any way he could. Legal or not. Lemke started his own escort agency, which is how he met Brandi Hungerford, and the two started dating.

Brandi had been out with Rick Chance a few times; he was very open with her about his wealth and showed her the briefcase of jewelry he carried around. When she told Rob Lemke about the briefcase he instantly saw dollar signs.

Lemke put together a plan for he and Brandi to steal Rick's briefcase full of jewelry, but their first attempt was a failure. Rick had met Brandi for Mexican food before they went back to his house. The plan was for Brandi to call Lemke and tell him to come to his house and rob him, but Rick and Brandi had spent the evening smoking pot in his $3 million Paradise Valley home and when she called Lemke, she was too high and mumbled into the phone that she couldn't remember the street he lived on.

Throughout the summer of 2002 Brandi left Rick several messages, most of which he didn't return. Brandi and Lemke thought Rick may have become suspicious of her. The unanswered calls would later become a trail of evidence for police to use against her.

In early August 2002, Rick and Brandi went out a few more times. After dinner on the evening of August 8, Brandi suggested they get a bottle and have some drinks at the Best Western hotel in Tempe. Brandi later recalled,

 "Rick probably thought he's gonna get sex."

After checking in at the front desk, Rick and Brandi entered room 317 and Rick lit a cigar while Brandi stepped into the bathroom. He had no idea she was in the bathroom calling Lemke to give him the room number. When Brandi emerged from the bathroom, she told Rick she would step out into the hall to get some ice from the ice machine. In the hallway, Lemke was waiting for her. He put on a black ski mask and gloves, took her keycard, and entered the room with a gun in his hand.

At 1:15 p.m. the following afternoon it was well past check-out time. A maid at the Best Western ignored the "Do Not Disturb" sign and entered room 317. Rick was face down on the floor, lying in a pool of blood.

When police arrived, they found a single shell casing, an orange pill, white powder and a burned stick of incense. Rick Chance had a single bullet wound in his throat. In his pockets were his identification, credit cards, some cash, two wrapped condoms, and the keys to his 2000 Mercedes. The briefcase with over $1 million in jewelry was missing.

The forensic evidence came easily. Brandi's keycard was left in the room with her fingerprints on it. Her fingerprints were also on the hair dryer. Surveillance video showed Brandi and Rick in the parking lot, at the front desk, and in the hallway of the third-floor room. Rob Lemke was in clear view of the security cameras just outside their door too. Police shared photos with the media, and the calls poured in.

Of the hundreds of calls that came in to police, one was particularly useful: A call from Brandi's mother who worked as an officer at the Maricopa County Estrella Jail. She had recognized her daughter on the local news channel and called Tempe police.

When police searched Brandi's cell phone records, it showed multiple calls to Rob Lemke. The Tempe police then searched Lemke's Tempe apartment and found jewelry tags that displayed Rick's brand.

It wasn't difficult to ascertain that Rob was originally from Washington State and already had a warrant out for his arrest. All law enforcement agencies between Arizona and Canada were alerted to be on the lookout for Brandi and Lemke.

Police were correct in assuming they'd run back to Washington State. Brandi and Lemke had fled to Tacoma, where Lemke knew someone who he thought would buy the jewelry from him.

Five days after the murder, Brandi was arrested in Tacoma without incident. Lemke was arrested just two days later. They were found with jewelry, a fur hat filled with more than $20,000 in cash, and several guns.

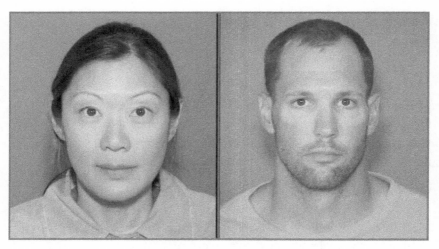

Brandi Hungerford & Rob Lemke

Brandi was charged with first-degree murder and was cooperative during her interrogation. She provided the murder weapon to police and fingered Rob as the trigger-man. The gun that killed Rick had been given to a friend of Lemke and hidden inside a pizza box.

Brandi told police that she had no idea Lemke planned to kill Rick. She said that after leaving the room she stood in the hallway for less than a minute before she heard a loud pop,

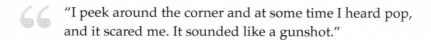 "I peek around the corner and at some time I heard pop, and it scared me. It sounded like a gunshot."

A witness in a nearby room, however, contradicted Brandi's explanation. The witness told police they heard her say,

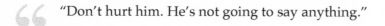 "Don't hurt him. He's not going to say anything."

The witness claimed that she then looked through the hotel door peephole and saw a man standing guard.

For her cooperation in implicating Lemke, prosecutors offered Brandi a lesser charge of second-degree murder, along with armed robbery, and conspiracy charges. She accepted the offer. Brandi Hungerford was sentenced to fourteen years in prison, serving part of her term at the same prison that her mother used to work. She was released in August 2016.

Rob Lemke fought extradition without success. When he was returned to Tempe to face charges, he eventually pleaded guilty and was handed a life sentence. He will be eligible for parole in 2032.

CHAPTER 8
THE TIGER PARENTS

"Tiger parenting" is a term used to describe a style of strict, demanding parenting, popular within the Chinese community. Every parent wants their child to achieve greatness of some sort, whether it be sports, the arts, or academia, but a tiger parent is a completely different animal. Tiger parents are obsessive with their child's success and push their influence on their children to the extreme.

A typical tiger parent would expect their child to attend an Ivy League school like Harvard, Princeton, or Yale. They also might regulate who their child dates, so they marry into a "good" family. Ultimately, their goal is to make sure their child gets a lucrative job such as Wall Street lawyer, investment banker or highly paid surgeon.

Huei Hann Pan and Bich Ha Pan were stereotypical tiger parents. Hann had immigrated to Toronto, Canada as a refugee and his wife Bich (pronounced "Bick") followed shortly after. The two married after their arrival in Canada and got jobs working for an auto parts manufacturer. By the late eighties, they had two children, Jennifer and Felix.

Hann & Bich Pan

The Pans led an extremely thrifty life, saving as much as they possibly could. By 2004 they had $200,000 in the bank and owned a nice-sized home in a suburban neighborhood. Their sole extravagancies were their cars, a Mercedes and a Lexus. Their main objective was to save enough to send their kids to the best schools and make sure they were eligible for any possible scholarships. They wanted to make absolutely sure that Jennifer and Felix lived a more plentiful life than they did.

Their first born, Jennifer Pan, showed potential at an early age. By the age of four she was already taking piano lessons, proving to be exceptional. In her elementary school years, she started figure skating. Some evenings Bich and Hann would keep her up practicing until 10:00 p.m. —and then homework until midnight.

At graduation from middle school Jennifer was expected to be valedictorian of her class, but was turned down. She was devastated and her parents even more so. The pressure on Jennifer was immense—more than a girl in her early teens could handle. She told her friends that she would just put on her "happy mask," but deep down she was suffering and began cutting her forearms with tiny cuts.

Jennifer attended high school at Mary Ward Catholic Secondary School in Toronto. The school was known for its unique self-directed learning program with uncommonly high academic standards. Jennifer fitted in well and got along with almost everyone. Her parents monitored her after-school activities closely in which she became an avid swimmer and practiced Wushu, a Chinese form of Kung Fu. In band class, Jennifer excelled at playing the flute.

Though she was an accomplished ice skater, her skills began to slip. A second-place in a skating completion just wasn't enough for her demanding parents and her confidence began to slip. At one point she was an Olympic hopeful in figure skating, but those hopes were quashed when she tore a ligament in her knee.

In earlier years Jennifer was a straight-A student, but by the end of ninth grade her grades in everything but music had slipped considerably. Knowing that a C or even a B wasn't going to sit well with her parents, Jennifer got creative. Armed with her old report cards, gluestick, scissors, and a quick trip to Kinko's she was able to create the straight-A report cards that her parents expected. But she knew she would have to improve her grades before the final two years of high school if she wanted to get into college.

Jennifer's activities out of school were closely monitored by her parents. Even into her twenties, she had never been allowed to go out with friends without close supervision. She had never been drunk or gone to a nightclub. She felt as though she was missing out on her childhood and the controlling nature of her parents infuriated her.

In her junior year of high school Jennifer traveled with the school band to Europe playing the flute. When the band played an auditorium that allowed smoking Jennifer had an asthma attack. A fellow student and trumpet player, Daniel Wong, took her outside and calmed her down.

Daniel was a chubby, funny, and happy-go-lucky kid. He was also a part-time pot dealer. When he took the time to take care of Jennifer, it impressed her, and it wasn't long before they were dating. But of course, she would have to hide the relationship from her parents.

Jennifer Pan & Daniel Wong

By the time senior year rolled around, Jennifer's grades still hadn't improved and she had continued forging her report cards. She had already been accepted to attend Ryerson University the following year, but when she failed her calculus class Ryerson dropped her. Not only was she not going to be going to University, she wasn't even going to graduate from high school with that failing grade.

Nervous that her parents would find out, Jennifer continued forging documents. As far as they knew, she was going to Ryerson. She told them she would take two years of science and then would transfer to the University of Toronto's Pharmacology program, just as her father had planned. Her father, Hann, was ecstatic and bought her a new laptop for school.

Jennifer forged receipts for tuition and a $3,000 scholarship, bought used textbooks, and left every morning for school. But instead of going to school, she took the bus downtown and hung out at cafes and public libraries all day. She studied scientific subjects and filled her notebooks with notes as if she was attending class. She also spent time with Daniel, who was attending York University. She taught piano lessons when she could and worked part-time days at the pizza place where Daniel worked as the kitchen manager.

When Jennifer arrived home in the evenings, she made up elaborate stories about her lessons, teachers, and other students. She told very few friends of the huge lie she was telling her parents, knowing that if friends knew it may eventually get around to her parents.

Eventually Jennifer convinced her parents to let her move in with her friend Topaz three nights a week. Topaz lived closer to campus and she wouldn't have to make the long commute every day. But this was just another lie on top of all the others. She actually moved in with Daniel and his parents. His parents constantly asked to meet with her parents, but she made excuse after excuse.

After two years of lying to her parents about Ryerson University, it was time for her to transfer to the University of Toronto. She found someone online to print her a fake transcript.

Graduation from Ryerson was going to be tricky. Jennifer came up with an elaborate excuse that her graduating class was too large and students would only be allowed one guest. Rather than choose between her mother and father, she gave her guest invitation to a friend so that both of her friend's parents could attend.

Jennifer's parents still didn't even know that she had a boyfriend; if they had known, they would have forbidden it. Though she lived with Daniel three nights a week, she wanted to stay more. She told her parents that she was going to volunteer at Toronto's Hospital for Sick Children in their blood testing lab so she would need to stay in the city on the weekends as well.

This was the first time that her parents suspected her of lying. Her father knew that if she was working at the hospital, she would need a uniform and a keycard, but she didn't have them. Hann convinced his wife Bich to follow her, but Jennifer knew she was being followed. Jennifer went to the hospital and sat in a waiting room all day until she was convinced that her mother was gone.

Her parents still knew that she was up to something and the next morning they confronted Topaz who broke the news to them that Jennifer had never lived there and was instead living with Daniel.

When they confronted her, Jennifer confessed. She told her parents that she wasn't volunteering at the hospital, she wasn't attending University of Toronto, and she was staying with Daniel. But she still didn't tell them that she had never attended Ryerson University and hadn't even finished high school.

Jennifer's father was beyond livid. His first instinct was to kick her out of the house, but her mother, who was much more lenient than her father, intervened. Her parents forbade Jennifer from leaving the house for two weeks. During her time at home, Jennifer's mother spent as much time as she could with Jennifer. Though her father had taken her phone away from her and insisted on no contact with Daniel or any friends, her mother occasionally let her have access to her phone.

In February 2009 Jennifer wrote on Facebook,

 "Living in my house is like living under house arrest. No one person knows everything about me, and no two people put together knows everything about me… I like being a mystery."

Eventually she got access to her phone and though she was forbidden from having any contact with Daniel ever again, she would sneak phone calls and texts, and she would occasionally sneak out of the house. Every chance she got between teaching piano lessons, she would sneak to Daniel's house.

Her parents eventually allowed her to retake her calculus class to get the one last credit she needed to get her high school diploma. Then she would need to apply for any school that would take her. Her father was convinced that it wasn't too late and she could still become a pharmacy lab technician or a nurse.

Meanwhile, Daniel was getting sick of all the sneaking around. She was twenty-four years old, but her parents had full control over her love life. Eventually Daniel broke up with her and started seeing another girl, Christine.

Jennifer grew insanely jealous and concocted an elaborate story to regain his attention. She told Daniel that a man had come to her door claiming to be a police officer and showing his badge. When she opened the door a group of men pushed their way into her home and gang-raped her. She then told him that the following day she had received a bullet in the mail. Jennifer told Daniel it was all a warning from his new girlfriend; she claimed Christine was trying to keep them apart.

By the spring of 2010 Jennifer had had enough. Her father was tearing her life apart, and she wanted it to end. She wanted her parents dead. In high school she had heard stories of a boy named Andrew Montemayor. The rumor was that he had robbed people at knifepoint and had once considered killing his own father. She contacted Montemayor but he wouldn't have anything to do with her plan, but told her that his roommate Ricardo Duncan might be interested. According to Jennifer she paid him $1,500 that she had earned from teaching piano but then never heard from him again.

Jennifer and Daniel were texting again, and she shared her thoughts with him. She explained that her parents were worth about $1 million and if they were out of the picture she was set to inherit $500,000. If her parents were dead, she and Daniel could live their life with no sneaking around and they could finally be happy.

During his weed-dealing days Daniel had met a guy named Lenford Crawford who went by the nickname "Homeboy". Daniel thought that if anyone knew how to hook something like that up, it would be Homeboy. Sure enough, he did. Daniel set up a meeting between Jennifer and Crawford and they agreed on a price. Crawford told her the going rate was $20,000, but for a friend of Daniel he would only charge $10,000. Jennifer agreed and said that once she got her inheritance it wouldn't be a problem.

Crawford gave Jennifer an iPhone and a SIM card. This phone and SIM would be used strictly for when they spoke and would then be destroyed after the deed was done.

Though Daniel knew of the plan and knew Jennifer's deepest, darkest secrets, he was still in love with Christine. He told Jennifer he wanted out of the plan. She texted him:

> Jennifer: "So you feel for her what I feel for you, then call it off with Homeboy."
>
> Daniel: "I thought you wanted this for you?"
>
> Jennifer: "I do, but I have nowhere to go."
>
> Daniel: "Call it off with Homeboy? You said you wanted this with or without me."
>
> Jennifer: "I want it for me."

The next day Daniel confirmed it was all still going to happen.

> Daniel: "I did everything and lined it all up for you."

Despite Daniel professing his love for Christine, his flirtatious texts still continued in the days after.

In early November 2010, Crawford texted Jennifer,

> "I need time of completion. Think about it."
>
> She replied, "Today is a no go. Dinner plans out. We won't be home in time."

Eventually Crawford and Jennifer agreed on a date; Monday, November 8.

At 9:30 p.m. on Monday night, Bich Pan had just returned home from a night of line dancing with her friends. Her husband Hann had retired early and was already in bed. Jennifer's younger brother Felix was away at college, and Jennifer was in her bedroom watching television. Bich kicked off her shoes and filled a footbath with warm water to soak her feet and watch some TV in the living room before going to bed.

At 9:35 p.m. Jennifer came downstairs, asked her mother about her night, kissed her goodnight, and discreetly unlocked the front door. She then went to her bedroom, and spoke on her iPhone for three and a half minutes.

At 10:02 Jennifer turned an upstairs bedroom light on, then one minute later turned it off. That was the signal that the door was unlocked. Jennifer then sent a text:

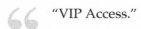 "VIP Access."

Moments later three men came through the unlocked front door: Lenford "Homeboy" Crawford, David Mylvanganam, and Eric "Sniper" Carty. All had guns drawn.

One man ran up the stairs to the room where Hann was sleeping and put a gun in his face. He demanded that Hann go downstairs where another man was watching over Bich.

Bich and Hann spoke to each other in Cantonese, wondering what they wanted when one of the men yelled,

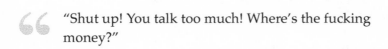 "Shut up! You talk too much! Where's the fucking money?"

Hann assured him he only had $60 in his wallet and Bich pleaded with her assailants, "Please don't hurt my daughter."

The third man, Carty, went up the stairs and met with Jennifer outside of her bedroom. Jennifer handed him $2,500 in cash and showed him another $1,100 that her mother kept in her nightstand. He then tied her arms behind her back with a shoelace and led her downstairs with her parents.

The men took Jennifer back upstairs and tied her to the stairway railings while they took her parents downstairs to the basement.

Moments later, five shots rang out. Hann was shot twice. Once in the face and once in the shoulder. Bich was shot two times in the back and once in the head. Though Bich died instantly, Hann was bleeding profusely but still alive. After eighteen minutes in the house, the three men left through the front door and left Jennifer alive upstairs.

Jennifer's Samsung flip-phone was tucked into the waistband of her pants. Despite being tied with her hands behind her back, she pulled the phone out, flipped it open, and dialed 911.

 "Help me, please! I need help! I don't know where my parents are!... Please hurry!"

'What's your name?"

"My name is Jennifer."

"Someone just broke in?"

"Someone broke in and I heard shots like pop. I don't know what's happening. I'm tied upstairs."

"Did it sound like gunshots?"

"I don't know what gunshots sound like. I just heard a pop."

(screaming in the background)

"I'm ok! My Dad just went outside screaming."

"Do you think your mom is downstairs too?"

"I don't hear her anymore. Please hurry, I don't know what's happening."

The screaming that was heard thirty-four seconds into the 911 call was Hann Pan. Covered in blood, Hann crawled out of the basement and back to the main floor of the house. He then ran outside, screaming as loudly as he could. Nearby neighbors heard his screams and called 911 as well.

When police and emergency crews arrived to the home, they found Jennifer upstairs tied to the bannister just as she had said, her flip-phone laid on the floor next to her. Hann Pan was rushed to the hospital where he was put into a medically induced coma.

At 3:00 a.m. Jennifer was brought in for her first interrogation. She told police that three black males had burst into the house, had taken whatever cash they could find, and had shot her parents. Police asked her to explain how she managed to pull her flip-phone out of her waistband while tied to a bannister. She demonstrated that she reached around her waist, flipped the phone open with her thumb, and turned the volume all the way up.

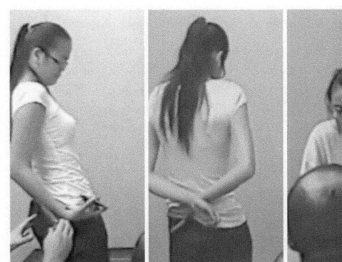

Jennifer Pan interrogation

She showed that making the call was possible, but still left a lot of unanswered questions. If it was a robbery, why did they leave so many valuable items in the house? Why did they not bring duffel bags or backpacks to carry what they had stolen? Why did they not take the Lexus or the Mercedes when the keys were there in plain view? How did they get in the front door so easily? If they had planned on killing two people, why leave a third as a witness?

The biggest question police had was: Why did Hann come up the stairs and run outside for help, when he knew his daughter was still in the house? Why did he not try to help her? Their questions would be answered a few days later.

Detectives set up twenty-four-hour surveillance on Jennifer and even followed her to her mother's funeral. During the funeral detectives noticed she had a lack of tears or emotion as they lay her mother in the ground.

When Hann awoke from his induced coma, his neck bone was shattered, bones in his face were broken near his eye, there were bullet fragments lodged in his face, and a bullet had clipped his carotid artery. Though he was barely alive, Hann remembered everything and had a story to tell that differed greatly from the story Jennifer told.

Hann told police that Jennifer's story was all lies, like everything else about her life. He said that when the men rushed in he was taken downstairs at gunpoint into the living room with his wife. When he looked for his daughter Jennifer, he saw her speaking in a friendly manner with a white man and walking around the house with him without any restraint.

Police had already interviewed Jennifer twice, but on November 22 brought her in for a third interview. Two hours into the interview Detective Bill Goetz began what is referred to as the Reid Technique.

The Reid Technique is a controversial interrogation procedure that was developed in the fifties to evoke a confession. It has been banned in most European countries because it involves deceptive techniques such as lying to the suspect about the evidence against them and invading their personal space. The procedure has been accused of leading to many false confessions, but it's still in use in most of the United States and Canada.

Using this technique, Goetz falsely told Jennifer that police used satellites and infrared technology to view activity within buildings and they had software that could tell if a person was lying.

Jennifer succumbed to the interrogation and admitted that she hired the men, but not to kill her parents. She told police she hired them to kill her. She claimed that she had tried to commit suicide many times in the past but had failed every time. She said she had hired a hit on herself, "I didn't want to be here anymore."

She told police that her parents wouldn't allow her to see Daniel Wong anymore and she wanted to end her life. She said the men were already outside the house when she decided to call it off, but they demanded the money anyway and burst into the house. She claimed that she couldn't pay them, so they shot her family instead.

The cops didn't buy her story; they arrested her and brought Daniel Wong in for questioning. Daniel confirmed that she was lying once again, as she did with everything in her life.

Jennifer Pan mugshot

Despite Jennifer destroying the SIM card, police were able to recover text messages from her iPhone and Daniel's phone to confirm her arrangement with the hitmen. Jennifer, Daniel, and the three hitmen were charged with first-degree murder, attempted murder, and conspiracy to commit murder.

Jennifer's trial lasted almost ten months, and she took the stand in her own defense for seven days, but it was no use. When she was handed the guilty verdict she initially showed no emotion. Once the cameras left the room, she burst into tears and shook uncontrollably.

Jennifer Pan was sentenced to life in prison with no chance of parole for twenty-five years. Daniel, Mylvaganam, and Crawford all got the same sentence. Jennifer was also given a non-communication order. She was no longer allowed to have any contact with the other defendants or anyone in her family.

When Carty's lawyer became ill, his trial was declared a mistrial and was postponed. In December 2015, Carty pleaded guilty to conspiracy to commit murder and was sentenced to eighteen years in prison with parole eligibility after nine years.

Hann Pan still suffers with his injuries and is unable to work. He released a statement after the trial which read,

> "When I lost my wife, I lost my daughter at the same time. I don't feel like I have a family anymore. Some say I should feel lucky to be alive, but I feel like I am dead too. I hope my daughter Jennifer thinks about what has happened to her family and can become a good honest person someday."

CHAPTER 9
MOM, I'M A MONSTER

J ust northwest of Denver and southeast of Boulder lies the suburb of Westminster, Colorado. The city of about 100,000 is a nice, safe place to raise a family. At least that's what the residents thought before May 2012.

On the Memorial Day holiday, a twenty-two-year-old woman was jogging around beautiful Ketner Lake, a fifty-acre open space with a one-mile trail that encircles the lake. As she ran along the secluded trail in the early afternoon, a man ran up to her from behind, grabbed her arms, and forced a cloth over her mouth. She could smell the distinct odor of chemicals on the cloth.

The young woman was lucky. Though she was terrified, she was strong enough to fight the man and got away to call police. She described the attacker as a white male, approximately five feet eight inches tall, with brown hair, an average build, wearing a blue baseball cap, black t-shirt, jeans, and sunglasses.

Westminster police developed a sketch of the attacker and obtained some DNA from the scene, but months went by and they weren't able to find any suspects.

Police had no idea the attacker was seventeen-year-old Austin Sigg. When Austin was just twelve years old his step-mother sent him to a faith-based therapist after finding porn on his computer. He wrote a note to his therapist,

 "I have an addiction to porn, and I would like to stop."

This wasn't just any kind of porn, though. Austin was addicted to child porn.

Austin Sigg

Austin went through therapy and his therapist encouraged his father to add parental controls to his computer, but as with any teenager nowadays, he easily circumvented it. From there, his addiction only escalated.

Austin later recalled,

 "… it took a hold of me and it just started growing. After I got done seeing my Christian therapist, psychiatrist, whatever you want to call it, I thought I had a grip for a little while and then it probably lasted not even a month and then I went back to it."

To his friends and fellow students, he seemed like a relatively normal kid. Friends said he was a bit of a goth kid, but well-liked, smart and "a total sweetheart." He had a collection of swords and knives, but came across as a regular kid into music and video games. His classmates, however, had no idea about the crazy thoughts that were swirling in his head.

Austin left high school early to attend Warren Tech, a local technical school, and get his GED high school equivalency. He then enrolled at Arapahoe Community College. He wanted to put high school behind him and pursue his obsession: Mortuary science and crime scene investigation.

In addition to his porn addiction, Austin had an obsession with dead bodies and decomposition. He took dead rats home from school so he could study them in various stages of decomposition.

Austin's father was a wealthy business owner, but had a long criminal record. Robert Sigg had a federal conviction for bank fraud and various other charges including assault, burglary, domestic violence, distributing drugs, DUI, and resisting arrest.

By the time Austin reached seventeen, his child porn obsession had progressed to include violence and death. On his iPhone, Austin kept photos and videos of children, bondage, rape, and human dismemberment.

On October 5, 2012, five months after the Ketner Lake jogger was attacked, ten-year-old Jessica Ridgeway started her walk to school just like any other day.

Jessica was excited to become a teenager. Only three more years. She loved to play waitress and cheerleader; she loved math, and her favorite color was purple. She was known for her purple glasses and the tiny gap in her front teeth.

Jessica Ridgeway

Jessica's mother worked the night shift from 10:00 p.m. until 7:00 a.m. so she was able to see Jessica off to school in the morning before she slept during the day.

Normally Jessica walked to school with a young boy down the street and called the boy's father at 8:25 a.m. to let them know she was on her way. Jessica kissed her mother goodbye, put on her black puffy coat, and at 8:30 a.m. headed out the door. Though the boy only lived a few houses away, Jessica never arrived there. The boy's father assumed Jessica's mother had decided to drive her to school.

When Witt Elementary School realized Jessica had not shown up for school they called her mother, Sarah, but because of her work schedule, she was still asleep and the call went to voicemail.

When Sarah Ridgeway woke at 4:00 p.m. and heard the voicemail, she immediately went looking for Jessica along the route to school. She checked her friend's homes, the nearby parks, but there was no sign of Jessica.

 Sarah Ridgeway told the media, "… and then you get a pit in your stomach you don't want any parent to experience in their entire life. When you know your child has been taken."

Jessica's terrified mother reported her missing at 4:30 p.m. and the search started immediately. Police questioned school faculty and went door-to-door along her route to school, hoping for any leads.

Volunteers and firefighters joined in the search and an amber alert was issued at 9:15 p.m. By morning there were over a thousand people searching for Jessica, resulting in one of the largest searches in Colorado history.

Police sent divers into Ketner lake while sniffer dogs and helicopters searched the area, but there was no trace of Jessica. Despite their efforts, the first forty-eight hours came and went with no clues.

On Sunday, October 7, six miles away, a man found a backpack in his yard. Not having heard the news of the missing girl, he posted on a local social media page about it and mentioned that it contained a key chain with the name Jessica Ridgeway. Others in the group informed him that was the name of the missing girl, and he turned the backpack over to police.

Inside the backpack investigators found Jessica's purple glasses and the clothes she was wearing when she left for school that morning. Her clothes were soaked in urine. DNA analysis of the backpack revealed the DNA of someone other than Jessica. Most likely it was the DNA of her abductor. When the DNA was put through databases, it revealed that it was also a match to the DNA from the person who attacked the jogger on Ketner Lake.

Five days after Jessica had gone missing, maintenance workers were working in Pattridge Park Open Space when they noticed something that seemed strange and out of place. In a patch of tall whisky grass was a large black garbage bag. When workers opened the bag, they found a tiny human torso.

Pattridge Park was nine miles southwest of Jessica's home in the town of Arvada. Arvada police and Westminster police worked together with the FBI under floodlights throughout the night processing the scene.

The torso was missing the arms, legs, and head and had been wiped clean, but not clean enough. Police were able to retrieve DNA from the torso. It matched the backpack and the Ketner Lake jogger.

The next morning, investigators announced the devastating news. The torso was indeed the remains of ten-year-old Jessica Ridgeway.

A sense of anguish and terror gripped the community of Westminster and the surrounding cities. Parents took time off work to make sure their children made it to school safely. The city that once left doors unlocked and kids played free had instantly lost its sense of security.

Jessica Ridgeway's funeral was held on October 16, and her favorite color purple was predominant. Over 2,000 people attended. Her mother wore a purple ribbon in her hair, mourners released purple balloons, and Colorado Governor John Hickenlooper wore a purple shirt as he spoke and expressed the sadness of the entire state of Colorado.

In the days after Jessica's death over 700 local residents gave voluntary DNA samples. One of those samples was seventeen-year-old Austin Sigg. He had been studying crime scene investigation and was confident he had left no trace, so he voluntarily allowed investigators to swab his cheek. Incredibly, Austin's DNA sample was mishandled. His DNA was mistakenly returned to police in a batch of samples that were not a match.

Three days after the funeral, on October 19, Westminster police asked the public for help. They had found a small cross near the torso in Pattridge Park, which was possibly part of a necklace. Police were asking for anyone that may have seen the cross before to come forward, and they were in luck.

Cross found at the scene

A woman called detectives and reported that a friend of hers, Mindy Sigg, had a son who wore a cross similar to the one shown on the news and lived less than a mile from Jessica's home.

When police interviewed Austin Sigg, he was calm and answered all questions asked of him. He told police he was sleeping on the morning that Jessica disappeared.

Though he was calm during the questioning, after the interview he was on edge and told friends at Arapahoe Community College that he felt "sick and wobbly." Austin was certain that the FBI had matched his DNA to the samples taken from the torso and the backpack. On the night of October 22, Austin was panicking, and so slept with his mother.

The next day Austin told his mother, "I am a monster and need to be punished." He explained what he had done, and his mother called Westminster police. The following are excerpts from Mindy Sigg's 911 call:

 Mindy Sigg: "Hi, um, I need you to come to my house… um, my son wants to turn himself in for the Jessica Ridgeway murder."

911: "And what's going on there. Ma'am, are you there?"

Mindy: "Did you not hear me? He just confessed to killing her."

911: "I know. I want you to tell me what's going on. Can you tell me exactly what he said?"

Mindy: "That he did it and gave me details and her remains are in my house."

The 911 dispatcher then asked to speak to Austin.

Austin Sigg: "I don't exactly get why you're asking me these questions. I murdered Jessica Ridgeway."

911: "Okay."

Austin: "There is... I have proof that I did it... there is no other question. You just have to send a squad car, something down here."

Austin Sigg also admitted to attacking a jogger at Ketner Lake. He was then asked if he had weapons.

Austin: "I have knives in my room, um, and we own a few guns, but... I'm giving myself up completely, there will be no resistance whatsoever."

The dispatcher talks again to Mindy.

911: "Is Austin still there with you?"

Mindy: "Yeah, I'm hugging him (crying)."

911: "Okay, you guys are hugging? Okay, you definitely did the right thing. You tell me when the officers get there, they're coming to your front door, okay?

(The complete sixteen-minute 911 call is available in the online appendix at the end of this book.)

Investigators questioned Austin Sigg for hours while he explained in horrific detail how he abducted and murdered Jessica Ridgeway.

Austin had been hiding in the back seat of his Jeep on the morning of October 5 as Jessica was walking to school. Though he claimed Jessica was chosen at random, he had parked near her house and knew that she would have to walk past his vehicle as she walked down the street.

As she passed his Jeep he leapt out of the back seat and grabbed her. Jessica screamed, but nobody heard her screams.

Using zip ties, he bound her wrists and ankles and threw her in the back seat, then drove down random side-streets. By the time they arrived at his house, the frightened ten-year-old had wet herself with fear.

Austin claimed that he sat with Jessica for two hours in his bedroom watching a movie and cartoons and she asked him over and over if he knew her mom. He then cut her hair and gave her clothes to change in to. He put her urine soaked clothes into her backpack. Initially he claimed he didn't sexually assault her, but later admitted that he did several times. She suffered considerable bruising from the force of the rape.

After he had repeatedly raped her, Sigg told her to face the wall. When she turned around he put zip ties around her neck in an attempt to strangle her. He told investigators that he "didn't have enough lever-age" with the zip ties and they cut into his hands. He then tried strangling her with his bare hands, but after three minutes he realized his hands just weren't strong enough. Eventually he filled the bathtub with scalding hot water and forced her head underwater, drowning her.

Sigg went on to tell investigators that he shoved the small cross into her vagina and dismembered her body, using a small knife and a saw. He cut her arms, legs, and head off. Police didn't release full details of the dismemberment, but Sigg told detectives that the whole process fulfilled a sexual fantasy for him.

He cut her hands and feet into small pieces and flushed them down the toilet. He then removed her internal organs, put them into containers and labeled them. He kept her skull and organs in a small crawl space in his home.

Sigg told police that afterwards he sat looking at her body,

"All I could think of was, 'Oh god, what have I done?'...
There is no better word to describe what I have done
than evil."

At only seventeen years old at the time of the murder Sigg could not be
charged as an adult and wasn't eligible for the death penalty or life in
prison because the Supreme Court determined those penalties are
cruel and unusual punishment for minors. Instead, he was charged in
Juvenile court, but prosecutors wanted to make certain he would never
again see the outside of a prison.

The counts against him piled up. He was charged with nineteen
counts, including first-degree murder after deliberation, three counts
of felony murder, sexual assault on a child, second degree kidnapping
and robbery, plus attempted murder, attempted kidnapping, and
attempted sexual assault for the Ketner Lake jogger attack. Sigg
pleaded guilty to all counts against him.

His defense argued that he was not mature and didn't understand the
acts he was committing, but the judge disagreed. On November 20,
2013 Austin Sigg was sentenced to forty years in prison for first-degree
murder plus an additional eighty-six years for the remaining eighteen
counts against him, ensuring he will never be released from prison.

On October 5, 2013, one year after her death, the city of Westminster
Colorado changed the name of Jessica's favorite park to the Jessica
Ridgeway Memorial Park. Throughout the park the sidewalks are
etched with Jessica's favorite knock-knock jokes and the children's
playground toys are painted her favorite color, purple.

CHAPTER 10
A GRISLY NEW ORLEANS TALE

Zach Bowen grew up like any other normal American boy. He was sociable and had an average number of friends. Nothing about him made him extraordinary. For the most part he led a normal American life. It wasn't until he turned eighteen that his life started to change.

Just after his eighteenth birthday, before he was legally allowed to drink, Zach met twenty-eight-year-old Lana Shupack in a New Orleans strip club. Though she was ten years older than him they dated and eventually married and had two kids together.

In order to support his new family, Zach decided his best option was to join the US Army. He enlisted in the 709th Military Police Battalion and was sent on a tour of duty in Kosovo and a second one in Iraq, spending time in Abu Ghraib. Back home, Lana sent him strip club photos of her and her coworkers.

Though he later almost never spoke of it, Zack experienced atrocities that left him with post-traumatic stress disorder. During the early days of his first tour a member of Zack's unit, a young female friend, Rachel Bosveld, was killed during a mortar attack in Baghdad. The death drained him mentally and the once happy-go-lucky man fell into a more somber tone.

Later in his military career, Zack became friends with a young Iraqi boy. When insurgents blew up the shop that the boy's family owned Zack fell into an even deeper depression.

Zack had been promoted to sergeant and when it was time to leave the military his commanding officer gave a recommendation for an honorable discharge. But much to Zack's disappointment he was given a general discharge, making him ineligible for GI Bill education benefits. In addition to his depression, Zack felt cheated for his service in the military.

By the time Zack returned to New Orleans, his marriage had failed. Though they didn't divorce, he and Lana separated and Zack took a job as a bartender in the French Quarter. It was during that time that he met Addie Hall who also worked as a bartender in the trendy area of New Orleans.

Zack & Addie

Addie was artistic and free spirited. She wrote poetry and occasionally taught dance classes. She was described by her friends as "a mean drunk," and "… a wonderful person, except when she wasn't." According to her friends, Addie had been molested as a child and was a victim of several abusive relationships; she also suffered from bipolar disorder.

Zack and Addie moved in together and started their tumultuous relationship. Both were heavy drinkers and drug users, and Addie was known for her abusive temper. Together the couple had a passion for both drinking and fighting. When they were drunk or high on cocaine Addie could easily turn a minor argument into a raging inferno.

Zack and Addie became an iconic couple during Hurricane Katrina. While the rest of the city had evacuated and camped out in the Louisiana Superdome, the two decided not to vacate. They stayed in their apartment that they rented above the Voodoo Spiritual Temple on Rampart Street and drank their way through what seemed to be the end of the world. The national news media interviewed them and their story was featured in the New York Times.

They seemed to thrive on the lifestyle that the hurricane brought. To them it was like a camping trip. No electricity and plenty of booze. They didn't have to work, they could drink all day, and they didn't have any bills to pay. Addie would occasionally flash her breasts at passersby just to make sure the police regularly patrolled their street.

Zack & Addie

In early October 2006, a year after Hurricane Katrina, the two twenty-eight-year-olds got into one of their epic fights. Addie was convinced that Zack had been cheating on her. On October 4, she approached the landlord of their apartment and asked to have Zack taken off of the lease. Knowing Addie's explosive temper, the landlord refused, tried to calm her down, and suggested that she try to patch things up with Zack.

Two weeks later on October 17 at 8:30 p.m. a man looking out the window of his hotel room at the Omni Royal Orleans Hotel in the French Quarter noticed a man's body on the roof of the adjacent parking garage.

Police arrived to find the body of Zack Bowen face down on the roof. His body was mangled and lifeless, clearly having died from the impact, but police were unsure if he had been pushed or he had jumped. Small cigarette burns were found all over his body. When police searched his pockets looking for identification, they found a note that said:

"This is not accidental. I had to take my own life to pay for the one I took.

If you send a patrol to 826 N. Rampart, you will find the dismembered corpse of my girlfriend Addie in the oven, on the stove, and in the fridge along with full documentation on the both of us and a full signed confession from myself.

The keys in my right front pocket are for the gates. Call Leo Watermeier to let you in.

Zack Bowen."

When police arrived at the Rampart street apartment, the first thing they noticed was the temperature. The air conditioner was running full-blast. It had been turned down to sixty degrees, presumably to slow the rate of decomposition.

The walls of the apartment had been spray painted with red paint,

"Please call my wife. I love her."

"I'm a total failure."

"Look in the oven."

"Please help me stop the pain."

On the stove was a pot with Addie's charred head in it. In another pot were human hands and feet. A roasting pan inside the oven contained arms and legs. All were burnt beyond recognition. Potatoes and carrots were cut up on a cutting board next to the stove. Investigators noticed what seemed to be Cajun seasoning on the limbs, but from the burnt condition of the body parts, it's believed his intention was not to eat them. It's assumed Zack cooked the body parts in an attempt to remove the tissue from the bones for easier disposal.

137

In a large plastic garbage bag inside the refrigerator was the torso of Addie Hall.

Addie kept a journal and Zack had filled in the last eight pages. It was a confession in horrifying detail of how he had killed his girlfriend.

> "Today is Monday 16 October 2 a.m. I killed her at 1 a.m. Thursday 5 October. I very calmly strangled her. It was very quick."

> "Halfway through the task, I stopped and thought about what I was doing. The decision to halt the first idea and move to Plan B (the crime scene you are now in) came after a while. I scared myself not only by the action of calmly strangling the woman I've loved for one and a half years, but by my entire lack of remorse. I've known forever how horrible a person I am (ask anyone)."

The note mentioned that he had had sex with her body several times after strangling her and would drink in the apartment with her body until he passed out. He went to work as usual. When he got home from work, he moved her body to the bathtub and dismembered her with a handsaw and a kitchen knife. When police arrived, the bathroom had been thoroughly cleaned.

In his suicide note, Zack also explained the cigarette burns on his own body. He had burned himself one time for each year of his life as a punishment for his failures.

Zack Bowen had demons of his past war experiences and there's no place like New Orleans for a demon story. In the years afterwards, the house at 826 N. Rampart became a tourist attraction, infuriating the couple's friends and family.

The Rampart Street apartment above the Voodoo Spiritual Temple

Eight years after the murder/suicide, a documentary was made called "Zack and Addie." The film featured a woman named Margaret Sanchez. Margaret was a friend of both Zack and Addie and spoke of her relationship with the couple and of the nightmares she still had in the years after. She hypothesized that Addie may have killed herself rather than Zack killing her.

On June 6, 2012, in a disturbing twist to the story, Margaret Sanchez and her boyfriend Terry Speaks walked into a New Orleans strip club called "Stilettos" and asked about getting a threesome with one of their dancers for a private party. Unable to find a willing girl, they went to another bar called "Temptations." There someone pointed them in the direction of a young girl with purple hair named Jaren Lockhart. They told the couple she was desperate to make some money.

She was indeed desperate and quickly said yes to their proposition. Jaren was seen on security cameras grabbing her belongings from the dressing room and primping herself in the mirror, then she exited the building with the couple. She was seen with the couple a few additional times on Bourbon Street security cameras, then she was never seen alive again.

Jaren Lockhart's dismembered body parts washed ashore days later on various beaches in Mississippi. There were mutilated areas where tattoos had been, which was an attempt to hide her identity.

Terry Speaks & Margaret Sanchez

When Sanchez and Speaks were arrested Speaks' computer had recently been wiped clean. His car reeked of cleaning products. In e-mails between the couple they spoke of a rare celestial phenomenon called the Venus Transition, when Venus passes directly in front of the sun, that happened at the exact time of the murder.

Cadaver dogs reacted to scents in the couple's back yard, shrubbery, burn pile, and a trash can. Inside the burn pile, investigators found remnants of women's underwear and pieces of a cell phone. Several parts of Jaren Lockhart's body were never recovered.

During the trial the forensic pathologist explained her death and dismemberment in graphic detail. Members of the jury were seen openly weeping.

Terry Speaks was convicted of second-degree murder and sentenced to two life sentences. One day later Margaret Sanchez pleaded guilty to manslaughter, obstruction of justice, and conspiracy to obstruct justice. She was sentenced to forty years in prison.

CHAPTER 11
THE ALLIGATOR THEORY

At the southwest corner of Georgia where it meets the border with Florida, the Chattanooga and Flint rivers join to form Lake Seminole. The lake was artificially formed by the Jim Woodruff Lock and Dam in the fifties. From there, the water flows 500 miles south through the Apalachicola River toward the Gulf of Mexico.

The shallow water was full of stumps from trees that were there before the lake was formed. The stumps created problems for boaters that used the lake for fishing and duck hunting. But that didn't discourage thirty-one-year-old Mike Williams. Every chance he got, he would make the fifty mile drive from Tallahassee, Florida to go to his favorite duck-hunting spot.

Mike got his first taste of duck hunting when he was fifteen. In high school Mike was a jock. He was a star football player, student body president, and was active in the Key Club. North Florida Christian School was also where he met the love of his life, Denise Merrell, who was a cheerleader at the same school.

Denise and Mike dated, and after high school Mike went on to Florida State University in Tallahassee where he majored in political science and urban planning. He worked his way through college as a property appraiser where his boss, Clay Ketcham, said he was the "Hardest-working man I ever saw."

Mike & Denise Williams

Mike and Denise married in 1994 and in 1999 had a baby daughter they named Anslee. By 2000 Mike had built a real estate business and was making over $200,000 a year.

December 16, 2000 was a special day for Mike and Denise. It was their sixth wedding anniversary. They had plans to celebrate that evening, but Mike wanted to start the day with a quick trip to the lake for some duck hunting. It was mid-December and very cold and stormy, but he was determined to get some hunting in. Mike woke up early, grabbed his gear, loaded up his Ford Bronco and towed his boat out to Lake Seminole before dawn.

Leaving that early in the morning, Mike should have been home long before noon, but when he hadn't returned home that afternoon Denise was frantic. Mike wasn't answering his cell phone, so she called her father who then called Mike's best friend, Brian Winchester. Together, the two men drove out to Lake Seminole late that afternoon to look for Mike.

When they arrived at the boat launch where he usually parked, his Bronco was nowhere to be found. They searched the area, and just before nightfall they found his Bronco and boat trailer parked seventy-five yards away at a muddy boat launch that he normally would never use. It would have been very unlike Mike to park there when his normal boat launch was available. As darkness fell, the wind picked up, and the temperature dropped to nineteen degrees. The wind and pouring rain made a further search impossible, so they waited until morning.

The next day Denise's father, Brian Winchester, and the Fish and Game Department continued their search for Mike. That morning they found Mike's boat about 300 yards from the boat launch. Strangely, it was 300 yards in the opposite direction that the strong winds had blown that night. Inside the boat was a shotgun still in its case, although it wasn't the shotgun that Mike normally used for duck hunting. They also found hunting equipment and duck decoys, but there was no sign of Mike.

Searchers assumed that Mike's boat may have hit a stump in the lake and that he had been thrown overboard with his hip-wader boots on. Divers were sent to search the murky lake; helicopters scoured the lake from the skies, hundreds of man hours were put in by several law enforcement agencies. Days turned into weeks and weeks turned into months, but Mike had simply vanished.

Stumps in Lake Seminole

Because the lake was filled with stumps and his hip-waders were missing, law enforcement assumed that Mike had fallen overboard and drowned. His boots had most likely filled with water and pulled him under. The lake was also known for being alligator infested and it was believed that after he drowned he had been eaten by alligators. The case was treated only as a missing persons case.

Six months later a hunting cap was found floating on the surface of the water. Police thought it might have belonged to Mike Williams and sent divers into the area. In the same area they found his hunting vest, his still-working flashlight, his hunting license, and his pair of hip waders.

In the state of Florida, a missing person can only be declared deceased if they've been missing for five years. But only eight days after Mike's belongings were found in the lake, Denise Williams successfully petitioned the state to have his death certificate issued. With the valid death certificate she was now able to collect Mike's two life insurance policies totaling over $1,500,000.

As the years went by, Mike's mother, Cheryl Ann Williams, wasn't buying the accidental death theory. She saw several gaping holes in the "official" story and started her own investigation.

Cheryl wanted a criminal investigation opened into his disappearance, but Mike's widow, Denise, threatened to cut off access to her grand-daughter, Anslee, if she did. Ultimately, Cheryl lost access with her granddaughter and pursued the death of her son.

The first thing that stood out to Cheryl was that none of the items found six months after Mike's disappearance seemed like they had been submerged for six months. The hat and jacket were pristine and free of mud or algae. The hip wader boots had no teeth marks—nothing to indicate an alligator attack. Even his hunting license was still legible after spending a supposed six months in the murky lake.

She also contacted alligator experts that supplied her with an impor-tant fact. Alligators don't feed in temperatures below forty degrees, they go into a state called brumation. Similar to hibernation, alligators become lethargic and their metabolism slows down significantly. They dig themselves into a bank of the lake and go dormant until the weather gets warmer. The temperature when Mike disappeared in December was well below freezing. There was no possibility that he could have been eaten by alligators.

Additionally, alligators don't eat people whole. When alligators do attack humans, they bite, chew, and tear the bodies. There are always pieces left to be found. In the history of Lake Seminole there had been a total of eighty deaths there. Mike's death would have been the only one in which a body had not been found.

There were other inconsistencies Cheryl found. Mike's boat was full of gasoline when it was found. If he had fallen out of the boat while it was running, the boat's motor was designed to circle endlessly until it ran out of gas.

Mike's friends also verified that he would never have worn his hip waders while driving the boat. He would only put them on once he reached a hunting spot.

The most significant sign for Mike's mother was the fact that his widow, Denise, was issued a death certificate after just six months and awarded the life insurance claim. There were two policies, one of which was for $1 million written just six months before he vanished. The insurance agent that sold him the policy was his best friend, Brian Winchester.

Five years after Mike's disappearance, Brian Winchester and Denise Williams were married.

This solidified Cheryl Williams' suspicions. Mike Williams was not in that lake. She knew it. She spent years trying to get investigators to take a second look at the case.

Every Sunday Cheryl could be found in Bradforville holding a giant "Missing" sign on the side of the road in the hope that someone might see his face and remember something. She took up donations and paid for huge billboard signs, flyers, posters, and websites. Nothing seemed to help.

Cheryl never gave up. She sent over 240 letters to the then-Governor of Florida, Rick Scott. Every single letter went unanswered.

She regularly placed full-page ads in the Tallahassee Democrat newspaper:

An open letter to Governor Rick Scott:

 Dear Governor Scott,

> Fifteen years ago, today, December 16, 2000, my son, Mike Williams, supposedly drowned in Lake Seminole, Sneads, Florida, while on a solo duck/hunting trip.

> After a two-week search of the lake, Mike's body was never found. I was told by Florida Fish and Wildlife Conservation Commission Officers, that my son fell out of his boat, drowned, and was eaten by alligators.

> Governor Scott, there is only one problem. Alligators do not eat in cold water. They hibernate! It would have been

physiologically impossible for an alligator to eat anything, much less a 5'10" 180 lb. man.

Mike was declared dead six months after he disappeared when (planted) evidence surfaced in the lake. His wife collected millions of dollars in life insurance, and then married his best friend.

It took me three and a half years to get a criminal investigation into Mike's disappearance, because of this investigation I lost access to his daughter.

FDLE has been the lead investigating agency since February 2004. I still do not know what happened to my son. His case is now considered an active cold case, nothing is being done to find Mike or his murderers.

In May 2012, in a face-to-face meeting, in front of witnesses, I was told by an FDLE investigator, "Ms. Williams, you no longer have an investigation because you don't do things the right way!" In other words, Governor Scott, I talk too much.

Governor Scott, I have written a letter to you every day since you took office. You do not see my letters because they are sent over to FDLE, the very agency I am complaining about.

Governor Scott, would you please appoint a Special Prosecutor from another part of the state to investigate my son, Mike's disappearance? As a parent yourself can you image the undying agony of not knowing where your daughters are for the past fifteen years, while simultaneously being lied to, ignored, and being called crazy by law enforcement officials, when the facts clearly prove otherwise?

Please help me find my son,

Cheryl Ann Williams

Cheryl's efforts fell on deaf ears, but she never gave up hope.

By 2016 the marriage between Denise and Brian Winchester was falling apart. Things had begun to sour in 2012 due to Brian's sex addiction, and Denise filed for divorce in 2015.

On August 5, 2016 just before the divorce was to be finalized Winchester told a friend that he thought the police were "after him" and that once she divorced he was convinced that she would,

 "say something about this guy who died 10 or 12 or 15 years ago."

Brian Winchester hid in the back of his wife's car and waited for her to arrive. When she got into the driver's seat she felt a gun barrel jammed in her side as he climbed over the seat.

Winchester grabbed her phone and told her to drive. He told her that because she had blocked his text and refused to take his calls, he had no choice. He held her against her will for over an hour until she finally pulled into a drugstore parking lot and parked next to the front door. He threatened suicide if she divorced him, telling her he had nothing to live for. Eventually she talked him down and agreed to not tell the police he had kidnapped her.

After he released her Brian apologized for what he had done and she drove straight to the police station. Brian Winchester was arrested for kidnapping, domestic assault, and armed burglary. Two of the charges were felonies. Denise asked for a restraining order and claimed she was so distraught that she hadn't been able to eat or sleep for weeks. Winchester was held without bond.

Mike's mother was elated with the news of Brian and Denise's breakup and after sixteen years it gave her new hope that she might be able to find out what had happened to her son,

 "Brian's not going to let Denise run around alone with all that money. I'm praying he doesn't commit suicide; I'm praying he'll tell us what actually happened."

She added that she was alone among her family in holding out hope that her son was still alive.

Brian Winchester sat in jail for over a year awaiting trial. During the trial the prosecuting attorney told the media that he hoped that the case would help solve the disappearance of Mike Williams, but there was no mention of Mike at all during the court proceedings.

Finally, in December 2017, Winchester was sentenced to twenty years in prison for the kidnapping plus another fifteen years of probation. The day following Brian's sentencing, the Florida Department of Law Enforcement called a press conference. They had found the body of Mike Williams.

After seventeen years, Mike Williams' remains were found buried at the end of a dead-end road just five miles from where he grew up, forty miles from Lake Seminole.

The body had actually been discovered two months earlier in October. As part of a plea deal, they had waited until after Brian Winchester's sentencing to announce it.

Florida Department of Law Enforcement brought thirty workers to the area to work sixteen-hour days for five days without even telling the workers what they were looking for. The search was to be kept confidential and workers were told it was a training exercise. The work involved digging nine-foot-deep holes with a backhoe and building dams and pumping water to keep the nearby mucky Carr Lake from destroying their work. Investigators searched through massive stacks of mud and found 98% of Mike Williams' bones. DNA from the bones matched that of his mother.

On May 8, 2018 Denise Williams was arrested as she was on her way to her daughter's nineteenth birthday. She was charged with first-degree murder, conspiracy to commit first-degree murder and accessory after the fact. Remaining details were kept confidential until court.

Brian Winchester & Denise Williams

Prosecutors argued that Denise Williams conspired with Brian Winchester to kill her husband as early as nine months before his death. At court prosecutors played an audio recording of the police interview with Brian Winchester after his kidnapping arrest. Brian confessed to killing Mike Williams in cold blood, but claimed the whole thing was Denise's idea.

Brian Winchester took the stand to testify against Denise where he told the court he had been having a relationship with Denise ever since high school. They both married other people, but continued their affairs off and on and frequently double-dated with their spouses. He explained that in 1997 their affair "snowballed" and they began a steady affair for the last three years of Mike's life.

Winchester explained that because of Denise's religion, her family would never forgive her for a divorce. Instead, she plotted to kill her husband. Denise suggested several methods of getting rid of him, such as faking a boating accident in the Gulf of Mexico for both her husband and Brian's wife, Kathy. But Brian didn't want his children to grow up without their mother. Other ideas involved a robbery at Mike's work, but they eventually agreed to make it look like a hunting accident.

On the day he disappeared, Brian invited Mike to Lake Seminole for a morning of duck hunting. Once they were out on the water Brian waited until Mike put on his hip-wader boots and pushed him out of the boat, assuming he would sink to the bottom. But Mike didn't sink. He held on to a tree stump. Brian finished the job by circling the stump in the boat and shooting Mike in the face with a shotgun.

With a shotgun blast to the face, the story of a boating accident wouldn't work. Winchester then pulled Mike's body out of the lake, left the boat and belongings, and drove forty miles away to bury Mike's body near Carr Lake.

Though there was no physical evidence linking Denise Williams to the murder, that didn't stop the jury from coming back with a guilty verdict on all charges.

The following February Denise was sentenced to life in prison. Cheryl Williams addressed the media only to say that justice had finally been served. Denise was allowed to sign over the remainder of the insurance money to their daughter Anslee in order to avoid prosecution for insurance fraud. As part of the agreement, no part of the insurance money was to be used for Denise's legal defense.

CHAPTER 12
THE KIČEVO MONSTER

Kičevo is a mountain plateau city of a little over 20,000 inhabitants. Throughout the years the area has changed hands many times, once belonging to the Byzantines, then conquered by the Ottomans, Serbia, Yugoslavia, and is now called Macedonia. Not much happens in Kičevo. It's a halfway point between the capital and fancy resorts on Lake Ohrid. Other than a pit-stop, there's not much reason to stop in the slow-paced town.

Though the area has seen its share of warfare throughout the centuries, it generally wasn't a place that was known for violent crime. Daily life in Kičevo was mundane and boring. Nothing much happened that was newsworthy. That was until three women between the ages of fifty-six and sixty-five were beaten, raped and strangled between 2005 and 2008.

The slayings were exciting news for Vlado Taneski. He was a mild-mannered journalist in his early fifties, frustrated with the lack of reportable news in the area. News of the brutal murders kept local residents riveted to the newspapers and Taneski's articles that covered them. He seemed to have an uncanny inside knowledge of the murders and an extreme eye for detail that kept residents buying papers.

Vlado Taneski was born in 1952 and raised in Kičevo to parents who were strict conservative disciplinarians. When his eldest brother left home, his parents disowned him and never spoke to him again. They did the same to his older sister. Vlado's father was a World War II veteran who worked as a security officer while his mother was a custodian at the local hospital. Both were extremely strict parents who often took a belt to their children whenever they misbehaved.

Vlado attended a technical high school, and after graduating took a job at a local factory. He was active in the local communist youth programs which allowed him to travel to central Croatia to attend political school where he studied journalism. In 1973 Vlado met his future wife at a poetry reading. He was twenty-one; she was nineteen, and both shared a love of literature. After four years of dating, the couple married and soon had two boys.

Vlado Taneski

By the time he and his family returned to Kičevo in 1980, Vlado was more educated than most people in the city and factory work was beneath him. His wife had finished her law degree. He initially worked for Radio Kičevo, then advanced his career to become a journalist. He was a staff reporter for Nova Makedonija (New Macedonia), the largest daily newspaper in Macedonia, based in the capital city of Skopje.

Though his father was a loner, and he had a tumultuous relationship with his mother, Vlado moved his parents in with him and his family.

Vlado's wife later recalled,

"His mother took her younger son's abandonment very hard. Then her daughter, Trajanka, went to work in Skopje. Vlado was the only child in the household left to take care of his parents. So when I married him, we both decided to stay and live with them."

Over time, Taneski became a very talented writer. Besides his journalistic writings he also wrote poetry, short stories and several novels. As technology progressed, he remained nostalgic, longing for the old days of communism as opposed to capitalism, and preferring a typewriter and paper over computers.

Living in a small town outside of the capital and his penchant for nostalgia both took a toll on his career and Vlado was passed up for many articles. He was assigned to cover stories taking place in his own small town. With such a quiet town, this didn't leave much.

By 2003 his full-time staff position at the newspaper had been eliminated and Taneski only worked as a freelancer, selling a story whenever he could.

Though his parents lived in his home, Taneski's father spent much of his time alone at the family summer cottage several miles away, and in August of that year he hanged himself in the cabin. Just four months later his mother accidentally overdosed on sleeping pills.

Taneski's life had reached a low point, but journalistic work was suddenly about to pick up in Kičevo.

In November 2004 a sixty-one-year-old retired custodian, Mitra Simjanoska had gone missing. She lived in the same neighborhood where Taneski had spent his entire life and he covered the story for the newspaper.

Theories swirled throughout the town about Mitra's disappearance. She was known to have many lovers. Had she made a man jealous? Did she run off with someone? In January 2005, the townspeople received some answers. As a man was looking through an abandoned construction site he came across the body of a woman in a large nylon bag. She had been dumped naked into a shallow hole in the ground.

Though Mitra had been gone for two months, her body showed only a few weeks of decomposition. She had obviously been kept alive some-where. She had been raped, strangled, and her hands and feet were bound with a telephone cord.

Police were quick to find suspects. Just a month earlier in the nearby village of Malkoetz an elderly man had been robbed, raped, and murdered. The killers had tortured him by placing objects in his anus and took heated fireplace tongs to his penis. Two men in their twenties were charged with the murders.

Because the killing of the old man was similar to Mitra's death in that it involved extreme torture, the two men were charged with her murder as well. They pleaded guilty to killing the old man, but insisted they had nothing to do with the killing of Mitra Simjanoska.

In Vlado Taneski's article titled "Surgical Gloves for a Monstrous Murder" he wrote,

"In handcuffs and with searching eyes, 28-year-old Ante Risteski and his friend Igor Mirčeski, accused of a horrible double homicide in Kičevo and Malkoetz, walked into the courtroom. They stared vacantly at the ceiling and from time to time whispered, as if to them-selves: it's all over and now we'll pay for our crimes."

The two young men were tried, convicted and sentenced to life behind bars, but there were still unanswered questions. Mitra's body was found with traces of semen, but the DNA from the semen didn't match either of the men sitting in jail for the crime.

Later that year, to make ends meet, Taneski's wife took a job with the Ministry of Education in Skopje, seventy miles away. She moved to Skopje and took their youngest son with her while the eldest son went abroad to study. Taneski had spent his life with a house full of family and suddenly found himself completely alone. He took the time to start using a computer for work and often spoke of selling the two Kičevo homes, but that never happened.

In November 2007 another woman from Kičevo, Ljubica Licoska, went missing. Like Mitra, Ljubica was also a custodian, an older woman, and coincidentally lived in the same neighborhood as Taneski.

Ljubica's body was found three months later near a gas station. She had been subjected to the same types of torture. She was found wrapped in a plastic bag, bound with a telephone cord, and had been raped and strangled. Pathologists determined that the body had only been dead for a few days, but she had been missing for three months. Again, this meant that she had been kept alive somewhere and endured three months of rape and torture.

When the people of Kičevo realized the similarities between Ljubica and Mitra, rumors started to swirl that the two men who were locked up may not have been the killers.

People also pieced together similarities to an older case predating the others. Another elderly woman had gone missing in May 2003. Like Mitra and Ljubica, Gorica Pavelska was a seventy-three-year-old retired cleaner who also lived in the same neighborhood. When she went missing most people thought she had possibly gone to work in Skopje, but now there were rumors that all three cases were linked.

On February 6, 2008, Taneski's story was the top story in the Morning Herald,

 "Rumors abound. While the police are working on the case, the majority of people in Kičevo think that this

murder is related to the double homicide in Malkoetz and Kičevo, when two older citizens were killed for a very small sum of money."

Taneski also speculated that Ljubica had possibly been hit by a car and rather than the driver taking her to the hospital he had decided to kidnap and torture her.

 He reported, "The Kičevo police have not announced a suspect yet, but, according to our sources, the investigation is on its way to solving the case."

Just three months later another body was found. Zivana Temelkoska was a sixty-five-year-old custodian at a local school. Again, she was from the same neighborhood as Taneski and the other victims with the same profession. Zivana's body was found near a soccer field on top of a trash heap. Her body was placed inside a plastic bag wearing only her nightgown. She had been savagely raped, bound with a phone cord and strangled.

Zivana had five broken ribs and thirteen cuts on her skull. She had been raped with a glass bottle and several other items including a vial of aftershave, cotton balls and gauze. Like Mitra, pathologists were able to retrieve semen from her body.

Unknown body wrapped in plastic

Taneski had interviewed police, detectives, neighbors and the victims' family members. His front-page article on May 19 read,

 "The people of Kičevo live in fear after another butchered body has been found in the town. The corpse strongly resembles one discovered 20 kilometers outside Kičevo last year and there is a possibility that these monstrous murders are the work of a serial killer."

"Both women were tortured and murdered in the same fashion, which ruled out the possibility that there could have been two killers. The Ochrid serial killer murdered three people [in 2007] but his victims were all street-based money exchangers and his motive was to rob them."

"The motive of the Kičevo monster remains unclear. Both women were friends and living in the same part of town. Police have a few suspects who they are inter-rogating."

"The latest body was found in a rubbish dump. It had been tied up with a piece of phone cable with which the woman had clearly been previously strangled."

"Officials from the Ministry of Interior say that they have several suspects, all of them from Kičevo. They were interrogated and released. There is confirmation that traces from the murderer have been found on both victims, and those are now being analyzed."

Realizing they had a serial killer on their hands, police developed a psychological profile of the killer. The murders were all planned well, and the killer showed an extreme amount of control. Their profile showed that the killer was likely a strong, middle-aged male with above-average intellect. They also believed he was sexually frustrated, most likely since childhood. From the killing they knew that his sexual frustrations had grown into sadomasochism. They also believed that the killer acted alone.

Next to Zivana's body, police found an old jersey with blood traces on it. The blood type was B positive - not hers.

Police interviewed over 150 men and eventually narrowed the list of men down; their next step was to test them for DNA that could match the semen samples. One of the suspects was Vlado Taneski himself.

Vlado had known all the victims. They all knew his mother and worked as cleaners, just as his mother had. But the thing that caught police's attention were his articles published in the newspaper. Taneski seemed to have information about the killings that had not been released to the public. Specifically, he reported that the telephone cord that was used to bind Zivana was also used to strangle her. Based on his knowledge of this information, Taneski was arrested on June 20, 2008.

After his arrest, independent forensic labs confirmed that his DNA matched the semen that was found on two of the victims. They also confirmed that they found seven hairs near Ljubica's body that belonged to Taneski. The old jersey found near Zivana's body belonged to him and the green nightgown she was wearing belonged to Taneski's mother, suggesting that he dressed the victims as his mother before raping and killing them. When police searched his house and summer cottage, they found some of the victims' clothing.

During more than twenty hours of interrogation, Taneski was mostly silent. The questions he did answer were mostly vague claims that he couldn't recall.

Due to lack of space Taneski was transferred to the jail in the nearby town of Tetovo and placed in a cell with three other inmates. The cell had two bunk beds and a separate bathroom. Inside the bathroom was a large white bucket.

At 2:00 a.m. on June 23, one of the cellmates alerted guards when he found Taneski on the bathroom floor. His head was in the bucket of water, and his hands were to the sides. Guards tried to revive him, but Taneski was pronounced dead.

Inside his pockets were three items: a round trip train ticket to Skopje that he had purchased before he was arrested, several pills of the anti-depressant Paxil, and a signed note that read,

 "I have a note under the pillow on my bed."

The note under his pillow was a suicide note proclaiming his innocence,

 "I have not killed the women. I am proud of my family."

The sudden death of Taneski left more questions than answers. The ability to hold one's head in a bucket long enough to drown is nearly impossible, but his body showed no defensive wounds that would

indicate he was forced into the bucket. There were also no signs of a struggle.

Bucket in prison cell

Conspiracy theories of the case spread throughout Macedonia. Was he a victim of waterboarding? Were the police protecting the real killer? His military record shows his blood type was O positive, which was different to the blood found on the old jersey. Ultimately, there was no motive for the police or other cellmates to want him dead. The police wanted to see him tried in court. The only person to benefit from Taneski's death was Taneski himself by avoiding a lifetime in jail.

TRUE CRIME CASE HISTORIES

VOLUME 5

TRUE CRIME
CASE HISTORIES

VOL. 5

12 Disturbing True Crime Stories

JASON NEAL

INTRODUCTION

Those of you familiar with my previous books in this series know that I always start off with a quick word of warning: real true crime isn't for everyone. Television shows and newspaper articles often gloss over the shocking details because it may be too grisly for the average viewer or reader.

When researching these stories, I commonly use actual police reports, court documents, and first-hand descriptions. Some of the details can be disconcerting. I do my best to not leave out any of the details in my books, no matter how depraved they may be. My intent is not to shock, but to show precisely how twisted the mind of a killer can be.

That being said, if you are overly squeamish, this may not be the book for you. If you're okay with it, then let's proceed.

Volume Five of True Crime Case Histories features twelve new stories taking place over the past fifty years. As with some of my prior books, I've focused on a few stories that happened near where I've lived or stories that I remembered being in the news as they were happening. With those stories, it wasn't until I had fully researched them that I realized how macabre they really were.

In this book, you'll read about a young, intelligent man that would rather kill his entire family with a crossbow than tell his girlfriend that he had been lying to her. You'll also read of the suburban housewife that endured thirty years of an abusive relationship before smashing her husband's skull with a hammer.

There's the story of the Amish man, tormented by the threat of Hell, that killed his wife because he thought she was the devil. There's also the Roman Catholic priest that ritualistically butchered a nun, stabbed an upside-down cross into her chest, and anointed her with her own blood.

Three stories in this volume take place in Washington State, one of which is of a young girl that ran away from her Seattle home in the 1970s. For thirty years, her parents believed she was a victim of Ted Bundy, until the real killer was finally caught. In another, a sexual sadist fancied himself a werewolf while he stalked and butchered his prey in unspeakable ways.

The stories in this volume are shocking and disturbing, but they're also true. These things really do happen in the world. We may never understand why killers do what they do, but at least we can be better informed.

I am constantly looking for new stories for future books and I prefer stories that can't already be found all over the Internet. Since the last volume, several of my readers have sent me murder stories that they remembered happening in their hometowns. In many of these cases, the stories had gone largely unreported other than the original reports in local newspapers - these stories are exactly what I'm looking for. If you remember a story that happened years ago, has been forgotten, and you'd like to see it written about, please send me any details you can remember and I will do my best to research them.

Lastly, please join my mailing list for discounts, updates, and a free book. You can sign up for that at

TrueCrimeCaseHistories.com

You can also purchase paperbacks, hardcovers, and signed copies of my books directly from me at:

JasonNealBooks.com

Additional photos, videos, and documents pertaining to the cases in this volume can be found on the accompanying web page:

https://TrueCrimeCaseHistories.com/vol5/

Thank you for reading. I sincerely hope you gain some insight from this volume of True Crime Case Histories.

- Jason

CHAPTER 1
THE HOMESCHOOLERS

I t's not clear what life was like for Hana Alemu in Ethiopia, but it's hard to imagine it could have been worse than it became when the eleven-year-old was adopted by the Williams family in Sedro-Woolley, Washington.

———

Larry and Carri already had seven children of their own and wanted more, but her last pregnancy had left Carri Williams unable to bear more children. It had become a trend for homeschooling evangelical Christians in the mid-2000s to adopt needy children into their already large families. The families felt that it was a duty of their faith to rescue children that needed a good home and then homeschool them according to a conservative Christian curriculum. Other families from their Bible study group had adopted as many as eight children into their lives; Carri and Larry wanted the same.

Larry Williams worked from noon until midnight as a millwright for Boeing, while Carri stayed home to homeschool their kids. Carri had attended a women's retreat run by a ministry called Above Rubies. During the retreat, they spoke of the trend among evangelicals to adopt children from Liberia, a west African country experiencing political instability caused by multiple civil wars.

In 2008, the Williamses contacted Adoption Advocates International (AAI), a secular adoption agency based in Port Angeles, Washington. AAI was run by a woman named Merrily Ripley who had twenty children; three biological and seventeen adopted. Merrily informed Carri that there were two orphaned children in Ethiopia that needed a loving home. One child was deaf and Carri had studied American Sign Language before getting married, so it seemed like a perfect match.

To prepare for the adoption, the Williamses took a quick home-study course provided by AAI and filled out the necessary paperwork. AAI apparently missed the fact that Carri had left one section of the paperwork blank: the part about their beliefs on child discipline.

In the months leading up to the adoption, Carri and Larry saw a one-minute video clip of the children crying and begging for a good home. It was heart wrenching. Seven-year-old Immanuel was deaf and eleven-year-old Hana was slightly underweight at only 77 pounds.

Immanuel and Hana had been living in the Kidane Mehret orphanage in the Ethiopian capital city of Addis Abada. Both had been abandoned at an early age. Though they were not related, they were excited that they would soon become brother and sister living in the United States. Learning that their new parents lived in the idyllic countryside of the Pacific Northwest, Hana naively read *Little House on the Prairie* in preparation for her new, exciting life.

Hana Williams (Right photo in Ethiopia)

In the months after Hana and Immanuel's arrival in 2008, the Williams' post-adoption reports came to AAI as per the adoption agreement. According to the adoption agency, everything in the reports seemed normal and Hana had filled out to a healthier 105 pounds. However, in June 2009, the reports suddenly stopped. Although the adoption agreement stated that Carri and Larry would continue to send reports throughout the children's lives, technically they were under no legal obligation to file the reports. The adoption agency had no way of knowing the atrocities that were going on in the Williams household.

Larry and Carri Williams believed in a strict fundamentalist Christian lifestyle. In addition to homeschooling their children, almost all television and Internet access was prohibited. They believed women should never wear pants, only skirts or dresses and never swimsuits, and certainly never vote. The children were rarely seen in a public setting and only socialized with a select few like-minded families. Larry regularly preached to the children in the backyard of their rural five-acre property.

As for disciplining the children, the Williamses adhered to the teachings of a controversial book called *To Train Up A Child* by Michael and Debi Pearl. The book taught that the principles and techniques for training an animal and raising a child were the same. It instructed parents to begin spanking their children within the first few months of birth to "break their will."

In his book, Michael Pearl's argument for beating a child came straight from his interpretation of the Bible. Pearl believed that Proverbs 13:24 justified his beliefs:

 "He that spareth his rod hateth his son."

Pearl said,

 "A child properly and timely spanked is healed in the soul and restored to wholeness of spirit. A child can be turned back from the road to hell through proper spankings."

The book went into great detail of specific implements for parents to use; a wooden spoon, spatula, or the most popular weapon — a short length of small plastic plumbing tubing. This was a particularly well-liked implement because it could be easily curled up and kept available in a parent's pocket at all times. The book also taught parents to withhold food and put children under a cold outdoor garden hose as punishment.

The Pearls' book was extremely popular with fundamentalist Christian homeschoolers and, according to the author, sold almost 700,000 copies in the first seven years of its publication. The Pearls' No Greater Joy ministry generated upwards of $1.7 million tax-free dollars per year.

For the next two years, Hana's hopes of the American dream quickly washed away. Life with the Williams family was nothing like the *Little House on the Prairie* life she had envisioned.

Within months after Hana arrived in the United States, she began menstruating. This infuriated Carri, who told members of her knitting group that she had wanted to adopt "a little girl, not a half-grown woman." She complained that Hana was rebellious, telling her knitting friends, "I wouldn't wish her on anyone."

Friends and neighbors of the Williams family had noticed that Hana and Immanuel were often absent from public family outings, holidays, trips to town, or to church. On the rare occasion that they were brought to church with the family, one parishioner that knew sign language often attempted to sign with Immanuel, but Carri and Larry didn't want him communicating with anyone. One of them would quickly whisk the boy away before he had a chance to converse.

Neighbors noticed the seven children would be seen actively playing together at the front of the Williams' home, while Hana and Immanuel would be left standing alone near the driveway staring at their feet.

At home, the discipline was much worse than anyone could have imagined. Hana had Hepatitis B, which again infuriated Carri, who accused her of purposely smearing blood on the bathroom walls. Because of this, Hana was not allowed to use the bathroom in the house. She was only allowed to use a filthy outdoor portable toilet behind the barn that was only serviced twice a year.

The indoor shower was off limits too. Regardless of temperature, Hana's shower was a garden hose propped up with sticks in the front yard. Hana was often forced to use the cold makeshift shower while the other children watched from the windows of the warm house.

When Hana made any sort of complaint about the clothes that Carri had chosen for her to wear, she would lose her right to wear clothes at all, and given only a towel to wear for the day.

Hana had long braided hair that she was proud of. Her hair was the one thing she could take pride in and Carri knew it. The first spring of Hana's new life, she was told to cut the grass in the yard. When she finished, the grass was cut shorter than Carri had wanted it. As punishment, Carri shaved her head. She would later shave her head on two additional occasions.

The daily punishments had begun almost immediately after the children were adopted. Most of the time, Immanuel and Hana had no idea why they were being punished. It could have been for standing in the wrong place or getting an answer wrong on their schoolwork. They were never quite sure.

A few months after arriving in the United States, traumatized by the change of environment and daily punishments, Immanuel began wetting the bed. Carri and Larry were convinced he was doing it on purpose just to anger them. The boy was taken outside and was given a shower with the cold hose, then sent to sleep in the dark shower room.

To add to his trauma, Carri often teased him by running the plastic tubing she called her "switch" up and down his face. On one occasion, Larry hit Immanuel on the top of the head with his fist and caused blood to run down his face. That night, he was made to sleep outside and the other children were told not to sign with him.

The punishments themselves were often straight from the *To Train Up A Child* book and involved beatings with a piece of plastic tubing that Carri kept in her bra. Sometimes it was one of Larry's belts folded in half, or a long, flexible piece of glue stick. Other common forms of punishment that the Williamses adhered to from the book included denying food, denying clothes, forced outdoor sleeping, and cold outdoor showers.

The Williams' biological children were punished, too, but never to the severity of Hana and Immanuel. The adopted children were fed different meals than the biological children. While the other children had sandwiches, Hana and Immanuel would have the same sandwich, but with a glass of water poured over it. Sometimes they would get cold leftovers with unheated frozen vegetables. Almost always, the two children were forced to eat outside while the other children ate inside, regardless of the cold, rain, or snow.

Because of Hana's menstruation, Larry and Carri took the initial steps to change her official age. Carri told her knitting group that if they could get her age bumped up a few years, they could kick her out of the house sooner when she turned eighteen. When another member of the knitting group asked how the girl would survive in the outside world, Carri snipped, "It wouldn't be my problem."

In the three years that Hana lived with the Williamses, she went from sleeping alone in the barn behind the house, to being locked inside a bathroom with no light, to eventually being kept in a four-foot by two-foot closet for up to twenty-four hours at a time. Larry's recorded bible sermons and religious music played outside of the closet the entire time, depriving her of sleep.

In the afternoon of Wednesday, May 11, 2011, Carri sent Hana into the backyard as one of her daily punishments. It was a rainy spring day and the temperature was in the mid-forties. When Hana, only wearing shorts and a t-shirt, complained that she was cold, Carri commanded that she do jumping jacks in the yard to stay warm. After a few hours alone outside, the children noticed Hana's lower lip quivering. She seemed unable to control her own movements, had fallen a few times, and eventually had trouble standing up at all.

Carrie went out the back door of the home and grabbed Hana by the arm and led her to the outhouse behind the barn. She continued to fall repeatedly, which infuriated Carri. She believed Hana was only trying to create attention. Unable to get her to stand, Carri left her lying alone in the yard.

Hours later, Hana's clothes were soaked. Carri set dry clothes on the back porch and yelled at her to come back inside the house. When Hana didn't return, Carri called on her two eldest sons. She gave the boys a length of plastic tubing and told them to hit her on her bottom for not following orders. Strangely, as the boys whipped her, she started to remove her own clothing and Carri called the boys back inside. By 5:00 P.M. Hana began throwing herself down on the pavement, gravel driveway, and grass. Her knees and hands began to bloody as Carri watched from inside the warm house. When she couldn't watch anymore, Carri turned away from the window and ignored Hana for the rest of the evening.

Near midnight, the seven biological Williams children giggled as they continued to stare out the window at Hana, who had removed all of her clothing and was still uncontrollably throwing her body around in a fit. She was wallowing in the mud and pounding her own head into the ground. They watched in amusement as Hana was experiencing what's known as "paradoxical undressing." In the final stages of hypothermia, the nerves can become damaged causing irrational behavior. This final stage of hypothermia tricks the mind into thinking it's extremely hot, causing the person to remove their clothes and attempt to burrow themselves into the ground.

When Hana finally stopped moving, one of the daughters called their mother to come check on Hana. She was face-down in the yard with a mouth full of mud. Carri, upset with Hana's nudity, grabbed a bedsheet and wrapped it around Hana. She then instructed her boys to drag her into the house.

First Carri called Larry, who was driving home from work. When she hung up, she finally dialed 911.

"I think my daughter just killed herself.... She's really rebellious, and she's been outside, refusing to come in. And she's been throwing herself all around. And then she collapsed."

"Is she breathing?"

"I don't think so, no."

"How old is your daughter?"

"I don't know. We adopted her almost three years ago."

"You don't know how old she is?"

"She's somewhere between the ages of fourteen and sixteen. She was throwing herself all over the gravel, the yard, the patio. We went to bring her in. My sons tried to carry her in, and she took her clothes off. She's very passive-aggressive. I don't know how to describe it."

During the call, Carri sounded more annoyed than saddened or shocked. The 911 operator coached Carri through CPR, but it was no use. Hana was gone. When emergency crews arrived, Hana had a large lump on her forehead and she was covered in blood. Her hips, knees, elbows, and face had fresh red bloody markings from repeated whippings. She also had a stomach infection.

The postmortem examination of Hana's body revealed she was abnormally thin for just thirteen years old. At only five feet tall, she was emaciated and had gone back down to 76 pounds. She was lighter than 97% of girls her age and thinner than she was when she originally came from Ethiopia three years earlier. The official cause of death was hypothermia compounded by malnutrition and gastritis (stomach infection). It was determined that her body had been too thin to retain enough heat on the day she died.

When Child Protective Services knocked on the door of the Williams home the following day, Larry refused to let them in. Two weeks after Hana's death, the entire family were interviewed by detectives and Child Protective Services. All the children gave the same story, obviously coached by their parents: Hana was rebellious and "possessed by demons."

When Immanuel was interviewed, he told detectives, "People like Hana got spankings for lying and go into the fires of Hell." When Larry heard Immanuel give that answer, he immediately stopped the interview and took the children home.

Two months had gone by with no charges brought against the Williamses when Child Protective Services received an anonymous tip. Someone claimed that Carri didn't like her adopted children and Immanuel was being treated much like Hana. With that news, CPS worked with detectives and opened a formal investigation. All eight of the Williams children were taken into foster care. During a search of the house, police found a copy of the book *To Train Up a Child*.

Even after months in foster care, Immanuel was afraid of his foster parents and nervously apologized for every little mistake he made, even asking his foster mother why she wasn't beating him. He told his therapists of repeated nightmares and constantly worried that he would be the next to die. Immanuel was diagnosed with post-traumatic stress disorder.

That September, more than four months after Hana's death, Carri and Larry Williams were arrested on charges of homicide by abuse and first-degree manslaughter for the death of Hana, as well as first-degree assault of a child for the abuse of Immanuel.

Carri and Larry each faced a potential life sentence. Both posted bail of $150,000 each, but were given strict orders to not contact each other or any of their children — either directly or through third parties or other means. However, when Larry continued to send highlighted bible verses to the children, the prosecution believed them to be coded messages encouraging them to come to his defense. Larry Williams was arrested again and placed in a state jail where he remained for almost two years awaiting trial.

This wasn't the first time that the book by Michael and Debi Pearl, *To Train Up a Child*, had been linked to a child's death. Two other sets of fundamental Christian parents that employed tactics from the book had recently killed their adopted children: Sean Paddock and Lydia Schatz. The three deaths happened in different parts of the United States, but all were adopted, homeschooled, and beaten with a length of 1/4 inch plastic tubing, as recommended by Michael Pearl.

Seven-year-old Lydia Schatz's parents, Kevin and Elizabeth, held her down and beat her for nine hours with a piece of the tubing for pronouncing the word "pulled" incorrectly. Four-year-old Sean Paddock's mother Lynn Paddock smothered him in a blanket wrapped too tightly around him because she wanted to stop him from getting out of bed in the middle of the night. Like Hana, the abuse that eventually killed these children was just the tip of the iceberg.

At trial, Carri and Larry turned on each other. The couple sat at opposite tables in the courtroom, rarely looking each other in the eye. Larry testified that the discipline was all at the hands of Carri, while Carri testified that her discipline was at the instruction of her husband. Carri also admitted that she told her children not to talk to detectives about any of the abuse. The children, however, testified that lying was considered one of the most serious offenses in their household.

One of the Williams children, Joshua, confirmed that Hana had not been homeschooled or eaten meals with the other children for at least a year before her death. The child told the court that she would sometimes go two days without anyone speaking to her and none of the biological children liked her, "but it didn't matter because she was always in the closet."

Immanuel testified using sign language with the help of three interpreters. The courtroom was silent as he was asked what he thought happened to Hana. "I don't know" he signed. "She disappeared. I think maybe she's dead." He also testified that he was often beaten with a stick or plastic tubing until blood ran down his face, telling the court, "I would suffer with the pain until it eventually went away."

The biological children admitted that they were coached to tell authorities that Hana slept in the bedroom with them, when in fact she slept in a tiny locked closet. The jury was shown the closet that she slept in and were shown photos of the scars on Hana's body from repeated beatings.

Larry testified that he trusted his wife's discipline choices with the adopted children because she had done such a good job raising the other children. Carri rebutted that her husband was an equal participant in the discipline and even came up with some methods on his own, like hosing off Immanuel and locking him in the shower room after his bedwetting. She also testified that Larry was the one that installed the lock on the closet door.

During the trial, the defense attempted to argue that Hana was actually sixteen-years old rather than thirteen. If she had been sixteen at the time of her death, the homicide-by-abuse charge could not be applied as it only applies to children younger than sixteen.

Since there was no documentation of her birth from Ethiopia that proved her age either way, the trial was postponed to have Hana's body exhumed for examination. Tests on her teeth and bones, however, were inconclusive and experts couldn't confirm that she was sixteen.

The defense agreed that Larry and Carri may have been bad parents and their choices were bad, but they weren't killers and had no idea that their form of discipline would lead to the child's death.

After seven weeks of testimony, the jury didn't agree with the defense and both Larry and Carri Williams were convicted of first-degree manslaughter and first-degree assault. Carri was also found guilty of homicide by abuse and was sentenced to thirty-seven years in prison. Larry Williams was sentenced to nearly twenty-eight years and given credit for the almost two years he had been in jail awaiting trial.

CHAPTER 2
THE SUBMARINE CASE

For more than 100 years, Refshaleøen - a large industrial area in the port of Copenhagen, Denmark - was home to Burmeister & Wain, one of the world's leading diesel engine producers for large ships. The company thrived for 150 years, employing over 8,000 people until the global competitiveness of the shipping industry in the 1970s eventually caused the company to collapse.

Over 120 acres of dilapidated shipyard sat abandoned for the next decade or so. By the late 90s, the warehouses, with their rusted metal landscapes and cheap rents, became home to local aspiring artists and entrepreneurs.

The artificial island was only a quick ten-minute bike ride from the city center of Copenhagen. By the late 2010s, the area had grown into a vibrant, thriving hipster bastion. Over time, the starving artists were eventually pushed out by flourishing tech firms, craft breweries, and food vendors. Today, the area features many popular restaurants including Alchemist. Consistently rated one of the best restaurants in the world, it features $15 million decor and seats only forty guests for a five-hour meal at $700 a plate. The area is also home to the annual Copenhell heavy metal festival, featuring some of the largest names in heavy metal such as Ozzy Osbourne, Tool, KISS, and Iron Maiden.

One of the better-known entrepreneurs that had occupied the area was Peter Madsen, a Danish inventor, artist, and entrepreneur known to many as "Rocket Madsen." He was an eccentric, self-taught aerospace engineer who had built three submarines, several rockets, delivered a popular Ted Talk, and was working on a personal rocket designed for human travel in 2017 that he described as an, "intercontinental ballistic missile passenger ship." He was known as a charismatic dreamer that some thought of as an aspiring, small-scale Elon Musk or Richard Branson.

Peter Madsen / Kim Wall

Kim Wall was an independent journalist living in Copenhagen and thought Peter Madsen would be an excellent subject for one of her long-form articles.

Kim was exceedingly intelligent and eternally curious. To hear her friends describe the petite redhead as "a badass" was a gross under-statement. The ambitious thirty-year-old had written many articles that had taken her all over the world.

Born and raised in Sweden, Kim spent most of her adult life scouring the globe. She earned her bachelor's degree in international relations at the London School of Economics, then moved on to graduate with honors from Columbia University in New York with two master's degrees in journalism and international relations.

Kim's writings were certainly not fluff pieces. She wrote articles on foreign policy, social justice, climate change, nuclear weapons testing, gender, and pop-culture. Her stories took her all over the world, to places like Sri Lanka, North Korea, India, Australia, Haiti, Cuba, and Uganda. She believed that the best stories were not told from inside a newsroom; she needed to be in on the action. Her extensive client list included The New York Times, Harper's, BBC, The Guardian, Time, The Atlantic, Vice Magazine, Slate, The South China Post, and many others.

On the evening of August 10, 2017, Kim and her boyfriend Ole Stobbe were preparing to host their going-away party. In six days, they were planning to move from their home in Copenhagen to Beijing, China.

At 5:00 P.M. that evening, Kim received a text message from Peter Madsen inviting her to his nearby workshop for tea. She had been trying to get an interview with him for several weeks. If she wanted to get that interview before she left for Beijing, this was her last chance. She agreed and left for his nearby hangar warehouse.

Just thirty minutes later, Kim came back home. She grabbed a few things and told Ole she was going for a two-hour ride with Madsen on his Nautilus submarine and would have to miss the first few hours of their going-away party. The UC3 Nautilus was a fifty-eight-foot midget submarine that Madsen had designed and built himself.

Madsen told Kim that they could take a quick trip around the bay surrounding Copenhagen and she could interview him during the trip. She could even make it back for the last few hours of their party.

That Thursday evening, Kim left for the pier not far from their apartment where Madsen's submarine was docked. Just before 7:00 P.M., she texted Ole a photo of the Nautilus with the message, "I'm still alive btw [by the way]." As they cruised through the bay with the tower still above the water, she sent him another photo of nearby windmills. Moments later, as Ole was entertaining their guests at the waterside barbecue, he and their friends saw Kim waving from the tower of the submarine. Kim sent a final text to Ole, "Going down now! I love you!!!!!!" That was the last time they would see Kim alive.

For several weeks in 2017, an Australian filmmaker, Emma Sullivan, had been filming a documentary about Madsen and his group of engineers for Sky News. That evening, neither Sullivan nor Madsen's assistants had known anything about his meeting with Kim Wall. This seemed strange at the time, considering the close proximity they had all been in during the filming. However, in hindsight, it became clear that Madsen had purposely hidden the existence of Kim because he knew what was to come.

Kim should have returned by 10:00 P.M. that night, but there was no word from her and no sign of the submarine at the pier. The goodbye party had moved from the waterfront to a nearby bar, but when Ole returned home late that night and Kim was still not back, he was worried sick. Ole rode his bike around the island, searching for her in the dark, but found nothing. Frustrated and frightened, Ole called police just before 2:00 A.M. to report his girlfriend missing.

Peter Madsen & Kim Wall aboard the UC3 Nautilus Submarine

By dawn, the Danish Navy had issued a full-scale maritime search using two helicopters, three ships, and several private boats. There had been no distress calls issued the prior night. Finally, several hours later, the Nautilus submarine was spotted floating in the bay south of Copenhagen.

Witnesses on nearby rescue boats saw Madsen in the submarine's tower wearing his trademark military fatigues. He then disappeared inside the tower for a moment and a loud "whoosh" of air was heard coming from the sub. Seconds later, the submarine quickly started to sink and Madsen climbed out. It only took about thirty seconds for the sub to sink as he swam toward the nearby boats.

Madsen was rescued unharmed from the sinking vessel. But the question remained… where was Kim? Rescue boats brought him back to Copenhagen and dropped him at the dock. Television crews filmed him giving a thumbs-up as he stepped off the boat. Madsen told the waiting cameras,

 "I couldn't close any hatches or anything. But I guess that was pretty good because otherwise I still would have been down there."

There was no mention of Kim.

Police detained Madsen for questioning, but when he was asked of Kim's whereabouts, he looked confused. According to Madsen, he had dropped Kim off at the same pier that he had picked her up from. He said the two of them went on a quick cruise of the bay before he dropped her off, as planned, and decided to go back out in the submarine by himself.

The police didn't believe Madsen's overly vague story and suspected that he had intentionally sunk the submarine in an attempt to destroy evidence. He was arrested for preliminary involuntary manslaughter, "for having killed in an unknown way and in an unknown place Kim Isabel Fredrika Wall of Sweden sometime after Thursday 5:00 P.M."

That Saturday, Madsen was brought into a closed-door court session. When asked again about Kim, he changed his story. Madsen admitted that he lied when he said he had dropped her off at the pier. He then claimed that he was holding the submarine hatch open for her when he lost his footing and his hand slipped. The hatch fell on her head, crushing her skull and killing her instantly. He told authorities that he had panicked, pulled her body out of the hatch, and "buried her at sea."

If Madsen's story was true, police would know soon enough. Kim's body was bound to wash up ashore sooner or later, so police continued their search of the bay.

On August 21, eleven days after Kim went missing, a cyclist riding along the shoreline of Amager Island noticed something that had washed up on the shore. Upon closer inspection, the cyclist could tell it was part of a human body. It was a torso, missing the arms, legs, and head.

Using DNA from Kim's hairbrush and toothbrush, the torso was positively identified as that of Kim Wall. She had been stabbed fifteen times —fourteen of which were in and around her vagina. It was obvious that Kim's death was no accident. Prosecutors changed their charge against Madsen from involuntary manslaughter to murder and improper handling of a corpse.

Divers searched the area where the torso had been found and where the submarine had gone down. Over the course of the next month, Kim's head was located, as were both of her legs. All three were in bags with large pieces of metal to help weigh them down. They also found her orange fleece sweater, shoes, socks, and black and white skirt, along with a knife. All were packed inside another plastic bag with large pieces of lead.

Medical examiners found no fractures or wounds on Kim's skull, ruling out the possibility of her being struck on the head by the submarine hatch. It was determined that the likely cause of death was strangulation.

Despite the discovery of the dismembered body and no damage to her skull, Peter Madsen still insisted Kim had died from an accidental hit on the head. He had no explanation for the dismemberment or stab wounds.

Madsen sat in jail while detectives learned more about him and his strange proclivities. Although he was seemingly happily married, Madsen enjoyed his sexual freedom and was known for experimenting in various fetish groups.

When forensic detectives searched Madsen's computer and iPhone, they found over 140 video clips, many of which were "snuff films." Madsen had a morbid fascination of videos featuring simulated, animated, and actual death. The videos depicted women being beaten, strangled, and tortured. There were also videos of decapitation. His browser search history showed that he has searched the Internet for "beheadings" just before their ride in the submarine.

Madsen denied that any of the videos on the computer were his. He told investigators that the computers were often used by his office staff and an intern; he claimed that the videos could easily have belonged to any one of them.

When detectives interviewed Emma Sullivan, who had been filming the documentary about Madsen, she told them that in an interview just days prior to Kim's death, Madsen mentioned that he was, "worried that he might be a psychopath." He also spoke to her about his fixation of having sex on a submarine.

As the prosecution built their case against him, Madsen changed his story yet again. This time he claimed that Kim had died of accidental carbon monoxide poisoning while she was inside the sub and he was up on the deck. This new explanation was his excuse for why there was no damage to her skull. His theory was later shut down by the Danish Navy after their examination of the submarine showed no traces of carbon monoxide or CO_2.

Madsen also admitted to dismembering her and dumping the body parts in the sea. The charges against him were changed once again to murder, indecent handling of a corpse, and sexual assault without intercourse.

At trial the next January, Madsen entered a plea of not guilty. The prosecution read aloud a casual text that he wrote to his wife just moments after he killed Kim Wall.

"I am on a little adventure with Nautilus, sailing at sea by the moon, I am not diving. Kisses & hugs to the kittens."

The prosecutor queried Madsen on how he had the composure to send such a casual text after such a traumatic event on the submarine. Madsen replied:

"I know that my wife would worry. I couldn't think of much else than that there was a catastrophe on the submarine."

When asked why he decided to dismember and dump Kim's body if it was all just a tragic accident, Madsen said that he suffered a temporary "psychosis." He claimed that he dismembered her to,

"..save her family. It's something so horrible that I do not want to go into detail."

The prosecution pushed him to elaborate and Madsen told the court that it was an unbelievably insane situation which made him think of the movie Se7en, when Brad Pitt found his wife's dismembered head in a box at the end.

Eventually Madsen went into detail about the killing and how he needed to put Kim's legs into the toilet to stabilize her body as he sawed off her head. Madsen claimed,

"…it was very unpleasant and not planned."

He continued, explaining that he used a nineteen-inch sharpened screwdriver to puncture her body.

"Yes, I put some punctures in the body parts because I didn't want them to be inflated by gases. There's nothing sexual in the fact that the stab wounds were in and near her vagina. I understand why you might want to think there was, but there was nothing sexual in it for me."

Even the defense's witnesses couldn't deny his obsession with snuff films, murder, and where to hide body parts. A former "mistress" explained that he belonged to various sexual fetish clubs and had confided to her his "ideal murder" fantasy. This involved filming the murder of a woman while he and friends dismembered the body together.

She also recalled that he was kicked out of a BDSM (Bondage & Discipline / Domination & Submission / Sadism & Masochism) club for being overly creepy,

"not because he was too extreme, but because he was too passive. He seemed fascinated, but not turned on."

One witness told the court about a video that Madsen once showed her of a woman being strangled with a wire. Yet another witness testified that he had said Koge Bay would be, "a good place to dump a body because it was a busy shipping area and it would be difficult to use sonar."

The jury also heard testimony from psychiatrists that had questioned Madsen during his incarceration. During his sessions, he spoke of the dismemberment of Kim's body with no emotion.

 "What do you do when you have a big problem? You divide it into something smaller. A dead body does not deserve any special respect."

The psychiatrists agreed that Madsen had narcissistic and psychopathic traits, adding that he had,

 "a severe lack of empathy and remorse" and described him as, "extremely untrustworthy and a pathological liar."

Another witness testified that Madsen had repeatedly invited her onto the sub just two days before killing Kim. The prosecution used this information to help establish premeditation; they argued that Madsen had been actively trying to lure women to the submarine.

The prosecution also argued that Madsen showed premeditation when he brought along tools such as a nineteen-inch sharpened screwdriver and saws — tools that typically aren't needed on a submarine.

When the prosecution asked Madsen of his childhood, one of his answers was particularly bizarre: "I wanted to be a victim in a child porn film."

On March 8, 2018, Peter Madsen was found guilty of murder, indecent handling of a corpse, and sexual assault. He was sentenced to life in prison.

While in prison, on December 19, 2019, Madsen married Jenny Curpen, an eccentric Russian artist living in exile in Finland. Initially Curpen announced the marriage was part of an "art project" called "This is not the Peter we knew." She later claimed the marriage was genuine.

Emma Sullivan's documentary about Madsen, "Into the Deep," premiered at the Sundance Film Festival and was originally slated for an April 2020 release on Netflix, but the deal with Netflix has since been withdrawn.

CHAPTER 3
UNLUCKY 13

I t was a rainy Friday afternoon, April 13, 2012, when Brittany Killgore-Wrest began packing her bags. Brittany's online profile name was "13smyluckynumber," but this Friday the 13th was going to be anything but lucky.

Just three days earlier she had filed for divorce from her husband, Lance Corporal Cory Killgore. Cory had been a Marine stationed at Camp Pendleton just north of San Diego, but had recently been transferred for a tour of duty in Afghanistan, leaving Brittany alone in the small military town of Fallbrook, California.

As a teenager, Brittany had dreamed of marriage and wrote about it on her blog:

 "I want to be married. I want to love that person. But the divorce rate is so high."

She also wrote candidly of her insecurities and struggles with depression. Three years later she was married, but the marriage wasn't what she had hoped it would be. Both Brittany and Cory were only twenty when they married, but by the time they were twenty-two they mutually called it quits.

Brittany Killgore

Fallbrook was a small town that sat immediately east of the entrance to U.S. Marine Corps' Base Camp Pendleton. With a population of just 30,000 people, most of the town was comprised of military families. Brittany lived at the La Galiana de Cortez apartments in a small upstairs apartment just a short walk from the entrance to the base.

She had grown up in The Ozarks in Missouri, but her family had since moved to Pennsylvania. Once her divorce was finalized, she would have no reason to stay in the military town, so on that rainy afternoon she and her friend Channy Tal were packing boxes for her move to Pennsylvania.

That same afternoon, another of Brittany's friends, Elizabeth Hernandez, had stopped by the home of Dorothy Maraglino and Louis Perez to return a camera charger she had borrowed. In casual conversation, Elizabeth mentioned that her friend Brittany was moving away from Fallbrook. She told Dorothy that she was planning to take her to the marina in San Diego and treat her to a Hornblower dinner cruise before she left.

Dorothy was familiar with Brittany. In fact, she had a deep hatred of the girl. Although she barely knew her, Dorothy often called Brittany "the disease" or "the herpes."

Dorothy was in a polygamous open relationship with U.S. Marine Staff Sergeant Louis Perez, a sixteen-year veteran of the 3rd Marine Aircraft Wing stationed at Camp Pendleton. The couple had agreed that they were free to see other people, but despite the open relationship, Dorothy felt threatened by Brittany Killgore. Brittany was young and beautiful; Dorothy believed she was too flirty with forty-five-year-old Perez. She often asked Elizabeth why she hung out with Brittany at all and once jokingly told her, "I could get rid of her for you."

Dorothy Maraglino and Louis Perez's relationship was far from normal. The fact that their relationship was polygamous, however, may have seemed like the most "normal" part of the relationship. The two lived as "Master" and "Slave" in a twisted BDSM (Bondage & Discipline / Domination & Submission / Sadism & Masochism) relationship.

For years, Perez lived as the dominant (Master) of the household, while Dorothy lived as the submissive (Slave). Dorothy was also a "switch," meaning she was submissive to Perez, but would also be a dominant (Mistress) to her own slaves. Together, the two of them took part in their BDSM lifestyle with their live-in slave Jessica Lopez.

Each participant in the three-way relationship had their respective BDSM names; Louis Perez was "Ivan," Dorothy Maraglino was "Dee," and Jessica Lopez was "Rosalin."

Within the household, Dorothy established strict written rules including the "House Manual," "Perfect Slave Checklist," and a "Slave Contract." Dorothy (Dee) also had a contract that professed her as the sole property of Perez (Ivan). The contract, entitled "Deed to Dee," was signed in Dorothy's bloody thumbprint. The vanity license plate on Dorothy's truck read, "IVNS KTN" (Ivan's Kitten).

Dorothy Maraglino controlled everything that Jessica Lopez (Rosalin) did in life—both inside the home and out. Jessica wore a red dog collar at all times with a heart-shaped dog tag engraved with the text "Rosalin - Property of Ms. Dee" and ate her meals out of a dog bowl. Louis, however, as Dee's master, had control over both Dorothy and Jessica.

Louis Perez was a sadist. He lived to inflict pain on others. In prior relationships, he had choked his partner every time they had sex, either with his hands or with a leather belt. Occasionally he suggested having his slaves kidnapped by strangers, held prisoner, and tortured. Knives and chains were common sex toys in his relationships. Perez kept videos of himself beating women as they begged him to stop. One such video showed him beating a woman into unconsciousness.

On another occasion, Perez and Dorothy acted out an abduction fantasy where they picked up a young woman in a parking lot and took her to their "dungeon" in the basement of Dorothy's home for BDSM "play."

Later that rainy Friday at 4:38 P.M., Louis Perez knocked on the door of Brittany's apartment as she and Channy were packing boxes. It surprised Brittany to see him, considering she barely knew him, and she asked how he knew where she lived. He replied, "I asked around."

Perez explained that he had purchased two tickets for a Hornblower dinner cruise later that night and wanted to know if she'd like to go with him. It was an odd request, considering they weren't close friends. There was a twenty-three-year age difference and she knew he was in a relationship. Brittany was noticeably uneasy about the proposition and politely declined his offer, explaining that she needed to pack boxes for her move. Perez wrote down his phone number and handed it to her: "Call me if you change your mind."

When Perez left the apartment complex, he sent a text to Dorothy reading, "That wasn't successful." She replied, "Tomorrow is another day."

Just minutes later, Perez got a text message from Brittany. She wanted to know if he knew anyone that could help her with her move. Perez was quick to reply, "Party with me tonight & you'll have five guys there in the morning."

Still uncomfortable, Brittany messaged him saying that she would love having help with her move, but felt weird partying with him because she knew he was in a relationship with Dorothy. He replied, "She's ok with it, here's her phone number. Give her a call."

Brittany sent a brief text to Dorothy who immediately called her back. On speakerphone, Brittany's friend Channy heard the conversation. Dorothy encouraged her to go on the dinner cruise with Perez. She told her they'd already paid for the tickets and explained that, as she was pregnant with Perez's baby, being on a boat would probably make her seasick anyway.

After hanging up with Dorothy, Brittany told Channy that she still didn't feel entirely comfortable with it and had no interest in Perez romantically, but really liked the idea of champagne and a three-course-meal sailing on a yacht beneath the Coronado Bay Bridge.

By 6:10 P.M., Brittany had changed her mind. She sent a text to Perez agreeing to go with him, to which he quickly responded, "Be ready at 7:30."

What Brittany didn't know was that the Hornblower dinner cruise left the dock at 7:00 P.M. - and the dock was an hour away from Fallbrook. There was no chance they would make it. But that didn't matter... Perez never had tickets, nor any intention on taking her on the cruise. He had other plans.

———

Brittany borrowed two evening dresses from Channy for the dinner cruise and decided on a dark purple one with a glittery purple flower pattern. Still feeling awkward about the situation, she gave Channy the cell phone numbers of both Perez and Dorothy. Just in case.

At 6:38 P.M., Brittany messaged Elizabeth Hernandez to let her know about her date with Perez. Elizabeth was confused; she had planned on being the one to take Brittany on the dinner cruise as a gift. She had even mentioned her intentions to Perez and Dorothy earlier in the day. She also thought it was strange because she knew that Brittany barely knew Perez.

Brittany received a text at 7:31 P.M. from Perez, "I'm running late, be there in five minutes. Can you meet me at the curb?"

Brittany replied, "At the curb? It's raining, you know. I'd appreciate it if you drove into the complex."

"It's not. I don't want to miss our boat," Perez responded.

He knew there were security cameras throughout the complex and wanted to avoid them, but drove through anyway. At 7:36 P.M., surveillance cameras showed his white Ford Explorer entering the complex. One minute later he texted, "I'm here."

At 7:39 P.M. Brittany messaged another friend, Jessica Perry, that lived in her same apartment complex:

"I'm going on a dinner cruise with Louis Perez tonight. I might stop by to see you when I get back."

One minute later, the apartment security cameras showed the Explorer leaving the apartment complex with Brittany in the passenger seat.

Just ten minutes after Brittany left the apartment complex, Channy received a one-word text message from Brittany's phone. It simply read, "Help."

At approximately the same time, Perez messaged Dorothy: "Kitten?"

The message gave Channy Tal a sudden twinge of fright. She immediately replied to Brittany, "What? R U okay?" There was no reply, so she messaged again, "Brittany are U okay? I am freaking out here." Still no reply. Channy messaged one more time before she finally got a reply at 8:05 P.M., "Yes, I love this party."

Channy knew the reply was not genuine. Brittany would never have used the word "Yes" in a text message - she had always just used "Yeah."

After trying to call Brittany several times with no answer, Channy sent another message demanding her to call back, "Call me back now! I need to hear your voice."

At 8:07 P.M., Channy received another text, "In a few. hot guys." Channy was certain this wasn't Brittany and insisted that she call her immediately. At 8:09 and 8:10, Channy received two short phone calls. Both calls were only a few seconds long with loud music in the background. The calls were followed by another text message, "Its ok. music too loud."

Over the next several minutes, Channy contacted Brittany's other friends, Jessica Perry and Elizabeth Hernandez. After trying Brittany's phone with no answer, Elizabeth called Perez's girlfriend, Dorothy. Dorothy Maraglino told Elizabeth she knew nothing about a dinner cruise and hadn't spoken to Brittany at all that day. An obvious lie.

At 8:40 P.M., Jessica Perry called Perez, who answered the call. He told Jessica that he and Brittany had driven to downtown San Diego and went to The Whiskey Girl club in the Gaslamp District. He told her that Brittany had met a couple of Marines there and he'd left her there. Jessica Perry knew this couldn't possibly be true - that would have been completely out of character for Brittany. The truth was that she never made it out of Fallbrook.

Louis Perez and Dorothy Maraglino took efforts to cover their tracks. Dorothy had worked for a cell phone company in the past and knew that cell phones were traceable. She instructed Perez to drive toward downtown San Diego with Brittany's phone. During the drive, he sent text messages to her phone reading, "Where are you?" and "Your friends are calling me worried." He also messaged Dorothy asking how her night was going, to which she replied, "Just having a quiet night at home."

At 10:10 P.M., Channy tried to call Brittany one more time. When she got no response, she sent a text, "Should I just call the cops?" Channy received a text reply, "I'm ok." Perez then dumped Brittany's phone on the streets of downtown San Diego.

As he drove back to Fallbrook from San Diego, Perez called Brittany's friend Jessica Perry. Trying to establish an alibi, he told her he had been driving around the Gaslamp District looking for Brittany, but finally gave up.

Saturday morning was agonizing for Channy, Elizabeth, and Jessica Perry. There was still no word from their friend. Jessica called Dorothy and told her she knew she had lied to her. She knew that she had spoken to Brittany the previous day. Nervous, Dorothy stammered an excuse and handed the phone to Perez. He hadn't planned his alibi very well and mumbled several conflicting scenarios of what had happened the previous night.

Channy and Elizabeth went to Brittany's apartment, but there was no trace of her and they called the Sheriff's department. When the Sheriff's deputy called Perez he was clearly startled, but offered to come to Brittany's apartment to talk.

When Perez arrived at the apartment, Channy and Elizabeth were still there speaking to the deputy. Perez claimed that when he had picked Brittany up that night, she had already been drinking and was very flirty with him. Channy and Elizabeth immediately rebuffed this and let the deputy know that this was a lie. Perez claimed that he had left Brittany at a club in the Gaslamp District where she flirted with a few Marines. He said that when he couldn't find her, he texted her before he left and she replied with a text saying, "I'm okay."

The deputy's suspicion grew when he asked Perez to show him the text on his phone, but the text wasn't there. There was also the question of his white Ford Explorer parked outside; the bumper and running board of the vehicle were caked with mud. The deputy asked for his consent to a voluntary search of the vehicle and Perez agreed. Inside the vehicle was an AR-15 assault rifle which had been stolen from Camp Pendleton and was illegal in California. Perez was arrested on the weapons charge.

That Saturday afternoon, Brittany's mother, Michelle Wrest, got a phone call from her daughter's cell phone. A stranger on the other end of the phone explained that a homeless man had found her phone on the streets of San Diego and was attempting to sell it. Brittany's mother was unaware that her daughter was missing, but assumed the worst and called authorities.

On April 15, deputies began their search of the home at 317 East Fallbrook Street where Louis Perez, Dorothy Maraglino, and Jessica Lopez lived. Maraglino and Lopez stood in the front yard and watched. When police arrived the following day to continue the search, Maraglino and Lopez were gone, as was Maraglino's truck. Detectives noticed that several items that were in the house the previous day had been removed.

Law enforcement throughout Southern California were alerted to be on the lookout for Maraglino's Nissan Titan with the license plate, "IVNS KTN." Meanwhile, forensic teams were analyzing Perez's Ford Explorer. Inside his SUV police found blue latex gloves, a large piece of clear plastic sheeting with smeared blood on it, a plastic bag, and a stun baton. Brittany Killgore's DNA was found on the plastic sheeting and latex gloves. Perez's DNA was found on the strap and handle of the stun baton, while more of Brittany's DNA was found on the prongs.

The morning of April 17, Maraglino's truck was spotted in the parking lot of the Ramada Inn near the San Diego airport. According to the front desk, room 105 was registered to Dorothy Maraglino. When police knocked on the door, there was no answer, but officers could hear faint sounds. It sounded like the light cries of a woman.

When the door was forced open, they found a half-naked woman wearing only a red skirt and combat boots. She was bleeding from several deep, self-inflicted wounds on her neck and wrist. The bedsheets were soaked with blood. Several large knives and an ortho-dontic scalpel were found near the sink next to an empty bottle of Chambord liqueur. At the foot of the bed was a red dog collar with a tag that read, "Rosalin. Property of Ms. Dee." It wasn't Dorothy; it was Jessica Lopez, Dorothy's slave. Lopez was rushed to the hospital and subsequently arrested.

In the room was a clothes hanger above the vanity desk with a note clipped to it that read, "PIGS READ THIS!" Below the note were three envelopes. One was addressed to "Master Ivan," another to "My parents," and the third to a local television station. Each envelope contained a copy of a seven-page suicide note penned by Lopez.

In the suicide note, Lopez claimed it was her that killed Brittany, not Perez or Maraglino, stating, "You've got the WRONG FUCKING PERSON!" The letter claimed that Maraglino and Perez were asleep upstairs while she alone murdered Brittany. She described Brittany as a "miserable cunt" that came between Perez and Maraglino and went into detail of how she killed her.

According to Lopez, she used a Taser to knock her down, then restrained her legs and wrists before gagging her mouth. She then claimed to have tied a rope around her neck where she repeatedly applied and released pressure until she was dead. She then attempted to dismember her body with power tools, washed her body with bleach, and dumped her on the side of a road near Lake Skinner. Offi-cers were immediately dispatched to the Lake Skinner area.

Lopez's letter went on about her love for Dorothy Maraglino, her mistress. Using the hotel's surveillance cameras, police were able to see that Maraglino had been in the room when Lopez wrote the notes. Lopez took the first copy of the note to the hotel receptionist to make the copies. Maraglino left the hotel that morning and boarded a plane to Virginia.

Certain statements in the note, however, made no sense. Lopez wrote that the murder happened after 11:15 P.M. From the string of text messages, police already knew that was unlikely. Lopez also claimed that Brittany, who didn't drive, "suddenly appeared" at the house at 317 East Fallbrook Street unannounced and demanded sex from Perez.

Later that day, a maintenance worker clearing brush about a mile south of Lake Skinner found the nude body of Brittany Killgore dumped in a ditch.

The bruising on Brittany's wrists revealed that she had been bound with handcuffs. Five small marks on the left side of her face were an exact match for the pins of the stun baton. Deep postmortem wounds on her knee showed that someone had unsuccessfully attempted to dismember her body parts with a power saw.

The cartilage surrounding her trachea had been crushed. By examining the hemorrhaging in her eyes, the medical examiner could tell that pressure had been applied and released repeatedly over a long period, just as Jessica Lopez wrote in her suicide note. Ultimately, the cause of death was ligature strangulation.

As lead detective Brian Patterson drove to the spot where the body was dumped, he received a call from Dorothy Maraglino who was still on the run. Attempting to establish an alibi, she told him that she and Lopez were home that night and rented "The Adventures of Rin Tin Tin." Patterson, however, was more interested in the flaws in both Perez's and Lopez's stories. When he questioned her on the inconsistencies, she hung up.

Two days after they found the body, police searched Maraglino's house once again. This time they found the roll of plastic that Lopez mentioned in her note and a blade from a reciprocating saw.

Detectives also found several BDSM photos, videos, documents, sex toys, and bondage equipment. One document recovered was a "release of liability" form. It was a contract stating that Dorothy Maraglino agreed to voluntarily endure Louis Perez's beatings, whippings, and asphyxia, and that he held no responsibility in the case of "injuries or loss of life."

They also found a document in which Maraglino released her anger to Perez, encouraging him to "deliver justice on her behalf." The letter, riddled with strange spellings, was written by Maraglino on the day Brittany had been murdered,

 "I Dee do hereby give to Ivan all my grudges and revenge from my birth till now. I release my anger and entrust justice into Ivan's hands. I accept Ivan will decide, design, and dispense the measure of restribution he deems appropriate to my enemies, tormentors, and violators." (Signed, "Dee")

Another document read, "Please consider accepting this gift. I leave all methods of retribution to you. Please distroy them all. Rape the women. Destroy their reputation. Take their posessions. When you deem, take their last breath. I release all I carry from my rapist, abuseas, and tormentors to you. I'll join in where you direct me and allow, but I realse my own will and agenda in these matters." (Signed "Kitten")

Yet another document written by Maraglino detailed a fantasy she had of coming up behind a person and slitting their throat.

Other items found in the house included nylon rope with hairs embedded in it, duct tape, plastic bags, a rope and pulley system, a Black & Decker saber saw, and a red Skill saw.

Dorothy Maraglino was arrested on May 10, 2012, and returned to San Diego. Perez was still in custody on the weapons charge. All three suspects were charged with first-degree murder, conspiracy to commit kidnapping, kidnapping, torture, and attempted sexual battery by restraint.

With the three defendants in custody, the prosecution began their analysis of the evidence to prepare for trial. Detectives found profiles for both Perez and Maraglino on BDSM websites BMEhookups.com and TSRnetwork.com where "Ivan" described himself as "Lord and Master," and Dee as "slave, lover, confidant and partner." On another website, he wrote,

 "I am lord and master, dom and daddy of my house. My slave, Ms. Dee, is a slave to no one, but myself."

Dee's profile described herself as "an Alpha slave to Master Ivan."

Their profiles showed that they were looking for additional sex slaves and other couples to join their family: "We have a poly home in which I own two slave girls. Life is good." ("Poly" is referring to a polyamorous relationship involving multiple sexual partners, in this case one which is open to new individuals.)

Dorothy Maraglino was pregnant with Perez's baby when police arrested her. Perez requested that when the baby was born, she give custody to a friend of his named Becky Zagha. Zagha visited both Perez and Maraglino in prison regularly before the baby was born and Maraglino agreed to give custody of the baby to Zagha.

According to Maraglino, the agreement was that she would continue to live in the San Diego area and bring the child in for weekly jail visits. When the baby was born, however, Zagha took custody of the baby and moved to central California. The prison visits stopped. Maraglino tried in vain to regain custody of the child and give custody to her family on the east coast, but the courts sided with Zagha.

On one of Zagha's visits to Perez, he admitted to her that "everybody had a role to play that night, including myself." Although Perez later claimed he was referring to the cover-up, not the murder, that statement would later be used against all three of them in court.

The prosecution had a dilemma: Jessica Lopez's confession letter was an important piece of evidence, but her intention was to exonerate Perez and Maraglino. Introducing the letter into evidence was risky. They needed to establish that the letter was evidence of Lopez's guilt, but also prove that it wasn't evidence that Perez and Maraglino were innocent.

Another document that detectives seized was initially thought to be useless as it was written in some sort of code. Using a Forensic Document Examiner and the FBI Cryptanalysis Unit to decipher the code, it revealed a detailed plan to kidnap, torture, and murder a friend of Jessica Lopez.

Over 3,000 jury summons were mailed throughout San Diego county. During jury selection, potential jurors were warned of the unspeakable horrors they would hear of during testimony. During the jury selection process, many potential jurors broke down in tears and asked to be relieved of duty.

The murder trial started on September 8, 2015, and all three defendants were tried together. The prosecution was careful not to take Lopez's admission of the murder as absolute truth and never indicated who exactly was responsible for Brittany's death. Instead, they placed equal blame on each defendant.

Ultimately, it was cell phone records that were the key piece of evidence against the three of them. Cell phone data showed that Brittany did not show up at Maraglino's home unannounced, as Lopez claimed. The text messages that were sent to Brittany's friends that evening were all sent from inside Maraglino's house. Video evidence from the apartment complex also proved that Perez picked her up that evening and she never made it out of Fallbrook: she was taken straight to their home at 317 East Fallbrook Street.

During the trial, Perez took the stand in his own defense. He admitted that he tricked Brittany into believing they were going on a dinner cruise. He also admitted that he took her cell phone to downtown San Diego and dumped it. He denied, however, the accusation that he dumped the phone to give Maraglino and Lopez more time to clean up the crime scene.

Each defendant eventually turned on the other. Jessica Lopez claimed she was just playing the role of the obedient slave and her only crime was writing the suicide/confession letter to protect her master and mistress. Dorothy Maraglino claimed that because she was pregnant, she had put all of her BDSM activities on hold. She claimed that she only helped cover up the crime and that Lopez was the sole killer. Perez also blamed Lopez, citing the confession letter. He argued that he only helped with the cover-up.

The trial lasted six weeks and the jury deliberated for three days. Eventually the jury found Dorothy Maraglino, Louis Perez, and Jessica Lopez each guilty of first-degree murder, torture, and kidnapping. Perez and Maraglino were also found guilty of conspiracy to commit kidnapping.

The death penalty was initially considered, but later ruled out. All three received two life sentences in California state prison without the possibility of parole.

Dorothy Maraglino writes on prisonwriters.com of her complaints of the California prison system, bemoaning her bunkmate's body odor, the bad food, and her suicide attempts. Maybe she should have thought about what prison might be like before she snuffed out the life of an innocent girl. If you'd like to read her rants, a link is provided in the online appendix at the end of this book.

Years later, the house at 317 East Fallbrook Street fell into foreclosure. It later sold to a couple in their thirties for $212,000 who had no idea that there had been a savage murder in the house. Unfortunately, there was nothing they could do once they found out and kept the house despite its brutal history.

CHAPTER 4
DIVINE JUSTICE

The 1970s were a scary time in the Pacific Northwest - especially if you were a young, cute, teenage girl. It seemed that every month there was news of another young girl that had gone missing.

In January 1970, seventeen-year-old Patricia Garrison was murdered as she drove home from her part-time job at SeaFirst Bank in Olympia, Washington. The killer had cut her scalp twenty times with a knife and stabbed her three times in the chest, once in the back of her shoulder, and eight more times on her arms and legs. He then dumped her in front of St. Peter's Hospital, where she clung to life for thirty-two hours before succumbing to her wounds.

Eight months later, three children were playing in a remote wooded area just north of Olympia when they discovered a human skull. The kids kept it as a secret for a day at their clubhouse before telling the police. Near where they found the skull, Thurston county deputies uncovered a shallow grave that had been scavenged by animals. In addition to more bones, they found a piece of scalp with long dark blonde hair, a pair of blue jeans, white sneakers, and a polka-dot swimsuit.

Neighboring Pierce county officials suspected right away that it was the body of a missing thirteen-year-old, Laura Lea Burbank. Laura had been on her way to a pet shop when she had disappeared two months earlier. Detectives already had a suspect — an employee of the pet shop, David Fisher, who had promised to show her some baby raccoons.

Fisher was known to have a predilection for young girls and his wife had found a pair of young girl's underwear in their home. Police quickly arrested Fisher and he was later convicted and sentenced.

Just a few months later, another young Olympia girl, fifteen-year-old Valerie Goode, was shot to death by a stranger in her own home. Over the next several years, many more girls disappeared and were later found butchered.

Some, like nineteen-year-old Debbie Potter who was killed while leaving her job as a waitress at the China Clipper restaurant, were never solved. Several more in the Olympia area - like Lynda Healy, Donna Manson, Susan Rancourt, and Roberta Parks - were later confirmed to be victims of the notorious Ted Bundy.

Though she was only fourteen years-old, Kathy Devine was struggling with the reality of becoming a young adult. She had fought with her young boyfriend and naively assumed that the end of the relationship was also the end of the world. She had cousins that lived in Portland, Oregon, and decided to run away from home. Her plan was to hitch-hike from her home on Aurora Avenue North, Seattle, and make her way down to Oregon to stay with her cousins for a while. On November 25, 1973, Kathy packed a small bag and left her mother a note, ending it with, "P.S. Don't worry mom, I'll be back."

Kathy's mother reported her daughter missing to Seattle police immediately after she left, but runaways were common in the seventies. The police informed her that young girls usually come home on their own after a few days and it would be best if she just wait it out.

Less than two weeks later, a young couple were cleaning the campground at Camp Margaret McKenney park just south of Olympia. At the edge of a clearing they found the partially clad body of a young girl. Her clothes had been cut with a knife. When police arrived, they found the young girl face-down in the rain. She had been strangled, sodomized, and her throat had been slit. The wound at her throat had been disturbed by animals and the stage of decomposition told medical examiners that she had been there for at least a week. The lack of blood at the scene indicated that the location was a body dump; she had been killed elsewhere.

There was no wallet or purse found at the scene and nothing to identify who the girl was other than the clothes she was wearing. On her body, detectives found a suede coat with a fake fur trim, a white blouse that had been cut open, and dark blue denim jeans that had been cut up the backside. The jeans had a dragon patch on the left rear pocket. She was wearing one brown "waffle stomper" boot, but the other boot was missing. On her ears were a pair of gold cross earrings, and on her fingers she wore a Florentine friendship ring and a blue-green zircon ring.

The location of the campground was very remote. It was more than five miles from Interstate 5 and about fifteen miles south of downtown Olympia, off a rarely traveled side-road flanked with a dense fir and pine forest. Thurston county police assumed the killer must have known the area as it wasn't the type of place a person would just randomly happen upon.

When police showed the items of clothing on the nightly news the following evening, Kathy's older sister Sherrie recognized the dragon patch right away. She knew the family's worst nightmare had come true. Dental records confirmed that the dead girl was Kathy Devine.

Thurston county detectives worked together with Seattle police to attempt to retrace Kathy's steps as she left Seattle. One of Kathy's friends told police they saw her getting into a truck in Seattle near her home, while another friend claimed to have seen her with her boyfriend a few days after she went missing. The first step for investigators was to talk to the ex-boyfriend.

Since he was underage, Seattle police spoke to the parents of Kathy's ex-boyfriend and his parents allowed them to interview the boy. He confirmed that he and Kathy had broken up on November 25, but that this was the last time he had talked to her. Police searched his home and he agreed to take a polygraph. He passed the polygraph and a search of the home provided no clues. The young boy was cleared.

When the news of Kathy's death was released to the public, tips came in from all over the state. One tip in particular seemed odd: a neighbor of the Devine family claimed that he had witnessed Kathy's murder, but when police asked him for more details, he remained silent. With a search warrant in hand, detectives searched the man's home. In the man's house they found several newspaper clippings about the murder. They also found a knife covered in blood which was approximately the same size as the knife that would have been used to slice Kathy's throat. The blood, however, proved to be animal blood, and the man was cleared as a suspect. He was just a bizarre man fixated on the case.

Another tip unfortunately went unnoticed. Police received a call from someone that worked at Restover Truck Stop south of Olympia. The man said that he had suspected a co-worker was stealing from him and looked in the back of his pickup truck. The man claimed that he looked under a tarp in the back of his truck and saw a sleeping bag covered with blood, as well as a small single waffle stomper boot. The following day, the truck was completely and mysteriously burned in a fire. Sadly, the tip was not followed up on at the time.

Detectives were left with only a few clues: the clothes she was wearing and DNA that remained from a vaginal swab. Unfortunately, in 1970 the use of DNA as a crime-solving tool was more than a decade away.

Days turned to months and months stretched into years, but there were no new clues. Although the case was going cold, the Thurston county detectives kept the file open. Other young girls were still dying in the area.

In the years that followed, the world became aware of one of the most notorious serial killers in history — Ted Bundy. By 1975 the sociopath had kidnapped, raped, and brutally murdered numerous young women in the same area that Kathy was killed. Bundy's prey were almost always a certain type of girl; young, with long, straight hair parted in the middle. Kathy fit that description to a T.

After his arrest and conviction, Ted Bundy eventually confessed to thirty murders, many of which happened in the same area around Olympia. It was widely believed that Kathy was another one of his victims.

With days left before he was to be electrocuted, Thurston county detectives visited Ted Bundy in prison. With nothing left to lose, they hoped that he might confess to the murder of Kathy Devine and put an end to the mystery. However, they were surprised by his answer. He flatly denied it.

Though many still believed that Bundy did it, detectives knew better. Although Kathy was a similar age and the murder happened in the same area of the country as Bundy's killings, it didn't fit his style. Bundy often beheaded his victims, but Kathy was not beheaded. Also, Kathy was last seen getting into a truck, whereas Bundy usually drove a Volkswagen Bug and used a sling or a crutch to make himself seem helpless.

Kathy's family, however, spent the next twenty-nine years after her death believing that Ted Bundy had killed their daughter and had gone to his grave with the secret.

By 2002, there had been massive advances in crime fighting with the use of DNA. In 1998, the FBI had developed the Combined DNA Index System (CODIS) and made it available at a national level.

The Washington State Patrol Crime Lab was tasked with going through cold cases from the 1970s when Kathy Devine's case eventually came up. Detectives had saved the DNA from the crime scene for twenty-nine years and forensic scientists ran it through CODIS. There was a hit: William Earl Cosden Jr.

In 1966, nineteen-year-old William Cosden Jr. had just returned from an eleven-month tour in Vietnam to live with his parents in St. Mary's county, Maryland. Cosden had been injured during combat and given a medical discharge as a "highly decorated" Marine, but in hindsight he may have just had a propensity for killing.

Kathy Devine, William Cosden (1966), & William Cosden (2002)

Just months after his arrival back in the states, Cosden attended a dance in the tiny town of Leonardtown, Maryland. Cosden had his eye on a certain girl: twenty-two-year-old Helen Patricia Pilkerton. At the end of the evening, Helen made the biggest mistake of her life. She accepted a ride home from Cosden.

The following morning, two teenage girls found the lifeless body of Helen Pilkerton in a nearby creek. She had been badly beaten, stabbed, and raped with a pool cue. Cosden was quickly arrested for the crime.

The murder trial revealed what Cosden had experienced in Vietnam. The defense argued that his traumatic experiences caused him to develop "homicidal tendencies" and, because of these tendencies, "his conduct was directly and proximately traceable to his combat experience in the United States Marine Corps." Their plan was to plead insanity.

According to court documents, Cosden,

"participated in the killing of over 200 of the enemy in a single operation… In which he distinguished himself as a fighter." Military doctors noted that he, "suffered from an uncontrollable urge to shoot his fellow Marines."

Despite attempting to choke another patient, Cosden had been released from the Military hospital in Philadelphia only to return to Maryland and murder Helen Pilkerton.

The defense proved that Cosden was not guilty by reason of insanity and he was acquitted of his murder charge. He was sent to the Clifton T. Perkins State Hospital for the Criminally Insane, but within three years authorities believed he had miraculously recovered and Cosden was set free.

After his release in early 1973, Cosden and his parents moved to Washington state where his father purchased the Restover Truck Stop just south of Olympia on Interstate 5. Cosden worked for his father at the truck stop, the perfect location to prey on young girls.

Not long after his arrival in Washington state, Cosden murdered Kathy Devine. It's believed that she had hitchhiked from Seattle down Interstate 5 to the Littlerock/Maytown exit where she encountered Cosden working at his father's truck stop.

After Kathy's body was found, Cosden went completely undetected for two more years until Nov 30, 1975, when twenty-four-year-old Beverly Pearson was on her way home from work in Olympia and stopped to get gas. She often stopped at the Restover Truck Stop and was familiar with Cosden. It was a particularly cold and snowy night and, once cars left the main Interstate, the roads were extremely icy. Cosden offered to follow Beverly home that night in his truck to make sure she made it home safely, but she politely refused. She didn't live far and knew the icy roads well.

As she left the truck stop and continued her drive home, Beverly noticed Cosden's headlights behind her. He had followed her anyway. Suddenly, his headlights swerved off the road and his truck slid off into the ditch. Beverly stopped her truck and slowly reversed to see if he needed help. Cosden asked her to get behind the wheel of his truck and try to drive it out of the ditch while he pushed. That's when he made his move; Cosden struck her over the head with a large rubber mallet, pushed her into his truck, and drove off.

Still conscious, Beverly pleaded for her life, "Please don't hit me again!" She told him that she knew him and she knew his family, trying to communicate with him on a personal level.

Cosden pulled onto on an old logging road, stopped the truck, and raped her twice. Through it all, Beverly calmly kept talking to him, trying to make him understand that she was a human. She asked him personal questions and mentioned that they were neighbors. She begged for her life.

Her plan worked and Cosden eventually drove her back to her truck, sparing her life. Beverly was the stepdaughter of a police detective. As soon as she got home, she called police and reported the sexual assault. For the rape, twenty-nine-year-old Cosden was tried, convicted, and sentenced to forty-eight years in prison and was to receive extensive psychiatric treatment.

Cosden sat in prison for twenty-six years before the Washington State Patrol Crime Lab linked his DNA to Kathy Devine's murder. When confronted with the evidence against him, Cosden admitted he had sex with Kathy but claimed it was consensual and that he didn't kill her.

During the murder trial, jurors weren't allowed to hear about his past rape conviction or his prior murder trial and insanity plea. Despite this disadvantage for the prosecution, Cosden was found guilty of first-degree murder and sentenced to life in prison.

On June 23, 2015, William Earl Cosden Jr. died of a sudden heart attack while in prison.

CHAPTER 5
THE AMISH KILLER

I n the early 1990s, Rockdale Township was a tiny area in the northwest corner of Pennsylvania with only about 1,000 residents, many of which were Old Order Amish. However, in the years since the tragedy of March 18, 1993, much of the Amish community of Rockdale has moved away from the area in an attempt to escape the horrific legacy of Ed Gingerich.

Ed Gingerich was born in 1963 in Norwich, Ontario, Canada, into an Old Order Amish family. The Amish way of life was ever-changing. While they were slow to adopt modern technology, they would eventually adapt under certain circumstances.

The Amish people believed in a simplistic, uncomplicated way of life: plain clothing and traditionalist Swiss/German Anabaptist Christian beliefs. Many of the modern conveniences that most of us see as a part of everyday life were not allowed by the Amish. Hard work, family time, and face-to-face conversations were cherished. Any person that was not Amish was referred to as "English," regardless of their actual ethnicity.

As a teenage boy, Ed Gingerich worked in his father's wood shop with the simple machines that the Amish allowed themselves. Through the years, he became increasingly curious about more complicated machinery and devices that were not allowed in the Amish faith. Frustrated with the simple life, Ed eventually grew defiant and rebellious. He complained about having to constantly do mundane chores and lost any interest in going to church.

Early on it was obvious to others that Ed wasn't the same as the other Amish people in the community. Most Amish children would marry by their late teens, but when Ed had not found a match by his early twenties, Bishop Rudy Shetler - who was the leader of the community - had a solution. His niece, Katie Shetler, also had yet to marry and her faith in the Amish life was unwavering. The Bishop and members of the community believed Katie would be a good influence for the troubled young man.

Ed Gingerich

Katie saw potential in Ed. She felt sure that she could change his ways and fell deeply in love with him. Though Ed was reluctant, the Bishop pushed the couple into marriage. Many of the elders of the community didn't trust Ed, but they hesitantly approved the marriage in hopes that Katie could bring him back to a more traditional way of life.

Katie and Ed were married on December 2, 1986, in an uneventful Amish ceremony with ordinary plain clothes and no wedding rings. Ten months later, the couple had their first child, Dannie, but neither fatherhood nor married life seemed to interest Ed.

Ed's work provided him brief contact with English people from outside the Amish community. Through a man named Dave Lindsey, he learned about the fascinating world outside of his tiny perspective. Dave was a devout evangelical Christian and told Ed stories of Satan and Hell. Dave explained to Ed that if he continued to follow the Amish faith, he and his family would burn in Hell for all eternity.

Shortly after the birth of their son, Ed grew more and more lethargic and fell into a deep depression. He spoke less and less often and, when he did, it was usually to whine or berate his wife. Katie often had a hard time getting him out of bed to go to work.

Frustrated, Katie went to her uncle, Bishop Shetler, for help. Although Ed was clearly showing signs of depression, the Amish people had very little experience with mental health issues. Further complicating matters, the Amish didn't believe in the healing powers of modern medicine – instead, they were convinced that God alone had the power to heal.

Bishop Shetler presumed Ed's problems were physical and took him to Merritt Terrell, a chiropractor in nearby Cambridge Springs. Believing it would purify his blood, Mr. Terrell's "prescription" was to give him scalp massages and have him eat blackstrap molasses.

Three more years passed by. Ed and Katie had another son, Enos, and a daughter, Mary, but his depression only escalated. Eventually his anger became physical and family members noticed Katie doing her best to hide her bruises.

At work, Ed spent more time with people from outside the Amish faith and he drifted further and further away from the community. Eventually, he confided to Katie that he had doubts about the Amish faith and was worried that the whole family would be banished to Hell.

JASON NEAL

By the spring of 1992, Katie and Ed's brothers Atlee and Joe sought psychiatric help for Ed when he began to hallucinate. He told his wife he saw giant rabbits. He would howl like a wolf and spit on the ceiling, claiming there were eyes all over him, watching him. He began ranting that God and Satan were fighting for his soul; he jumped out of their second story house window and ran down the dirt road.

Though it was against the Amish way, twice the family called 911 and had him hospitalized. On one occasion, it took seven men to hold him down and hog-tie him in order to get him to the hospital, but when they untied him he flailed about, smashing medical equipment.

Eventually, Ed was diagnosed with paranoid schizophrenia and given anti-psychotic drugs to calm him. Many of the Amish townspeople just believed that Ed was paying the price for his sinful ways. God was punishing him.

Ed took the drugs but complained about the side-effects. He said they made him walk around in a stupor and he was unable to think straight. The Bishop and the elders of the community made a decision to let him stop taking the drugs, but the hallucinations and voices in his head continued.

On March 18, 1993, Ed threatened suicide, ranting that Satan was trying to steal his soul and that he thought Katie was the devil. There was a wedding planned that evening and he was upset that Katie believed he wasn't well enough to attend. Ed asked an English neighbor to take him to the chiropractor once again.

Early that evening after the chiropractor visit, Ed woke from a nap, walked into the kitchen, and punched Katie in the face in front of their six-year-old son Dannie. Katie fell to the floor and yelled for Dannie to run and get help. Dannie ran over a mile to Ed's brother's house while Ed calmly walked out to the back porch and put on his work boots. Their other children, Mary and Enos, stayed in the room to witness the horror that was to come.

224

Ed's younger brother Daniel raced to the house on horseback. When he opened the door, he saw Ed sitting on Katie's body with a look of insanity on his face. Katie's head was a mush of skull and brains on the floor. He had stomped her head into a pulp of nothingness.

Daniel claimed that he saw the devil standing next to his brother and was scared for his own life. Terrified, he ran down the road to a non-Amish neighbor's house to call 911.

Meadville police arrived at dusk to find Ed Gingerich covered in blood, walking calmly down Sturgis Road. He was carrying his daughter Mary in one arm and his son Enos was walking by his side, holding his hand. Ed was immediately taken into custody.

When police entered the house, they realized that Ed had disemboweled her while his brother ran for help. Her torso was cut from her throat to just below her navel and all of her organs had been piled to the side of her body. He had gutted her like a hunter would gut a deer. Police and EMT workers later said the mess on the floor wasn't even recognizable as human.

———

Late that night, detectives began interviewing Ed.

 Ed: "I'm just like in a tunnel."

Detective: "I want to try and understand this. Exactly what happened. Why you killed Katie."

Ed: "Because, for some reason, I felt… what is going to happen after we die? For some reason, I think we could still save her."

Detective: "No, we cannot. I've seen Katie and we cannot save her. Katie is dead and you know Katie is dead."

Ed: "Yeah, I know. Why did I kill her? I felt it was a gain."

Detective: "A gain for who?"

Ed: "A gain for us people."

Detective: "All the people?"

Ed: "Yeah, not just my religion."

Detective: "Maybe you can explain to me why you felt that you had to remove Katie's brain and work your way from the brain down. Explain that to me."

Ed: "You know how we, the human beings were made?"

Detective: "Yeah. From the top down?"

Ed: "That's right. I had it in my mind that if I worked from the top down... I'm so lost, I don't know what to say."

Detective: "We're getting away from why you felt that you had to kill Katie."

Ed: "To get rid of the devil."

Detectives interviewed Ed for more than an hour, most of which was nonsensical ramblings about how he thought Katie was the devil. Half of the time he was aware that he had killed her, but at other times he seemed to have no recollection of the night at all.

Ed Gingerich was the first Amish person to ever be charged with murder, but at trial was found, "guilty of involuntary manslaughter but mentally ill."

Had he been found guilty by reason of insanity, Gingerich could have been allowed indefinite hospitalization, but the conviction only carried a maximum of five years. Ed served his sentence in the State Correctional Institution in Mercer, Pennsylvania, and he was given credit for the time he had already served awaiting trial.

After serving the full five-year sentence, thirty-four-year-old Gingerich was free. Because he was not found to be insane, his ongoing treatment was his own responsibility. Almost sixty members of the Brownhill Amish community signed a petition requesting his permanent commitment to a mental hospital, but their pleas fell on deaf ears.

 "We like Ed Gingerich but absolutely don't trust him and are seriously afraid of him."

While the Brownhill Amish community wanted to see him in a mental institution, other Amish communities were happy to see him released and welcomed him, thinking they could help him. They believed he was sorry for the things he had done and required forgiveness to repent his sins. After his release, Ed was accepted into an Amish mental health facility in Michigan. However, after an episode where he had stopped taking his medication, he was again moved to a psychiatric unit in Indiana where he could receive constant supervision.

Throughout the years, Ed desperately wanted to reconcile with his children and family. It was all he thought about. In 2007, he returned to Crawford county and rented a house near the Brownhill Amish community.

Still diligently taking his meds and seeing a psychiatrist and caseworker regularly, Ed reconciled with his two brothers and his two sons. Mary, however, lived with her grandparents and was forbidden from seeing her father.

Word eventually got around to the Brownhill community of Ed's reconciliation, which resulted in the "shunning" of his sons who had become teenagers. Shunning is a decision made by the church to exclude a person and cease interaction for not following the rules set by the church.

Though reconciled with his sons, Ed was desperate to reconcile with his daughter Mary, who was now seventeen and looked very much like her mother. In April 2007, while she was riding in a buggy, Ed and his brothers abducted Mary and took her to a relative's home in the neighboring McKean county. The Brownhill community worried that

Ed plotted to kill his daughter, but after spending five days with her father, she was returned safely.

Ed was arrested for the abduction and pleaded no contest. He was sentenced to six months of probation and fined $500. The following year, Ed was arrested again when he was caught deer hunting with a rifle. His felony conviction prevented him from owning or using a firearm. Ed again pleaded guilty and served three more months in jail.

Although they loved their brother, Ed's brothers Joe and Atlee reconciled with the Brownhill community. The community would only accept them back if they stopped seeing Ed. Ed moved in with another cousin in another town, but when their English neighbors protested against a killer moving into their area, he was again asked to leave.

With nowhere left to turn, Ed moved in with the attorney that represented him at trial, George Schroeck. George and his wife Stephanie lived on a farm in nearby Cambridge Springs. Although Ed worked on the farm and continued taking his anti-psychotic and anti-depressant drugs, he was still extremely depressed. The Schroecks said Ed never had an episode while living with them, but was lethargic about having no contact with his family.

On the morning of January 14, 2011, Ed Gingerich went out to the barn to feed the horses, but when he hadn't returned five hours later, Stephanie went out to check on him. Ed had hung himself from a rafter in the barn. In the dust on top of the bucket that he had kicked out from underneath himself, he wrote, "Forgive me please."

Although the Amish community had shunned Ed Gingerich in life, they forgave him in death. Bishop Rudy Shelter, Katie's uncle, preached at the funeral held at his brother Atlee's home. Amish people came from several states to attend. He lies buried next to his wife in the Grabhof Amish Cemetery.

CHAPTER 6
COLD STORAGE KILLER

A mong the popular beach towns along the Pacific coast, between Los Angeles and San Diego, lies Newport Beach. Located in the middle of Orange County, Newport Beach was known for its seven tiny manmade islands housing expensive mansions, many with their own docks and yachts as expensive as the homes. The area is protected by Balboa peninsula, a long stretch of land that encapsulates the islands and creates a natural harbor.

Although she didn't live in one of the mansions, twenty-three-year-old Denise Huber did live with her parents in an upscale neighborhood of Newport Beach. Her shoulder-length straight brown hair and striking blue eyes made her very popular with the boys. Denise first met Steve Horrocks when she worked at the Old Spaghetti Factory on the Balboa peninsula in 1987. Steve was a bartender and she was a waitress.

Though they weren't romantically involved at the time, four years later in 1991, Denise and Steve started dating. Steve still worked at the Old Spaghetti Factory and Denise had graduated from the University of California at Irvine with a degree in social sciences. The job market was tight at the time and she couldn't find a job in her field. She took another waitressing job at the Cannery Seafood restaurant and worked part-time as a cashier at The Broadway department store.

On the afternoon of June 2, 1991, Steve won two free tickets to see the singer Morrissey later that evening. The concert was being held at The Forum, a venue in Inglewood, nearly an hour north in Los Angeles county. Unfortunately Steve had to work that night, so he suggested Denise and his friend Rob Calvert go together. Denise was also good friends with Rob, so the two agreed to go to the concert together.

After the concert, Denise and Rob decided to stop for a drink at the El Paso Cantina in Long Beach. Once there, they called Steve and invited him to meet them, but he declined. He had just gotten off work and was trying to save money.

While having late-night drinks, Denise and Rob ran into an acquaintance of Denise's named Ross. Denise knew that Ross had had a crush on her for years. Ross asked Denise if he could speak to her privately outside. When Denise returned, she explained to Rob that Ross had asked her out and she'd turned him down.

Rob and Denise stayed at El Paso Cantina until they closed after 1:00 A.M., then drove toward home. Denise dropped Rob off at his home in Huntington Beach just after 2:00 A.M. and continued her drive.

The drive from Huntington Beach to Denise's home in the East Bluff neighborhood of Newport Beach ran along Highway 1, the Pacific Coast Highway. However, when her parents awoke the next morning, they realized that Denise never made it home that night.

Denise Huber

It wasn't unheard of for Denise to stay out all night. After all, she was twenty-three years old - but it was extremely out of character for her to not let her parents know.

Panicked, her parents - Dennis and Ione Huber - called Denise's friend Tammy Brown. Although Tammy had known that she had gone to the concert, she hadn't heard from her since. Tammy gathered several friends and, alongside Denise's parents, they both set out to look for her.

They had searched the whole day, but there was no sign of Denise. Just before sundown that evening, Tammy located Denise's car parked in the southbound lane along Highway 73, the Corona del Mar highway. It was just a few miles from her parents' home.

The gray 1988 Honda Accord had been abandoned. The right rear tire was flat, the windows were rolled down, and the doors were unlocked. The battery had been drained and it was evident that the headlights and emergency flashers had been on all night.

When police arrived on the scene, they found no sign of a struggle, no blood, and nothing to indicate there had been foul play. The stretch of highway was in a busy area with plenty of businesses nearby and several call boxes where she could have called for help, but didn't. Still, there was no sign of Denise.

Her keys, purse, and wallet were not found at the scene and there were no signs of tampering with the tire. The sidewall had failed and there were skid marks showing that it had indeed blown out. Everything indicated that she had pulled over and walked off of the freeway to find help. But one thing was troubling... there were no fingerprints in the car — not even her own. It was obvious that it had been wiped clean.

Despite the car being wiped down, police initially believed she had possibly run off with a boyfriend without notifying her parents. Dennis and Ione, however, knew this wasn't the case and were hit with an unescapable sense of dread. Their daughter had been taken against her will.

Although Robert Calvert, Steve Horrocks, and Ross - the young man that asked her out at the bar that night - were all initially suspects, they were all cooperative and had alibis. They were quickly eliminated.

Police were left with very few clues. They did what they could: they used helicopters to search the immediate area and trained dogs to find her scent, but were ultimately left with nothing to go on. She had simply vanished.

Denise's parents turned to the public for help. They raised $10,000 in donations to offer a reward for the return of their daughter. They placed a huge thirty-foot banner on the side of an apartment building that faced the freeway where her car was found. They were looking for any information at all from anyone that may have seen their daughter on the side of the road that night.

Giant aerial banners were pulled behind planes and they placed billboards all over the area. Tips came in, but nothing seemed to help.

Denise's parents never gave up hope. Her father's car became a rolling billboard. When he was in public and he saw a tall girl with long brown hair on the street, he would have to stop to see her face and make sure it wasn't Denise.

The story of the missing girl was run on both local news and nation-
ally, on Inside Edition and America's Most Wanted. At a loss for
options, the family accepted the help of unsolicited psychics, but
nothing helped. They even took the family dog to the scene where the
car was. According to Dennis, the dog "went crazy" and picked up her
scent. He followed the dog through a hole in the fence along the
highway and to a hotel room at the nearby Marriott Courtyard Hotel.
Police followed the lead, but this too was a dead end.

The Huber family hired a private investigator who clashed with detectives. The private investigator believed that Denise had been abducted
elsewhere and her car had been placed on the Corona del Mar Freeway
as a distraction. After all, Denise was traveling from Huntington Beach
to Newport Beach. She wouldn't have needed to go that far inland to
get home; she normally would have taken the Pacific Coast highway.

Three years went by with no additional clues. Police checked Denise's
dental records against every unidentified body that was found, but by
that point the likelihood of Denise ever being found dead or alive was
extremely slim.

Eventually, Denise's parents gave up hope and moved to North
Dakota. On the third anniversary of her disappearance, Denise's
mother told the Los Angeles Times:

 "As time goes by, I realize Denise is probably not alive.
Just to know and not have to wonder what happened
would be easier than this mystery."

Prescott, Arizona, lies halfway between the Phoenix Valley and the
mountains of Flagstaff. Its small-town, old-west feel was a welcome
respite from the scorching July heat of Phoenix. Elaine and Jack Court
were visiting the Prescott Swap Meet and looking to buy some paint
for their paint supply business when they met thirty-four-year-old
John Famalaro.

Famalaro was working as a self-employed house painter and had been selling paint at the swap meet. Famalaro told Jack and Eliane that he had much more paint to sell them and invited them to his home after the swap meet ended for the day.

When Elaine and Jack arrived at his house, they were a bit surprised. Famalaro was clearly a hoarder. Though he lived in a nice house located in the Prescott Country Club, it was cluttered with junk. From floor to ceiling, the entire house was filled with random items, deteriorating cardboard boxes, and hundreds of paint cans.

Elaine and Jack purchased the paint they needed and, as they left the property, they noticed a twenty-four-foot Ryder rental truck parked in the driveway. Weeds that had grown to waist-height around the truck made it obvious that it had been there for quite some time. Not only was it out of place parked in the driveway, but they noticed that there was a very long electrical extension cord leading from the house into the back of the truck.

Jack knew that truck rental companies didn't usually sell trucks to the public without painting over the logo on the side and asked Elaine to jot down the license plate number before she and Jack left. The couple assumed the truck was stolen and when they got back to Phoenix, notified a friend who was a Phoenix Police detective.

Jack and Elaine's assumptions were correct. When the Yavapai County Sheriff Department searched for the license plate, the truck had indeed been stolen. It was originally rented in California and never returned. The extension cord leading into the rear of the truck most likely meant that it was being used as a methamphetamine lab. Prepared for a drug raid, Sheriff's deputies paid a visit to John Famalaro's home.

When they opened the back of the Ryder truck, it looked similar to what Jack and Elaine had seen inside of the house. The entire truck was filled with paint cans and cardboard boxes. It wasn't the meth lab they were expecting, but detectives were curious to find what was at the end of the long extension cord.

Pushing aside the boxes and paint cans, the cord led to a large, fifteen-cubic-foot chest freezer at the very back of the truck. Police cut the thick masking tape that held the lid shut and opened it. Inside, they found something wrapped in large black plastic bags and a few smaller white plastic bags. All the bags seemed to be covering one large item. Initially officers assumed Famalaro was just storing a deer carcass that he had killed, but when they felt part of the black bag, they realized that what they felt was a frozen human arm.

Famalaro's Ryder Truck

As they peeled away parts of the plastic bags, they revealed the frozen body of a young woman. She was crunched into the fetal position with her hands cuffed behind her back. Her body was wrapped in black plastic bags and her head was wrapped in white plastic bags. Beneath the white plastic bags, duct tape covered her mouth and nose. The bottom of the freezer contained a frozen layer of bodily fluids. John Famalaro was immediately taken into custody and charged with first-degree murder.

Assuming the body had been frozen for some time, detectives knew that thawing it would cause rapid decomposition. In order to keep the body intact as long as possible for analysis, the entire freezer was brought to a forensics lab in Phoenix.

The body in the bags was naked except for rings on her fingers. Using a hairdryer, forensic scientists slowly defrosted her fingers first in order to get fingerprints. Slowly and carefully, they were able to get a set of perfect fingerprints before the decomposition made them unreadable. The prints were a match for Denise Huber. Further analysis showed that her skull had been shattered from blunt force trauma.

Armed with a search warrant, police searched Famalaro's home and the home of his mother, who lived next door. His mother, Anne Famalaro, owned both homes. Famalaro's mother was upset that the police were searching her homes and defiantly set up a lawn chair across the street from the homes. She spent the afternoon glaring at the police.

Inside Famalaro's house, detectives found two boxes marked "Christmas" but filled with contents that were anything but festive. The boxes contained the clothing that Denise Huber was wearing the night she went missing: her high-heels, driver's license, credit cards, lipstick, car keys, checkbook, makeup compact, purse, a set of handcuff keys, and a pair of Famalaro's jeans. Also inside one of the boxes was a Montgomery Ward department store receipt for the chest freezer. It showed that he purchased the freezer in California just days after Denise went missing.

Both her clothes and his were covered with blood. DNA later taken from Denise's bone marrow matched the blood on his jeans. Semen stains found on her clothing matched Famalaro's DNA. Denise's high heels had damage to the back side of the heels, a sign that she had been dragged from behind.

In the basement of the house they found a dungeon that Famalaro had built. Hanging in a closet was a Los Angeles County Sheriff's uniform, but Famalaro had never been a law enforcement officer. They believed he had been using the uniform to gain the trust of women before abducting them.

Also inside the home they found boxes of the same black and white plastic bags which Denise's body was wrapped in, along with a roll of duct tape. Further searches of the home produced a bloody hammer, a roofer's nail puller, and assorted guns and handcuffs. Forensic anthropologists reconstructed her shattered skull, showing that Denise had been beaten on the head with the nail puller thirty-one times. From pieces of white plastic embedded in the skull, they were able to determine that the plastic bags were over her head while she was being beaten.

John Famalaro

Detectives were troubled when they found more boxes containing women's clothes that didn't belong to Denise. They believed that this may not have been the first time and Famalaro had possibly done this before. Police brought in cadaver dogs that found a scent which lead straight to the basement. After days of excavating, however, the police found nothing.

One of the boxes marked "Christmas" had an address on it for a rented warehouse space in Laguna Hills, California, just twenty miles from Newport Beach. Detectives found that Famalaro had lived in Newport

Beach at the same time Denise went missing and was renting the warehouse space for his painting business.

When detectives entered Famalaro's former warehouse, they noticed a dark stain in the corner on the concrete floor and walls. Detectives sprayed Luminol on the floor and walls of the warehouse, a chemical agent that fluoresces when it comes into contact with the iron compound in blood. The result was positive for massive amounts of blood that matched Denise's DNA.

Prosecutors believed Famalaro posed as a Sheriff's deputy, abducted Denise when her car broke down on the Corona Del Mar freeway, and took her to his nearby Laguna Hills where he raped and bludgeoned her.

At trial, there was little doubt of Famalaro's guilt. The forensic evidence against him was undeniable. Forensic scientists testified that they found seven specimens of his sperm in Denise's body. He knew he was going down. Facing the death penalty, Famalaro's best chance was to play the sympathy card - maybe he could get life in prison rather than the death penalty.

Famalaro sobbed as the defense explained that he was a victim of mental and emotional stress brought on by his tyrannical mother and the sexual abuse he endured from his brother, a convicted child molester.

Famalaro's brother, Warren Famalaro, was a reluctant witness at the trial and testified that their mother had indeed pushed their ninety-year-old grandmother down a flight of stairs. However, he flatly denied sexually abusing his brother John. Warren told the jury that John was a frail, sickly little boy with a nervous twitch and was bullied as a child.

He went on to explain that their mother Anne bathed them until they were ten years old and paid specific attention to scrubbing their genitals, explaining that "her breathing changed... kind of escalated. It just felt like an energy surge of some kind for her."

He continued by saying that John would have extraordinary mood swings, "just powerhouse, beyond type-A, very top-end manic" and would swing to, "just barely able to breathe or keep his eyes open." He also said that when John's pregnant girlfriend left him and gave up their child for adoption, it "crushed and devastated" him. A main factor for why his girlfriend left him was John's mother, who had threatened to kill her.

Ultimately Famalaro was found guilty of first-degree murder, kidnapping, and sodomy. In September 1977, a jury of nine women and three men recommended that Famalaro be sentenced to death.

Executions in California were halted in 2019 and the last person executed was in 2006. As of the time of writing, John Famalaro currently sits on death row in San Quentin State Prison. Though capital punishment has not been abolished in California, it's likely that John Famalaro will die in prison.

CHAPTER 7
COERCIVE CONTROL

F ifteen-year-old Sally Jenny had never had a boyfriend before she met twenty-two-year-old Richard Challen. Barely old enough to call herself an adult, Sally quickly fell in love with the older boy.

Sally grew up in the 1960s in Surrey, England, just southwest of London. Her four older brothers were all in their teens when she was born and her father died when she was six, leaving her to be raised by her mother. Sally's mother didn't believe in higher-education for girls and thought it was good that she had met a man at such a young age.

Richard Challen was outgoing, energetic, and had a healthy sense of humor. As a boy, his passion for fast cars had gained him a reputation as a "petrol head." That obsession with automobiles led him to buy older cars, fix them up, and sell them for a profit. It wasn't long before he had opened his own garage, selling his cars and making a good living.

From the early years, Sally was committed to their relationship and would stop by his apartment after school to cook and clean for him. Richard, however, wasn't as committed and was still very much interested in other girls, often dating other women behind her back.

When Sally became pregnant at seventeen, Richard wasn't ready to settle down and told her, "It could be anybody's." Devastated at his response, Sally asked her older brothers to take her to London for a late-term abortion.

Later, Sally became suspicious that Richard was seeing another woman. When she questioned him about it, Richard displayed his anger by pulling her down a flight of stairs and throwing her out of the front door of his flat. From that point on, Sally thought twice about grappling with him in similar situations.

Despite everything, Sally happily stayed with Richard. He was the only man she had ever loved or even dated. In June 1979, after ten years of dating, Sally and Richard were married - but not before Richard made her sign a prenuptial agreement.

Richard worked long hours at his car dealership and, before long, they had two boys and moved into a large, beautiful home in the upscale area of Claygate, Surrey. From the outside, they seemed to be a normal, happy family.

Sally & Richard Challen

The couple often hosted dinner parties with other wealthy couples in the area. Richard was known for his sports cars, his favorite being his

Ferrari Berlinetta. Sally was known for her heavy drinking, chain smoking, and her excessive chatting. She loved to talk and gossip. However, Sally's faults wore on Richard and he began to berate and criticize her in front of their friends.

Richard liked to brag to his friends about how he would skirt the law. In 1991, he outran the police chasing him in cars and a helicopter while racing his motorcycle. Later, in 2006, he crashed his beloved Ferrari on a racetrack in Belgium. In an attempt to collect insurance money for the loss, he shipped the car back to the United Kingdom and made up a story about getting hit by a semi-truck. His plan didn't work, though, and resulted in a conviction of fraud and a one-year suspended sentence.

In addition to the public berating of Sally, friends and family really started to take notice that there were problems when Richard sent out Christmas cards. Rather than a normal family photo on the front of the cards, Richard arranged a photoshoot of himself with two nude women on the hood of his Ferrari. A similar Christmas card came the following year.

As their two boys grew into their teen years, Sally was the center of the family. Richard was either working long hours at the car dealership or off on a vacation with friends to watch Formula 1 racing. The boys recalled Richard constantly ridiculing their mother, calling her "thunder thighs." Or, when someone complimented her looks, his standard reply was, "You haven't seen her naked!"

On a trip to Los Angeles to visit one of Richard's oldest friends, the friend gave Sally a goodnight hug and kiss, just as he had done for years. Richard didn't take kindly to it. That night, he anally raped her and never spoke to the friend again.

Dinner would often be a point of contention. Had she cooked the right thing? Was it cooked properly? When Richard came home from work in the evening, the atmosphere at the family home changed. Everyone was on edge. Richard made rules for the household, whether he was there or not. The television was not to be used if he wasn't in the house. The same went for the telephones.

Richard and Sally's sex life consisted of whatever he wanted at the time; she didn't have a say in the matter. He would often tell her to go upstairs and "get ready" for him, which meant she needed to wash herself first because he claimed that she smelled. Sally became so self-conscious about it that she went to see a doctor to make sure she didn't have a problem.

Eventually, Richard didn't even try to hide his infidelities anymore. He carried several cell phones, frequented massage parlors, and hired escorts. Suspicious of him, Sally followed him to a brothel just minutes from where she was working at the time. When he exited the building, he saw Sally standing across the street and he ran. When his sons confronted him about his infidelities, he denied everything, telling them that their mother was crazy and drank too much.

When Sally took a job working for the Police Federation, Richard made a new rule: all the money that she made was to go to the running of the household. She was to buy the groceries and pay all the bills.

Eventually, Sally began to show signs of stress. She slept and ate less and less. At their dinner parties, she smoked more, drank more, and endlessly chatted. Within their circle of friends, the Challens became the couple to avoid. If they were going to be at one of the many dinner parties, other couples would cancel, wanting to avoid them.

In late 2009, when the brothel that Richard frequented was raided, it was revealed that it had been staffed with trafficked women. Sally couldn't take anymore and, in November 2009 after thirty-one years of marriage, she moved out. Sally still loved her husband despite it all, but she was a broken woman. She used the money that she had inherited to buy a small house near their family home.

Although it was a horrible life with Richard, she found that she couldn't live without him. Life with Richard was all that Sally had ever known. Over the next several months of separation, she started and cancelled divorce proceedings thirteen times. Eventually she gave up and begged him to take her back.

Richard wasn't opposed to getting back together, but if they were to reconcile, he had a set of terms that she would need to comply to. A "post-nuptial agreement." Sally would need to finalize the divorce and take only a £200,000 settlement (approximately $300,000 at the time). It was an insignificant amount compared to what she would normally have been entitled to. She would also need to agree to never speak to strangers when they went out together; he considered it rude and inconsiderate. She would also agree to stop smoking and never interrupt him when he was speaking. The demands were harsh and clearly only a ploy to get her to agree to take a much smaller settlement.

On a Saturday morning in August 2010, Sally met Richard at the family home only a few blocks from the small home that she had purchased earlier that year. Sally hadn't told any of her family, friends, or even her sons about the possibility that she and Richard may be getting back together. Their plan for the day was to clean the home and prepare to put it on the market. They were expecting to make about £1 million from the sale and had spoken of taking a long trip to Australia together to rekindle their relationship.

Despite the talk of reconciliation, Sally hadn't been herself. She laid awake the prior evening in a rage of jealousy. She had managed to get into Richard's email account and noticed that he had been chatting with a woman named Susan Wilce, who he had met through an online dating service. When Sally met Richard at the family home the next morning, it was all she could think of.

Richard said he wanted breakfast before they started cleaning that morning and suggested that Sally run to the store to get some bacon and eggs. As she left for the store, she had a feeling that Richard was trying to get rid of her. She stopped by her home and the store, then returned to the family home to make breakfast for Richard.

As she made breakfast, she had the opportunity to sneak a look at Richard's cell phone where she listened to a voicemail from Susan Wilce asking him to lunch. Her suspicions were correct. Sally made breakfast, placed it in front of Richard, and confronted him about the voicemail. Richard's reply was, "Don't question me, Sally." As he ate, she walked back to her handbag, pulled out a hammer, and struck him in the back of the head.

Sally had snapped. She had placed the hammer in her handbag when she went back to her own home minutes earlier. She beat Richard in the head with the hammer twenty times as he sat at the kitchen table. When he fell to the floor, she stuffed a dishtowel in his mouth to ensure he stopped breathing. She then tore down some old curtains from the home, wrapped his body in them, and wrote a note saying "I love you, Sally" which she laid on his body. Sally then washed the dishes and drove back home.

The next morning, after driving her son David to work, Sally drove to the southern coast of England. Beachy Head is known for its 550-foot white chalk cliffs which plunge down to the rocky coast of the English Channel below. Its massive cliffs make it one of the most popular suicide spots in the world and Sally intended to end her own life. She parked her car, walked to the edge, and called her cousin to tell her what she had done. A suicide prevention team pleaded with her for hours and eventually talked her away from the cliff.

After Sally was arrested and the forensic team had left the family home, their son David was left to scrub his father's blood splatters from the kitchen table and floor.

Ten months later at Sally Challen's trial, she looked like a completely different person. She was missing a front tooth, her hair was messy, and her fingertips were stained yellow from chain-smoking. The jury heard her police interview after she was arrested.

 "I just want to say that on Saturday when I went over there I took the hammer over there from my house. I wasn't thinking I'm gonna go there and I'm gonna kill Richard. I was thinking I'm gonna go there and there's a possibility... depending on what panned out."

"And the hammer's there and I just pick it up and I use it. I don't know why. I feel that if I can't have him, nobody else can. I don't want anyone else to have him if I can't have him."

"It all became clear that he was playing a game and something flipped inside my head and that's when I picked up the hammer and hit him over the head repeatedly. I don't know why I did it, I don't know why I had the hammer in my bag. I couldn't stop hitting him, I think it took him by surprise."

Sally pleaded guilty to manslaughter on the grounds of diminished responsibility, but not guilty to murder. The prosecution, however, saw it differently. The fact that she carried the hammer to the house just before she killed Richard showed premeditation.

The prosecution painted Sally as a woman obsessed with jealousy and suspicion. They showed that she had been hacking his emails, text messages, and voicemails. She had even counted his Viagra pills.

When questioned by the prosecution, her standard answer was "I suppose so," "I suppose I did," or "I suppose you're right." She didn't bother to put up a fight. The jury heard nothing of the verbal and mental abuse she endured during their thirty-one years of marriage.

After seven days of trial, the jury unanimously found Sally guilty of murder, not manslaughter as she had hoped. Before he issued her sentence, Judge Critchlow told her,

 "You found yourself being eaten up with jealousy at his friendships with other women. You didn't want that and, as you have said, decided that if you could not have him, nobody would. You are somebody who has killed the only man you had known and loved, and you will have to live knowing what you have done. In my judgement the appropriate sentence here is a minimum of twenty-two years imprisonment."

Sally Challen never spoke to her sons, friends, or family about the murder during her time in prison, but they all knew the way Richard treated her and his controlling abuse. They knew she had been a broken woman and had become even more so in prison.

Sally had sat in prison for eight years when her niece Dalla mentioned to her that she had found an organization called "Justice For Women." It was a feminist organization that represented women who had killed violent men as a result of domestic abuse.

In 2015, four years after her conviction, "Coercive Control" (controlling or coercive behavior in an intimate or family relationship) had become a crime in the United Kingdom. This meant that Richard's years of controlling behavior offered a glimmer of hope that her murder conviction could be reduced to manslaughter. After much persuasion, Sally wrote a letter to human rights lawyer Harriet Wistrich of Justice For Women.

 "Dear Harriet, I wrote as Dalla told me that you might be prepared to look at my case and let me know if there were any possible grounds of appeal against my conviction for murder. What I did was very wrong. I've always freely admitted that I did kill my husband Richard, but the full circumstances and history were not put before the jury."

Harriet Wistich took Sally's case and prepared for appeal. Together, they listed the abuses by Richard; the instance when he raped her in Los Angeles after his friend kissed her, the Christmas cards with topless girls, the times when he told her to "get ready" and wash up for sex, the post-nuptial agreement, his excursions to a brothel with trafficked women. The list went on and on.

Sally's friends, family, and two sons rallied around her to help with her appeal. Her lawyers argued that Richard's years of control and emotional abuse wore her down and led her to kill. They argued that

Sally suffered from an undiagnosed personality disorder at the time of the killing, which was confirmed by psychiatrists while she was in prison.

In a landmark case in the United Kingdom, Sally Challen's conviction was overturned and she was set free in April 2019. Despite all the abuse, Sally still says she loves and misses her husband very much.

CHAPTER 8
THE WEREWOLF BUTCHER

O kanogan county was the largest county in Washington state, lying at the upper-middle of the state along the Canadian border. In the center of the county was the town of Tonasket. With less than 1,000 residents, not much happened in the tiny town, let alone the nearby Aeneas Valley that stretches for miles in each direction around it.

About fifteen miles from Tonasket, Dana Davis lived in a small rural home with her four children. Though the home had no running water, no telephone, and only a generator for power, nine-year-old Penny Davis loved that it sat near the banks of Patterson Creek, where she liked to explore.

In the late afternoon of September 17, 1994, Penny had been playing along the river with her seven-year-old brother. Later that evening when the young boy came back home without his sister, Dana became worried. The boy told his mother that Penny had just walked off and didn't come back.

Dana searched the area up and down Patterson Creek for hours on horseback, but there was no sign of her. By midnight, she had lost hope of finding her daughter without help and drove the fifteen miles into town to report her missing. Penny had simply disappeared without a trace.

By morning a full-scale search was underway. Penny was a tiny girl with blonde hair, hazel eyes, and a small scar on her right knee. She had been wearing a flowery white t-shirt and purple stretch pants with bright yellow stripes. Police, firefighters, ambulance members, and sniffer dogs searched the area with local townspeople for days with no clues whatsoever.

Dana remembered that Penny had once skipped school with another girl from Tonasket, but when police checked with the other girl's family, no one had heard from her. Police initially assumed that Penny had just lost her way and they would eventually find her along the creek bed, but as the days went by and there was still no sign of her, it became clear that someone had abducted her.

Among the townspeople assisting with the search was twenty-four-year-old Jack Spillman. Spillman had dated Dana Davis off and on over the past two years and lived with the Davis family for a while. When Penny went missing, he was living about eight miles away. Although he had grown up in Tonasket, he had dropped out of high school in the ninth grade and was known to move around repeatedly, staying with whoever could lend him a room.

Police first noticed Spillman in the early morning hours on the night that Penny had gone missing. He was driving his big black Chevy pickup truck down Patterson Creek Road near the Davis's home. When asked what he was doing that night, he told police that he had heard Penny was missing and had been helping with the search.

Within a few days, Spillman had become police's prime suspect after they looked at his prior criminal record. Among his offenses were burglary, theft, assault, and malicious mischief convictions. However, what concerned detectives the most was his arrest for rape. Just one year earlier, Spillman and another local man offered a woman a ride home from a bar. Once they got her alone, his friend raped her while Spillman held her down. The woman escaped before Spillman had a chance to take his turn raping her and she reported the attack. Both men were arrested and charged, but she later dropped the charges.

Police questioned Spillman about his whereabouts when Penny went missing and he claimed he was at a house party. Detectives spoke to other attendees that confirmed he was indeed at the party, but had left for several hours around 5:00 P.M. When he returned, his clothes were covered with mud. Nothing about Spillman's story seemed to hold up, but they lacked any evidence to convict him and kept him under constant surveillance for several months.

Six months later in March 1995, two hikers alerted the Okanogan County Sheriff's Department when they found what they thought to be part of a human jawbone in McLaughlin Canyon, just twelve miles from where Penny Davis was last seen.

When detectives arrived at the remote location, they found a shallow grave. Buried just a foot below the ground was the body of a young girl. Though the level of decomposition kept the medical examiner from determining a cause of death, DNA evidence later confirmed it was the body of Penny Davis.

Her body had been eviscerated — she had been cut open from the vagina to the chest, revealing the organs inside. The body was posed nude inside the shallow grave with the legs spread. By analyzing insect activity around the body, they could tell that the grave they found her in was not the murder scene, nor her original resting place. She had been buried somewhere for at least two weeks before she was moved and re-buried in McLaughlin Canyon. They knew this because the jawbone had been found outside of the grave — the person moving the body was unaware it had fallen off. It would have taken at least two weeks of decomposition for the jawbone to have fallen away from the skull that easily.

Police had been watching Spillman in the months prior, but just before Penny's body had been found, he had moved two hours south to Wenatchee, Washington, in Douglas County. In a regrettable move, Okanogan County authorities did not alert Douglas County authorities that their prime suspect in an abduction, now murder, had moved into their county.

Jack Spillman

Police informed Dana Davis that out of over one hundred potential suspects, all had been eliminated except for Jack Spillman. Although they had no evidence to convict him, he was their primary suspect. They also told her of his criminal past and his prior rape accusation, but she still stood by him:

 "Jack is the kind of person who will walk away from an argument. That's not the kind of person that would brutally kill somebody."

In Wenatchee, when Spillman heard the news of Penny's body being found, he flew into an insane rage. He broke into the apartment of a woman that he knew lived with a young daughter. He'd had his eye on them for a while. While the family wasn't home, he broke into their house, took the young daughter's pet hamster, and mutilated it with a butcher's knife from the kitchen. Then, with the bloody hamster in his hands, he spun around in a circle, squeezing the hamster and spraying its blood all over the walls. He then took the bloody butcher's knife, stabbed it into the head of a stuffed panda bear, and left the house.

Since Spillman had moved to Wenatchee, the local police received numerous reports of local women being taunted and terrorized. The reports ranged from obscene phone calls to attempted rape. On one occasion, a woman called police and couldn't stop shaking because she was so terrified. In the middle of the night, Spillman had knocked on her front door, then ran around to the back door and knocked again. He then ran to the sides of the house and knocked all over the outside walls while she was alone in the house. When she walked outside to the side of her house, Spillman attacked her. He finally ran away when she kicked him in the groin and tore off a piece of his clothing. As Spillman ran, he called her by name and yelled, "I'll be back!"

On another occasion, as he was working as a roofer, Spillman would sit on the roof watching young girls below. One homeowner that was having their home remodeled found the family cat dismembered inside the home in a similar fashion as the hamster. It was later discovered that Spillman was responsible for that carnage as well. However, he ultimately had sadistic plans for more than just animals.

Ever since his arrival in Wenatchee, Spillman had been watching someone specific. He had his eye on fourteen-year-old Amanda "Mandy" Huffman. Amanda lived with her mother, forty-eight-year-old Rita Huffman.

Spillman first encountered Rita at the Igloo Tavern in East Wenatchee. She was walking through the bar toward a payphone when Spillman grabbed her arm and they had a brief exchange of words. It's unclear what was said, but it was obvious that something had pissed him off. He stormed out of the bar immediately afterwards without finishing his beer.

In the days after, Spillman creepily drove through the Huffman's neighborhood in his truck, watching Rita and her daughter. He sat in the bleachers at Amanda's softball games as she practiced after school. He watched both of them methodically for months before he made his move.

On the evening of April 12, 1995, Rita's adult daughter, Angie Zimmerman, had tried several times to call her mother, but got no answer. The next morning she tried again, but there was still no answer. Angie drove to her mother's house in the late morning and tried the front door, but it was locked. There was no answer when she knocked. Knowing that her mother always kept the back sliding door unlocked, she entered the home from the back.

When Angie walked in through the rear of the house, she went to her mother's bedroom to see if she was still asleep. What she found was an unimaginable bloodbath. Amanda's body was sprawled out on the bed, nude with her legs spread. A baseball bat had been shoved sixteen inches into her vagina. Like Penny, she had been sliced from her vagina up to her chest. The skin surrounding her vagina had been cut off and placed on her face. On the bedside table was a woman's breast, not Amanda's. Another was on the chest of drawers.

Angie was in shock and found herself unable to breathe. Without looking for her mother, she ran from the house and into the street screaming in terror. Unsure of what had happened, neighbors immediately called the police.

When police arrived to the scene, it was unlike anything they had ever seen. Douglas County Sheriff Dan LaRoche later told the media.

 "There's evidence of sexual mutilation, but I don't know if there's been any sexual assault. This is worse than any case we've ever had. All I can say is that there was very violent trauma. There doesn't appear to be evidence of a struggle or forced entry, but our visual search has been real brief. We just don't want to contaminate any blood or hair fibers that might be at the scene."

The body of Amanda's mother, Rita Huffman, was sprawled on the couch in the living room. Her nightgown had been ripped off and she had been cut from her vagina up to her chest. Both of her breasts had been cut off and she had thirty-one stab wounds on her chest, arms, legs, neck, and back. The skin around her vagina had been removed and shoved into her mouth.

Rita still wore a broken wristwatch which had stopped at 11:35 P.M. The detectives assumed the watch had been broken defending the knife attack and stopped at that time.

It was later determined that the removal of the breasts and skin around their vaginas was done postmortem — after they were already dead. The killer had spent hours in the home with the bodies after death. Rita died from her massive stab wounds and Amanda had died from a blow to the side of her head.

At 2:00 A.M. that morning, before the bodies had been found, Jack Spillman had been parked near a dumpster in the parking lot of a VFW hall when a police car approached him. As the officer approached Spillman he raised his hands, but at the time the officer was unaware that a murder had occurred just around the corner. Suspecting that he may be a burglar, the officer questioned him and let him go.

The next day, when detectives realized Spillman had been so close to the murder scene just hours after it occurred, they immediately took notice. Returning to the dumpster, detectives found a kitchen knife wedged in the bottom. The knife was covered in blood that matched the victims; it also matched a set of knives from the kitchen of the Huffman home.

Police then spoke to a neighbor that saw a black truck which matched the description of Spillman's parked in the nearby elementary school parking lot around 11:00 P.M. on the evening of the murder. The parking lot was in clear view of the back sliding door of the Huffman's home.

257

Jack Spillman was put under twenty-four-hour surveillance for two weeks while detectives gathered more evidence. When police watched him put more items into a dumpster near his house, they confiscated the entire dumpster and brought it back to the Sheriff's Office. Inside, they found a bloody ski mask that matched the DNA of Rita and Amanda, as well as his own. The blood of both victims was located around the mouth of the mask. Police later learned that he had drunk their blood during his rampage.

Two weeks after the murders, Jack Spillman was arrested. Police searched his home and truck and learned that he had left the gloves and clothes he was wearing during the killings on the seat of his truck. He had worn surgical gowns over his clothes during the killings and taped the gowns to his gloves and socks in hopes that he wouldn't leave any hair, fibers, or trace evidence at the scene. Fibers from the surgical gowns found at his home, however, were matched to fibers found at the scene.

While incarcerated in Washington State Penitentiary at Walla Walla, Spillman boasted of his crimes and told his cellmate Mark Miller horrifying details about the murders and his plans to become the "world's greatest serial killer."

Spillman had read of serial killers extensively and continued to read about them in the prison library. He told Miller of how he had taped the surgical gowns to his socks and gloves and said, in the future, he would shave his entire body as well so he wouldn't leave any trace evidence. He went on to explain that with future murders, he planned to remove the bed linens and burn them, or burn the whole house down if necessary.

He explained that he knocked his victims out with a baseball bat before violating and dismembering them. That explained the blunt force trauma to Amanda's skull that killed her. He told Miller that his ultimate sexual fantasy was to be anally sodomized by a large male while torturing and mutilating his young female victims. This fantasy was so intense for him that he claimed that he could bring himself to orgasm just thinking about it.

He also told of his fantasies of inserting objects into his victim's vaginas, cutting genitals and breasts, and drinking the blood of his victims, ultimately pulling out their heart during the attack and eating it.

Spillman told Miller that he thought of himself as a werewolf and that he wanted to build an elaborate labyrinth of underground caves to keep his victims alive and torture them at will.

He went on to explain that Penny Davis was not his intended target; he had wanted to abduct and kill her thirteen-year-old friend, but the girl was able to get away from him, so he took Penny instead. He threw her over his shoulder so as to not leave her footprints and eventually tied her to a tree. He was sexually aroused by torturing her, but when he stabbed her in the stomach, he was disappointed because she died almost immediately after. He went on to say that he had sex with her dead body, then placed her into Patterson Creek. When he realized she wouldn't sink, he buried her instead. He added that he exhumed the body several times and had sex with it to fulfill his necrophiliac fantasies.

Spillman's trial had been set for August 1996 and prosecutors planned to seek the death penalty, but in order to avoid the death sentence, he pleaded guilty to three counts of aggravated murder, robbery, and burglary. In April 1996, Jack Spillman received a sentence of life in prison without the possibility of parole, plus an extra 116 years.

CHAPTER 9
THE BLACK WIDOW

"The Black Widow" has been used as a moniker for numerous female killers through the years. However, when Canadian police in the tiny town of New Glasgow, Nova Scotia, notified the public that a serious potential offender was living in their midst, they were referring to eighty-year-old Melissa Ann Shepard.

In 2012, Fred Weeks was in his late seventies and spending his twilight years in a small retirement community when Millie Ann Russell (aka: Melissa Ann Shepard) knocked on his door. His conversation with the white-haired, rosy-cheeked Melissa was short and simple. She lived three doors down, had heard that he was widowed and lonely, and knew he was the same. That's all it took. Fred was instantly smitten.

Fred had lost his longtime wife just the year before and was excited to be in love again. It only took a few days before he asked Melissa to marry him. Fred called a friend who was a Justice of the Peace and the couple had an informal civil union ceremony in his living room. Afterward, they headed out for a romantic honeymoon in Newfoundland.

As Fred drove the car toward Newfoundland, his head became clouded and he couldn't think straight. Their trip involved a ferry journey and Fred thought that maybe he could rest a bit while the ferry sailed toward Newfoundland. However, by the time the ferry docked he had trouble finding his keys, needed to be reminded how to start the car, and couldn't figure out how to put the car into gear. By the following day, he couldn't put on his own shoes and needed a wheelchair.

When the couple returned to Nova Scotia, they checked into a bed-and-breakfast and Fred spent the entire night vomiting. The next morning, he fell out of bed and hit the wood floor. He needed to be hospitalized. Doctors tested his blood and found that he had ingested benzodiazepine, a tranquilizer used to treat anxiety. Melissa had been putting the drug in his coffee.

Police looked into the background of seventy-eight-year-old Millie Ann Russell and realized that they already knew her by several different names. Melissa Ann Russell was born in 1935 and, through several marriages, was known by the surnames Shepard, Stewart, Friedrich, and now Weeks. With the exception of her first marriage to Russell Shepard, all subsequent marriages ended in diabolical manipulation or death.

The many faces of Melissa Ann Shepard

Twenty-three years before meeting Fred Weeks in 1989, Melissa met forty-two-year-old Gordon Steward. Although his wife had died of cancer three years earlier, he was still grieving. Melissa was recently separated from her first husband and knew all the right things to say. Melissa and Gordon fell in love.

Gordon's family didn't think much of Melissa, though. After some digging, they realized that Melissa had been convicted of fraud more than thirty times using four different names and had served time in prison. However, Melissa convinced Gordon she had changed. That was the old Melissa. Although she wasn't yet divorced from her first husband, they flew to Las Vegas for a quick wedding and returned to Canada.

Almost immediately after the wedding, things started to fall apart. Suddenly Gordon was drinking more and more and their money supply was dwindling. When his drinking finally landed him in the hospital, doctors realized it wasn't just alcohol poisoning; there were drugs in his system, too.

In 1991, Melissa claimed that Gordon attacked her and threatened to rape her. He drove her out to a deserted logging road near Halifax. She told police that when he went behind the car to urinate, she stepped on the gas without realizing it was in reverse. She ran over her husband's head, then put it in drive and ran over him again before leaving the scene.

But her story had a huge hole. Gordon's toxicology report showed that he had enough drugs and alcohol in his system that he would have been unable to rape her, let alone drive a car. The level of drugs found in his system would have left him comatose; in fact, he would have died of an overdose had she not run over him.

Melissa was charged with the murder of her second husband, but only convicted of manslaughter and sentenced to six years in prison. Because of good behavior, she only served two of those years. The prosecution believed her motivation was monetary. After his death, Melissa was entitled to Gordon's pension.

When Melissa was paroled in 1994, she manipulated the public by passing herself off as a survivor of domestic abuse. Her new persona became a career for her and she was the focus of a documentary about abused women produced by the National Film Board, *When Women Kill*. She traveled throughout eastern Canada for speaking engagements, but the public eventually saw through her ruse. She knew it was time to start a new life, packed her bags, and headed for Florida.

Melissa met Robert Friedrich at a Florida Christian retreat in 2001. Like Gordon, Robert was grieving the loss of his wife of fifty-three years. Melissa believed that the Holy Spirit told her that he would be her next husband. Sure enough, just three days after meeting him, they were engaged to be married.

Robert's family protested the engagement, but he argued that he was getting older and didn't have much time left. Within a month they were married and set off on a five-month honeymoon, traveling throughout the United States. The honeymoon ended with an elaborate Caribbean cruise. By the time they returned to Robert's modest Florida trailer home, most of his $250,000 life savings had been depleted.

Within months of their return to Florida, Robert's sons living in Canada noticed a difference in their father. He began to have fainting spells and soon needed a walker. Several times he fell and required hospitalization. However, when his sons spoke to him on the phone and noticed his speech was often slurred, they grew suspicious and thought he was possibly being drugged.

The three brothers contacted an elder abuse agency in Florida that visited Robert and Melissa in their home. When the agency suggested that Robert should have twenty-four hour a day in-home nursing care or be admitted to a nursing home, Melissa flew into a rage.

She threatened to sue the elder abuse agency and left a rant on Robert's son's answering machine.

 "Hello Bob, this is Melissa Friedrich calling. I have something to share with you this morning. Your father and I are going to see a lawyer. We've made an appointment. Your father is going to change his will. He's going to leave all the money to me except for the portion he had set aside for you and your two brothers. And that portion now is going to go to the Christian retreat. And you guys are getting nothing! A big fat zero! So try that on for size and have a nice day!"

In mid-December 2002, after just fourteen months of marriage, Robert mysteriously died of cardiac arrest. Melissa quickly had his body cremated and collected $100,000 in insurance money. She was also awarded his home, which she promptly sold. His family were left with a partial insurance policy.

Robert's family believed she had intentionally caused their father to overdose on a prescription drug that was not prescribed to him. Though they filed a criminal complaint against her, she was never charged with a crime in that case.

Despite her reputation in Nova Scotia, Melissa moved back to Canada in early 2004. However, by November of that year police realized that she had been receiving government funds and benefits using two different social insurance numbers. When police showed up to arrest her, she had already fled back to Florida.

Back in Florida, Melissa joined a dating website where she struck up a relationship with Alex Strategos. On their first face-to-face meeting, Alex and Melissa went to a nice romantic dinner. After coming back to his condo, Melissa didn't waste any time. They slept together that first night, but when he woke in the middle of the night to use the bathroom, his vision was blurry and he felt dizzy.

Over the next two months, Alex was hospitalized eight times. Like the men before him, Alex's family took notice of his quickly faltering health and his dwindling bank account. When he was admitted to the hospital and tests showed that he had tranquilizers in his system, Alex soon required a wheelchair and was admitted to a nursing home. The family knew she was poisoning him.

While he was in a drug-induced stupor, Melissa had him sign power of attorney over to her. She depleted his bank accounts and was in the process of selling his condo when his family alerted police.

Alex later said,

 "She's a nice woman, she treated me alright until she started giving me drugs."

Melissa was charged with forgery, grand theft, and using a forged document. She had been feeding him benzodiazepine in his ice cream. She pleaded guilty and was sentenced to five years in prison. After her prison sentence, she returned to Nova Scotia in 2012 using the name Millie Ann Russell.

This brings us back to the earlier story of her fourth husband, Fred Weeks, who she met by knocking on the door of his retirement home. Fred survived their fateful honeymoon trip to Newfoundland and Melissa was arrested yet again.

Police found an enormous amount of lorazepam, temazepam, and several other tranquilizer drugs in her belongings. The prescriptions were from five different doctors and she had used several different identities to obtain them.

Melissa was charged with attempted murder, but was only convicted of a lesser charge of "administering a noxious substance." She was released from prison at the age of eighty after serving only two years, nine months, and ten days. The conditions of her release were set: she was barred from using the Internet or any device capable of accessing the Internet, must report any relationship with a man and allow police to inform that man of her past, and she must allow police to photograph her if she changed her appearance.

Upon her release, police issued a press release advising citizens of Halifax that "a high risk offender is residing in our community."

Within a month of her release, Melissa Ann Shepard was arrested again for using a computer to access the Internet in a public library, violating the terms of her release.

CHAPTER 10
THE CROSSBOW KILLER

Scarborough is a large, beautiful area on the northern edges of Toronto, Canada. It was a suburb known for its diverse cultures and the stunning bluffs overlooking Lake Ontario.

Brett Ryan led a nice life in Scarborough, living with his parents and three brothers. In high school he was popular, athletic, and a hit with the girls with his spiked and gelled hair.

After graduating high school in 1997, Brett attended University of Toronto and did well academically. However, by his fourth year of college he had gone through two break-ups that hit him hard. His studies suffered and he dropped out in 2003, before he was able to graduate. After taking a year off from school, he re-enrolled in 2005, but again failed to graduate.

The next summer, Brett took a part-time job as a house painter while his friends graduated and got jobs in their fields. Though he had failed academically, he still planned for the future and did his best to be a credit to society. He volunteered his time with SickKids, a local charity, and coached Little League. By the end of summer, his part-time painting job had become full-time.

Despite having a shoestring budget with his painting job, Brett had extremely expensive taste. He liked to party with his friends, drove a nice car, and spent exorbitant amounts of money on trendy clothes. Versace, Dolce & Gabbana, Gucci, and Prada were his mainstays. He liked to live like he had money, but it was all borrowed. By his mid-twenties, Brett had over $60,000 in credit card debt and no savings to speak of.

It was all good, though: Brett had a plan. On the afternoon of October 20, 2007, twenty-six-year-old Brett Ryan walked into the Canadian International Bank of Commerce, not far from his home, with a bundle of papers in his hands. His arm was in a sling and his face was wrapped in hospital bandages. Without saying a word, he handed the teller a note. The note was concise and to the point:

 "Stay calm. Have gun. Withdraw $4,000, large bills. No, no games. 60 seconds. Go."

Though he only walked out the door with $1,115, it was exhilarating for him and he wanted more. A few weeks later, he robbed another bank. Then on Christmas Eve, another. He was hooked.

Brett Ryan

Knowing the police were looking for a man with an arm sling and bandages on his face, Brett decided to up his game. He posed as an old man with a very realistic long beard, glasses, and a Gilligan-style bucket hat. He walked with a limp. Again, he would simply hand the teller a note asking for a few thousand dollars and walk out of the bank with cash in his hand. The media dubbed him "The Bearded Bandit."

From October 2007 to June 2008, Brett made off with approximately $54,000, even robbing his own branch. Police were able to get a fingerprint off of one of the notes he passed to a teller, but Brett had never been arrested and his fingerprints weren't in any of the police databases.

At one point, police had twenty-five officers watching various local banks. Eventually police caught a break and spotted his truck leaving the scene of a robbery. Detectives followed Brett for two weeks before making a move on him.

On June 20, 2008, police knew who they were looking for and followed Brett from his home as he drove toward the bank. They watched the twenty-eight-year-old get into his car at his home, but when the car reached the bank, what appeared to be an old man exited.

Not knowing he was followed, Brett limped into the bank. As he approached the teller window, he paused for a second and turned around. Maybe he had second thoughts, or maybe he knew he was being followed, but police were waiting for him and he was arrested.

Brett pleaded guilty to all eight counts of robbery and an additional eight counts of using a disguise with intent to commit an indictable offense. He seemed genuinely remorseful for his crimes and was intent on turning his life around. Many of his family and friends wrote letters explaining to the judge that with this one exception, Brett had always been a good person and volunteered much of his time. With no prior police record, a sympathetic judge sentenced him to prison for three years and nine months.

Brett's mother, father, and three brothers rallied behind him, supporting him emotionally while he was in prison. While incarcerated, Brett was a model prisoner and was determined to get his life back on track. After only a year in prison, Brett was granted parole in April 2010.

Upon his release from prison, Brett moved back in with his family. They were forgiving and supporting; Brett was appreciative. His creditors, however, were not as supportive. The money he had stolen had not gone to paying his considerable debt and he filed for bankruptcy.

With his felony conviction, he had some trouble finding work. All it took was a quick google search of his name for a prospective employer to find out about his past. Even with his house-painting business, clients understandably didn't want him inside their homes. Eventually Brett got a job as a server at a downtown restaurant.

In the winter of 2010, Brett met Kristen Baxter on a blind date set up by a mutual friend. Kristen's life was very different from Brett's and everything he wanted his to be. She had a good job as a physiotherapist and owned a nice condo overlooking the waterfront. She enjoyed traveling and exercise.

Kristen knew that Brett had been the Bearded Bandit, but it didn't matter. They were in love and, by January 2013, he moved in with her in her high-rise condo.

For a brief time, life was bliss for the young couple and Brett proposed to Kristen with a small princess-cut diamond ring. She accepted. Brett had enrolled again at the University of Toronto and was actively looking for work in the technology field.

Brett & Kristen

A year after he moved in with Kristen, Brett's father died. Although Brett had had some trouble in his life, his mother Susan trusted him and made him executor of his father's estate. Brett spent much of his time over the following months with her. He performed tasks around the home and took care of the family finances, just as his father had done for years. Though his mother paid him for his work, his financial situation was still falling apart and, in 2015, one semester short of graduation, he dropped out of school again. This time, however, he didn't tell his fiancée or family. Instead, he told them he had graduated.

Brett still looked for work and things began looking up in the spring of 2016, when he was hired by a Toronto tech firm. Brett was finally on his way to earning a decent wage with a legitimate company. Kristen, Brett, and his family celebrated his new job and his recent graduation, but just days before he was to start work, his new employer googled his name. There was no way they were going to hire the Bearded Bandit. The tech firm let him go before he even started.

Brett was devastated and couldn't bring himself to tell Kristen, his mother, or his brothers. He went on with his life as if he had taken the job. Every morning he prepared for work, kissed Kristen goodbye, and got on the subway. In the evening he would arrive home to tell Kristen about his day at work, but it was all a lie. He had literally been riding the subway back and forth all day.

By that summer, Brett's stress mounted. Their wedding was just around the corner in mid-September. The ceremony was to be held at the Ancaster Mill, a bucolic event space along a bustling brook serving farm-to-table entrées at $100 a plate. Brett had a weekend bachelor party planned with friends at Mont Tremblant, a beautiful mountain resort town near Montreal. Kristen and Brett had also been looking at houses to buy, as the condo was a bit small for them. The obvious problem was that Brett's bank account was practically non-existent.

Susan Ryan was proud of her young son. As far as she knew, he had finally gotten a college degree, had a good job, and within a month would wed a beautiful, successful woman. She was more than happy to help with his finances, but when Brett finally told his mother the truth and asked for more money, the support turned to anger.

When Brett's mother learned that he had stacked lie upon lie for the past year, she was livid. Not only had he not told his family, but more importantly, he hadn't told the fiancée that he was planning to marry in less than a month. Brett's solution was to have his mother throw more money at the problem and hope it would all work out without having to tell Kristen. However, that just wasn't an option for Susan and she gave him an ultimatum. Either he told Kristen, or she would.

For Brett, his mother's option was no option at all. He had worked hard to gain the love of his perfect woman and he wasn't about to let his mother blow it.

Due to his felony conviction, Brett was not allowed to purchase a firearm. Instead, he purchased a second-hand Barnett Recruit Youth 30 Crossbow. The crossbow was small and light, designed for young hunters, but still strong enough to kill. Unlike a gun, a crossbow could easily be purchased without any kind of paper trail.

In the days after the argument with his mother, Brett continued to do remodeling work at her home. As he brought his construction equipment into the garage, he stashed the crossbow and arrows (bolts) in amongst the other items.

In the days prior to August 25, 2016, Brett had taken his time to note all of the security cameras in his building, as well as the cameras between his condo and his mother's house. It was all very similar to the preparation he had attempted to take back in his bank robber days.

Assuming he might make a mess, that morning Brett wore an extra set of clothes beneath his normal jeans and shirt, despite the summer heat and humidity. Inside a duffel bag he packed his Bearded Bandit disguise: the wig and bucket hat. Also inside the bag, he had packed a few extra crossbow bolts. Brett grabbed the bag and walked down the fourteen flights of stairs in his building to avoid security cameras.

When Brett arrived at his mother's house, he pleaded with her one last time to not tell Kristen that he hadn't graduated and didn't have a job. She refused and told him again that she would tell Kristen herself if he didn't. Susan then called Chris, Brett's oldest brother, and asked him to come help with the situation.

Brett fumed with anger and panic. He stomped out of the house and into the garage while his mother followed. A crossbow takes time to load and with his mother in hot pursuit behind him, he didn't have the time he thought he would. He grabbed one of the crossbow bolts and shoved the tip, with its three sharp blades, into her cheek. He then pulled it out and shoved it into her ear.

Susan was still alive, but bleeding profusely and struggling for her life. Brett threw his mother to the ground in the garage, grabbed a piece of yellow nylon rope, and strangled her to death.

Knowing that his brother Chris was on his way, Brett cocked the crossbow and inserted the bolt. Ready to fire, he waited quietly behind the side door of the garage. When Chris entered the garage, he didn't stand a chance. Without a sound, Brett placed the point of the crossbow bolt at the base of the back of his neck and pulled the trigger. The blades pierced the base of his skull and laid to rest in his mouth, killing him instantly.

Brett dragged Chris's body next to their mother's body and placed an orange construction tarp over them. His clothes were covered in blood, but he was prepared. He was about to remove his outer layer of clothing and put on his wig and hat when he heard his youngest brother drive up.

Brett walked out of the garage door with a crossbow bolt in his hand as A.J. walked up the driveway. Brett knew his plan had failed and he would need to kill them all. He met A.J. in the driveway and drove a crossbow bolt into his neck.

Brett's final remaining brother, Leigh, had been napping in the house and heard the screams. Looking out the window of the house, he could see his brother A.J. lying on the ground and Brett with a bloody crossbow bolt in his hand. Leigh picked up the phone to call 911, but Brett was having none of that.

Brett and Leigh fought inside the house, breaking furniture and spreading blood throughout the house. Leigh was able to get the bolt away from him, but was hit in the head in the process. Eventually Leigh made it out of the front door of the house and saw that his brother A.J., lying in the driveway, was still alive. Before Brett was able to catch him, Leigh ran to a neighbor's house and screamed for them to call the police. He made a point to tell the neighbor repeatedly to have the police come, not just an ambulance.

Brett realized there was nowhere to run. Out of breath and covered in blood, he calmly grabbed a bottle of water from the refrigerator, sat down on the front steps, and waited for police to arrive.

Though A.J. was still alive in the driveway at the time, he only lasted a few minutes longer and was dead by the time paramedics arrived. When the police pulled up, Brett told them,

 "The guys in the garage are dead. Crossbow to the head. It was me."

Worried that Kristen may have also been a victim of Brett's madness, Toronto police rushed to their waterfront condo. Though Kristen

wasn't there, police were a bit startled and confused at what they found. Unsure what the items in their condo were, police evacuated the building and called in the bomb squad.

Inside the condo, they found Brett's MacBook Pro wedged against the wall with dumbbell weights. The screensaver had been turned off so the computer wouldn't go to sleep and the browser was open to YouTube. The cursor was hovering over the "play" button. Next to the computer was an oscillating fan set up with a digital timer. Duct-taped to the fan was a wooden spoon placed next to the "enter" key. The elaborate setup was just an alibi for Brett. When the timer went off, the oscillating fan would start and the spoon would hit the "enter" key, causing the YouTube video to play. Brett could have then said he was home watching YouTube videos when the murders occurred.

Two similar contraptions were set up with two additional oscillating fans and digital timers, one with an iPad and another with an iPhone. Each of those were set to send pre-written emails to friends at different times during the day. All this was for the purpose of establishing multiple digital fingerprints that he could later use as an alibi.

Though Brett went through all the trouble of configuring the elaborate alibi, he hadn't set the timers. He later explained that he had had a change of heart that morning and hadn't planned on killing his mother or brothers.

Brett Ryan pleaded guilty to second-degree murder of his mother, claiming that the crossbow was only to threaten her — not kill her. Because he had waited in the garage for his brother Chris to enter and killed him from behind, Brett pleaded guilty to the first-degree murder of Chris. In the case of the death of A.J., however, he had not expected him to show up and pleaded guilty to second-degree murder. He was convicted on all three counts, plus the attempted murder of his brother Leigh.

Brett received three concurrent life sentences for the lives he took, plus another concurrent ten-year sentence for the attempted murder conviction. He is eligible for parole in twenty-five years.

CHAPTER 11
MURDER IN THE SACRISTY

E ven as a little girl, Margaret Ann Pahl knew she wanted to be a nun. When she told her parents of her plans, they weren't surprised. After all, two of her aunts had been nuns. Margaret Ann felt it was her life's destiny.

Sister Margaret Ann spent her life as a nun and was seventy-one years old in 1980 when she was working at Mercy Hospital in Toledo, Ohio. Although she had trained as a Registered Nurse, her hearing was failing and she was nearing retirement. She worked as the caretaker in the Hospital Chapel. It was Holy Saturday, the day before Easter, which coincidentally fell on her seventy-second birthday that year. Sister Margaret Ann woke early that morning, had a quick breakfast, and went to the chapel to prepare the Eucharist for Sunday's Easter services.

On what should have been a happy day for her, Sister Margaret Ann was in a foul mood that morning. She was very particular about how she felt the religious services were to be conducted at the Chapel and she wasn't happy with Father Robinson's Good Friday service the day before. As she ate her breakfast, she told other chapel workers that she intended to speak to the Roman Catholic priest that day about how she felt about his sermon.

Sister Margaret Ann Pahl & Father Gerald Robinson

At 8:00 A.M. that morning, a young nun working in the hospital walked through the chapel and noticed a small folded cloth on the floor near the alter. It was strangely out of place. When she unfolded the cloth, she noticed that it was stained red with what seemed to be blood. At first she assumed someone had a cut themselves or had a bloody nose, but the stain itself had an odd shape. The nun set the cloth on a pew and walked into the nearby sacristy.

The nun immediately noticed that the polished gray marble floor of the small room was red with pooled blood. The motionless body of Sister Margaret Ann laid in the middle of the pool. Her clothes had been partially torn open and her legs were spread. An alter cloth filled with puncture holes and stains of blood had been draped over the body. In shock, the young nun screamed as she ran from the chapel to alert authorities.

Police arrived and found the sacristy, a small room just off of the alter where a priest would normally prepare for service, was filled with several gold chalices and crucifixes. Sister Margaret Ann's purse was also in the room, untouched. Robbery was clearly not a motive. When they removed the alter cloth, Sister Margaret Ann's body had thirty-one stab wounds in her neck and torso. Nine of the stab wounds on her chest formed an upside-down cross, as if the killing was some sort of ritual. Her forehead had been anointed with a smudge of blood -

an obvious mockery of the Last Rites of the Roman Catholic Church. Her arms had been folded across her chest and the body was surrounded by lit candles. Everything about the scene seemed ritualistic.

An examination of the body showed that Sister Margaret Ann had been stabbed with a long, thin knife of some sort, like a tiny sword. From the indentations in her bones, they could tell the knife had a diamond-shaped tip. The stab wounds, however, were postmortem. Though her body was filled with holes, the official cause of death was strangulation. She had been choked to death, the alter cloth placed over her body, then stabbed repeatedly through the alter cloth after she had died. Stains on the alter cloth and bloody marks on the marble floor gave hints as to the shape of the weapon that was used.

Police examined the small folded cloth that the young nun had found earlier near the alter. When they unfolded it, they noticed a smudge of blood that resembled the smudge found on Sister Margaret Ann's forehead.

The community was shocked at the randomness of the murder and the ritualistic implications. For months, hospital staff were scared to walk the halls alone and raised money for a reward for the capture of the killer. Local authorities also wanted the killer captured and the Lucas county government offered an additional $10,000 in reward money.

Detectives and the forensic team spent weeks at the hospital processing the crime scene and questioning staff. Among the people questioned was Father Gerald Robinson, the Jesuit chaplain at the chapel that had presided over Sister Margaret Ann's funeral just four days after her death. Another chaplain at the hospital had accused him of the murder without actual proof.

Forty-year-old Father Robinson was well-liked at the hospital and had spent years preaching to sick and terminally ill patients. Two weeks after the murder, detectives searched his apartment and found a small sword-shaped letter opener with a diamond pointed tip. It was a souvenir from the United States Capitol and had a round medallion on the top in the shape of the capitol building, about the size of a dime.

Detectives immediately thought it could have been the murder weapon and placed it into evidence.

Deputy Police Chief Ray Vetter was a devout Roman Catholic and familiar with Father Gerald Robinson. When Vetter found out that detectives were questioning a respected priest, he stopped the interview immediately and instructed the detectives to hand over all existing reports to him regarding the case. Reluctantly, detectives handed over their reports, several of which were never seen again. Chief Vetter told the detectives:

"It was probably some screwball off the street. She just happened to be at the wrong place at the wrong time."

The prosecutor's office and the detectives working the case made accusations that there was a cover-up involved, but with the Chief of Police against them, the case was eventually dropped for lack of evidence. Six years later Chief Vetter had retired, but by then the case had slipped through the cracks. It had gone cold – and it stayed that way for more than two decades.

Father Robinson worked at the hospital for another year after Sister Margaret Ann's death until he was appointed to be the pastor at three parishes in suburban Toledo. In the mid-nineties, he became chaplain at Flower Hospital and the Lake Park Nursing Home.

Twenty-three years after the murder of Sister Margaret Ann Pahl, the Toledo Diocese received several accusations from both grown women and men that claimed they were sexually abused as children by a number of priests in the Diocese. Although the accusations were all horrific, one in particular was especially disturbing and involved Father Gerald Robinson.

In 2003, a woman in her forties came forward with a story that was hard to believe. She claimed that as a child, she was forced to be part of "Satanic ceremonies" performed by several Toledo Roman Catholic priests. She told authorities that the priests had placed her in a coffin filled with cockroaches, forced her to eat what she believed to be human eyeballs, and let a live snake penetrate her. The priests told her it was "to consecrate these orifices to Satan."

She also told police that the priests had killed a three-year-old child, performed an abortion on her, and mutilated dogs in Satanic sacrifices. When the woman made these claims, she had no idea that Father Robinson had been a suspect in a murder investigation two decades earlier.

Three other people came forward with disturbingly similar stories of abuse by Toledo Roman Catholic priests. Some of the accusers were too young at the time of their abuse to recall all the details, but all of them said the abuse came from many priests — one they were sure of was Father Gerald Robinson.

The news of the alleged abuse reached the Toledo prosecutor's office and detectives realized Father Robinson was involved. This news prompted the case of Sister Margaret Ann's murder to be pulled from the files and a cold case unit was assigned. They were going to give the entire case a new look, from top to bottom.

About seventy police reports that were earlier buried by the former Chief of Police were recovered and analyzed. One particular piece of evidence that was researched was the smudge mark on Sister Margaret Ann's forehead and the blood mark on the small cloth left near the chapel altar. Using new forensic technology that hadn't been available at the time of the murder, the blood stains from the cloth and her forehead were matched to the U.S. Capitol medallion at the top of Father Robinson's letter opener. Another blood stain on the ten-foot long alter cloth was matched to the ribbed handle on the letter opener. To obtain additional evidence, the body of Sister Margaret Ann was exhumed.

In April 2004, twenty-four years after the killing, Father Gerald Robinson was arrested for the murder of Sister Margaret Ann Pahl. During his interrogation, he told investigators he was innocent. He said he had been shocked when the nun was killed in his chapel and shocked again when the other chaplain had accused him of the murder.

At Father Robinson's trial, the prosecution produced three witnesses that had seen him near the chapel at the time of the killing. In addition to presenting the evidence of the imprint of the U.S. Capitol emblem on the cloth and her forehead, a medical examiner specializing in blood stain evidence testified that eighteen of the additional blood stains could have come from the letter opener. Photos of the stains were shown to jurors so they could see how closely it resembled the U.S. Capitol medallion. The prosecution was also able to provide evidence that the tip of the letter opener was a perfect fit for an indentation in her jawbone.

A Catholic priest that was an expert on the occult testified that the killing must have been committed by someone with a deep understanding of Catholic symbols and church rituals.

The prosecution argued that Father Robinson had tried to humiliate Sister Margaret Ann in death by stabbing an upside down cross into her chest and anointing her with her own blood in a ritualistic killing. Prosecutors said Father Robinson had been angry about Sister Pahl's domineering personality and her complaints about how he had conducted a Good Friday service the night before the killing.

Father Robinson maintained his innocence and wore his priest's collar throughout the entire trial. His defense team tried to argue that not all the DNA at the scene linked to him. They proposed a theory that Anthony and Nathaniel Cook, a pair of serial killer brothers that had been in the area at the time, could have committed the murder. There was, however, no evidence to support that theory.

On April 24, 2006, after nine days of testimony, Father Robinson was convicted on all accounts. The conviction represented the first documented time in history that a Catholic priest had killed a nun, as well as the second conviction of a Catholic priest for murder. Immediately upon his conviction, the judge sentenced him to fifteen-years to life behind bars.

In prison, sixty-eight-year-old Robinson remained a priest, but was barred from ministry. He filed multiple applications for appeal, but all of them were denied. In May 2014, he suffered a heart attack while in prison and died in July of the same year.

Despite his conviction and multiple accusations of ritualistic abuse, many of Robinson's lifelong parishioners stood by him, refusing to believe in his guilt.

CHAPTER 12
DEVIOUS DIXIE

Halloween 1984 was like any other Halloween for most people, but not for thirty-year-old Mel Dyson. He was working late at the office of the accounting firm that he worked for in Huntington Beach, California. His career as a financial consultant had paid off well. He worked hard and had nice cars and a nice three-story condo in an upscale complex in the Huntington Harbor marina. Life was good.

Mel's wife Dixie Dyson, however, worked in Los Angeles doing data entry. Although it was only twenty-five miles away, the L.A. traffic made it too much to commute on a daily basis. She and their seven-year-old son stayed at Mel's mother's house in Carson during the week and went to their Huntington Beach condo on the weekends. However, that routine had only started recently. Mel and Dixie had been struggling with their relationship for the past few years. They had been on-again-off-again until recently, when they decided to rekindle.

They had been together for almost ten years and had one child together, but had never actually married. Although California has no common-law marriage rule, the couple considered themselves husband and wife and Dixie took his last name.

Mel and Dixie met when he was in his early twenties. Dixie was ten years older, but that didn't seem to matter. The two were an odd couple. Mel grew up as an only child in a tight-knit Filipino family. He was shy and quiet, whereas Dixie was a loud, brash, and stocky blonde with cropped hair. She grew up as an adopted child of a broken family and had been married and divorced twice before. However, despite their differences, they were inseparable. At least for the first four years.

The second four years of their relationship were rocky. Mel and Dixie broke up briefly and she took their son south to San Diego county. Those four years were like a Yo-Yo. Over and over, she moved back in with him, then moved out again. But in October 1984, the couple were trying to patch things up.

When Mel Dyson finally arrived home that Halloween night, he was shocked to find that his beautiful condo had been trashed. Although the condo was in a secure complex with only one entrance that required going through a manned security guard station, someone had obviously been in the condo. Drawers were ripped from dressers, clothes thrown all over the house, artwork removed from the walls, and furniture overturned. Two of his watches had been stolen, his checkbook was missing, and about $300 in cash was gone.

When police arrived, they found no sign of forced entry and the guard at the gate had no record of any unauthorized person entering the complex. A window screen on the third floor had been torn, but a third-floor window hardly seemed a likely entry point. A burglar would have needed a very large ladder to get to that window, not to mention they would have had to come through the guard gate. None of it made sense.

On Saturday November 17, less than three weeks after the break-in, Dixie spent the day running errands and getting her hair done at the hairdresser. On her way back to the condo, she picked up their seven-year-old nephew who had planned to have a sleep-over with their son at the condo that night. That evening after the two boys were put to bed, Mel and Dixie went to bed and made love just after 10:00 P.M.

Sometime during the night, Dixie woke up to the sound of her son coughing and walked into his room to check on him. She found the two boys sound asleep, curled up next to her son, and slept for a while.

When Dixie woke up again later to go back to bed with Mel, she walked into the master bedroom and was immediately attacked. A man wearing a nylon stocking over his head held a knife to her throat, threw her to the ground, and raped her. Though the attack happened in the master bedroom, she didn't see her husband.

After the attacker finished with her, he forced her downstairs into the garage and gave her orders to get in her car and drive him out of the condo complex. She followed his instructions and drove him inland to the intersection of Golden West Street and Warner Avenue, a busy shopping corner with strip-malls on all four corners. The rapist then exited the vehicle and ran away on foot, but before he left, he told her, "The last time was just a warning."

In a daze at what had just happened, Dixie drove back home to the condo. When she went back into the master bedroom, she noticed something she hadn't noticed while she was being raped. The entire bedroom was covered in blood and Mel was dead on the floor. His torso was a mesh of gaping stab wounds. Dixie rushed to check on the children and found them still asleep, unaware that anything had happened during the night.

When police arrived and Dixie told her story, they were instantly suspicious. She was cold and calm. She didn't act like someone who had just been raped and had her husband brutally murdered.

So many things about her story didn't add up. Dixie claimed the masked man raped her on the bedroom floor just a few feet from Mel's body. The room was covered in blood and the killer would have been covered in blood, but Dixie had no blood on her at all. In fact, while being raped, she didn't notice that Mel had been killed just a few feet away. When she was examined at the hospital, there was evidence that she'd had sex, but no evidence of violence or sexual trauma.

Like Halloween night, the only possible point of entry was the third-floor window. Again, a very unlikely scenario - but the most concerning fact was that the night guard working at the condo guard station had a completely different story to tell.

Dixie had told the police that she had driven the killer out of the complex at around 2:00 A.M., but the night guard logged the Dyson car leaving the complex at 1:30 A.M. Thirty minutes before she claimed and with only one person in the car, not two.

The guard also said that at 2:40 A.M., just twenty minutes before police arrived, a man of about forty-five and who called himself Carl drove up to the security gate with a woman that looked to be about thirty-five. They told the guard they were there to visit the Dyson family. The guard had called the Dyson home, spoke to a woman that answered, and gave them permission to enter. Dixie had no answer for any of this, claiming that the night guard must have been mistaken.

Dixie Dyson was immediately considered the prime suspect in her husband's death; their suspicions were magnified when she submitted claims on several life insurance policies that Mel had. She was due to receive approximately $140,000 in benefits.

In the months following the murder, police backtracked Dixie's movements over the prior years in an attempt to find evidence and build a case against her.

The last four years of Dixie and Mel's relationship had been tumultuous. They clashed almost constantly and for much of the time, Dixie had lived in San Diego county. During her time there, she had a relationship with a man named Enrico Vasquez.

Enrico was thirteen years younger than Dixie, but he was handsome and she was attracted to his bad-boy lifestyle. He grew up in rough neighborhoods of the Bronx, New York, and was a former Marine. Dixie fell for him hard. While she spent time away from Mel, she would use Mel's money to buy Enrico presents and spoil him at any chance she got.

A year after the murder, police received an anonymous call. According to the caller, Dixie Dyson had asked him to murder her husband. He told the police that she offered to pay him $10,000 once she received the life insurance money from Mel's death. The man said that he refused her offer, but knew that she had found someone else to do the job — her boyfriend, Enrico Vasquez.

Police believed that Dixie may have conspired with Enrico to kill her husband, but they had one problem with that theory. When shown a photo of Enrico, the night guard was absolutely certain that he was not the man that drove into the condo complex that night claiming to be "Carl." With a search warrant, police initiated surveillance of Dixie Dyson. All of her incoming and outgoing telephone calls were monitored and recorded.

In March 1986, using the federal search warrant, police intercepted a letter that she sent to New York City addressed to "E. Vasquez." In the letter Dixie said that an unidentified woman had offered to lend her money if she confessed:

 "She said I could have the money as long as I admitted to being involved in Mel's accident. Either I did it or know who did it, or arranged it. She said then her people would have some guarantee that I'd pay the money back or they could go to the police.

Let me tell you, I was tempted. But I got scared and said no. I couldn't lie about it. She really started pushing it. I could have $15,000, $50,000 or whatever I wanted as long as I confessed to something."

Dixie went on to say that someone named "Mike" told her to stay away from the woman — that it was a setup.

> "With the circumstantial evidence, if I admitted anything to anyone they could pick me up. Although he [Mike] did say it was entrapment and he thinks a jury would laugh them out of town. But he says they definitely don't have enough to arrest me or they would have.
>
> There's never a day that goes by that I don't think of you. I get mad at myself that you are still so much a part of my thoughts.
>
> My God babe, can't you see how hard this is on me? I've got to get out. I think now is the best time. They think I'm stuck here, they won't be expecting it. Once I get the money, I think they'll really be watching to see what I do with it.
>
> Isn't there anyone you know that can help me? Don't you have any connections with the mob or loan sharks or anyone? I just can't take any more of this mental and emotional pressure. Knowing they [the police] are out there, that they still want me. It's never going to end for me as long as they know where I am.
>
> Please please, please help me. I need you now more than ever. Find three people to loan you $5,000. Please!!! Take care and don't get careless. They [the police] are still out there."

Two years had gone by since Mel Dyson's murder and there had still been no arrests in the case. Dixie Dyson had placed claims on Mel's life insurance policies, but all three insurance companies had denied them. They weren't in dispute of whether there was payment due, but rather they disputed who the beneficiary was.

Mel's mother, Delores, was the executor of his estate and had alerted the insurance companies that Dixie may have been involved in her son's death. After speaking to the police, the insurance companies agreed.

Claiming that the police had maliciously persuaded the insurance companies, Dixie hired a lawyer and planned to sue Allstate Life Insurance, Prudential Life, Security Life Insurance, the City of Huntington Beach, and Detective Mason, the lead investigator on her case. She was suing for the original $140,000 in life insurance, plus another $250,000 in damages. The court case was due to begin December 3, 1986, but the day before the case was to begin, Dixie was arrested for first-degree murder and conspiracy to commit murder.

Knowing that Dixie had visited the hair salon on the day of Mel's murder, detectives paid a visit to her hairdresser. At first her hairdresser was reluctant to talk, but eventually she told detectives that Enrico Vasquez called the salon the day of the murder and spoke to Dixie. Phone records confirmed the call.

The second piece of crucial evidence in the case was a drug store receipt found in Dixie's purse on the night of the murder. The receipt was from a store on the corner of Golden West Street and Warner Avenue — the very same intersection that Dixie claimed she had taken the killer. The timestamp on the receipt placed Dixie at the very same intersection just hours before Mel's death.

Another receipt found at the scene showed that Dixie had paid for flowers sent to Vasquez just weeks before the murder with a message, "Is it too late to start over?"

Though police knew that Dixie wasn't the actual killer and that Enrico Vasquez was involved, there still wasn't a warrant out for his arrest. Dixie's arrest report only listed that there was an "uncharged co-conspirator" involved. Detectives announced that, "This murder is still very much under investigation."

In March 1988, Dixie Dyson stood trial for the murder of her husband. Although most of the evidence against her was circumstantial, none of her excuses made sense.

Using the drug store receipt, the prosecution placed her at the same intersection where she claimed to have dropped off the killer just hours before the death. They proved that she didn't call the police until more than two hours after he was killed. She couldn't explain the lack of forced entry, nor the fact that she had no blood on her despite being raped on the bloody bedroom floor. They also placed motive on Dixie by showing how hard she had fought for the insurance money after Mel's death.

The defense attacked her dead husband. They argued that Mel may have been embezzling from his employer. More than $8,000 had gone missing at his work in the months before his death and the company was now facing bankruptcy. They argued that the police should have investigated the angle that someone from his company may have ordered a hit on him. Dixie also claimed that Mel was both verbally and physically abusive to her.

The key witness for the prosecution was the condo night security man. He had carefully logged every car that came through the gate on the evening of the murder and none of Dixie's explanations seemed to fit.

The jury deliberated for only two hours before coming back with a guilty verdict. First-Degree murder and conspiracy.

The jury foreman told the media:

> "Too many things in her story just didn't make sense. We just thought an innocent person would have done things a lot different from the way she did them."

> "We read that letter very carefully. There were just too many things in it that bothered us. She'd want him to call her at a phone booth instead of at home. If you're

innocent, what would you care if the police overheard your conversation?"

Dixie faced an automatic twenty-five years to life, but before her official sentencing, she asked for a delay. She was ready to give up her accomplices. Without her attorney present, Dixie spoke to Dale Mason, the lead detective on the case. She knew that cooperation was her only chance of a lighter sentence.

Dixie told detectives that she had only planned the murder and asked her boyfriend Enrico to do the job for her. She told Enrico that with Mel gone, she would own the house, would have sole custody of her son, and would inherit $140,000 in life insurance.

Enrico wouldn't do it himself, but had a friend from New York City that would do it for a fee, George Ira Lamb. Days before the murder, Lamb had flown out from New York City and shared a nearby hotel room with Enrico Vasquez.

Dixie claimed that just hours before the attack, she met with Enrico and Lamb at a drug store on Golden West Street and Warner Avenue. From there, Lamb rode in the trunk of her car with her to the condo so the guard wouldn't see him on the way in. He stayed in the trunk until just after midnight, when Dixie went downstairs and turned on the garage light. That was his signal that he could get out of the trunk and come upstairs to kill Mel.

Dixie then watched as he murdered her husband. Afterward, they had consensual sex so that it would seem as though she was raped. After the murder, he climbed back into the trunk and Dixie drove him back to the same intersection.

To verify Dixie's story, police searched the trunk of her car. On the inside of the trunk they found a fingerprint that didn't belong to Mel, Dixie, or Enrico; they needed to find George Ira Lamb.

With the help of New York City police, Enrico and Lamb were tracked down and arrested in New York in the summer of 1988. Both were charged with first-degree murder and conspiracy and extradited to California for separate trials.

Dixie agreed to testify against both of her accomplices in exchange for a lighter sentence. Her twenty-five to life sentence was reduced to fifteen years to life.

During the three-week trial of George Lamb, Dixie told her story of how she and Enrico hired him to kill her husband. But Dixie had told stories before... most of them lies. The jury was having a hard time believing her.

Lamb's lawyers argued that seventeen stab wounds on a victim indicates a deep rage and hatred — not the work of someone that doesn't know the victim personally and just wants to get the job done.

Lamb's young wife and two-year-old son flew out for the trial, as did his great aunt, a New York State Legislator.

The jury deliberated for four days and came back with a not-guilty verdict for the crime of first-degree murder. For the charge of conspiracy, they delivered a guilty verdict. The jury believed that Dixie and Enrico had enlisted him to murder Mel, but he had changed his mind and didn't participate. They believed Lamb was involved, but Dixie's testimony could not be trusted.

Many members of the jury, however, didn't realize that the conspiracy conviction also came with a mandatory twenty-five to life sentence - the same as the murder charge. After the trial, five members of the jury took it upon themselves to petition the judge to allow Lamb leniency, saying they had no idea a conspiracy conviction held such a harsh penalty. The judge, however, denied their request, saying:

> "From what I see on the surface, Mr. Lamb is an upstanding young man. But this was a cold, calculated, first-degree murder straight up. They planned it, they got results."

Later that year, jurors at Enrico Vasquez's trial weren't so sympathetic. After seven days of deliberation, a jury convicted him of first-degree murder and conspiracy, which came with a mandatory twenty-five to life sentence.

In the end, Dixie Dyson was the mastermind behind her husband's death but, because of her cooperation with police, received a reduced sentence. Ultimately, however, she served a much longer sentence. In 2011, in a two-and-a-half hour deliberation, sixty-seven-year-old Dixie Dyson was denied parole.

TRUE CRIME CASE HISTORIES

VOLUME 6

TRUE CRIME
CASE HISTORIES

12 Disturbing True Crime Stories
JASON NEAL

INTRODUCTION

As with the previous volumes of True Crime Case Histories, I use this introduction space as a quick word of warning. The stories in this book represent humanity at its absolute worst. Pure evil. Television crime shows and news articles often skip the messy parts of true crime stories. The details are just too much for the average viewer or reader.

In my books, however, I don't leave out the details. I go through hours of research for each story. I search through old newspaper articles, court documents, first-hand descriptions, and autopsy reports. In my books I include details not to shock, but to give the reader a deeper look into the twisted mind of the killer. In the end, it's unlikely any of us will understand the motive of the criminals in these books, but the level of depravity will at least keep you turning pages.

That being said, if you are overly squeamish with the details of true crime, this book may not be for you. If you're okay with it… then let's proceed.

Volume Six of True Crime Case Histories features twelve new stories from the past several decades. There's the story of a young English man that had plans to become the UK's most notorious serial killer, but couldn't keep his mouth shut after his first kill and bragged to over twenty of his friends.

Another story covers a group of four young men who believed they could do anything they wanted because their lord Satan protected them. Satan apparently couldn't protect them from prison.

There's the story of a San Diego man who made it his life's mission to help young men avoid a life of crime. His good deeds resulted in his entire family being butchered by a boy he was trying to help.

Another killer, a father of eight children, lured women to his boat, raped them, and threw them overboard. Ingenious forensic science was eventually used to catch the killer.

One story of a young man that couldn't handle being rejected by his teenage girlfriend was suggested to me by a reader whose daughter had a close-call with the killer.

The twelve stories in this volume are shocking and disturbing, but they're true. These things really happen in the world. We may never understand why killers do what they do, but at least we can be better informed.

You may have heard of a few of the stories in this volume, but there are several I'm almost certain you haven't. My goal is to find stories that aren't already covered all over the Internet. Over the last few volumes, many of my readers have sent me cases they remembered happening in their hometowns. If you have any stories that are largely unre-ported, please send them my way. I thrive on digging through old newspapers and trying to research interesting stories.

Lastly, please join my mailing list for discounts, updates, and a free book. You can sign up for that at

TrueCrimeCaseHistories.com

You can also purchase paperbacks, hardcovers, and signed copies of my books directly from me at:

JasonNealBooks.com

Additional photos, videos, and documents pertaining to the cases in this volume can be found on the accompanying web page listed at the end of this book.

Thank you for reading. I sincerely hope you gain some insight from this volume of True Crime Case Histories.

- Jason

CHAPTER 1
LOST IN THE DESERT

A nyone that lived in the Phoenix, Arizona area in the nineties might remember Terri's Consignment & Design. The commercials were shown constantly on television throughout the Phoenix valley and featured Terri Bowersock and her mother, Loretta Bowersock.

Loretta had run a successful furniture store as a young woman. In 1983, she used her business acumen to help her daughter, Terri, start her own furniture consignment company with a $2,000 loan from Terri's grandmother. Terri's Consignment & Design stores featured "gently used" furniture at bargain prices. Within a few years, the stores were well known throughout the Phoenix area and Terri was making a fortune.

Despite growing up with dyslexia, Terri was a master at marketing her business and was awarded the title of Arizona's top businesswoman. Not long afterward, Avon awarded her their prestigious "Woman of Enterprise" award and she was featured on the Oprah Winfrey show in an episode featuring "unexpected millionaires."

Loretta and Terri Bowersock in one of their commercials.

Although Terri owned the business, Loretta also became wealthy and bought a large house in the Phoenix suburb of Tempe. As a single woman, however, the home was too large for her and she decided to rent out a room in 1986. Loretta placed a classified ad in the local paper reading, "Room for lease in nice home. Executive businesswoman." The first person to respond was a forty-nine-year-old man named Taw Benderly.

Benderly showed up to her home penniless and with nothing but the shirt on his back. He told fifty-one-year-old Loretta that he had literally just gotten off of a plane at the airport and had his bag stolen. Loretta felt sorry for him and let him stay.

Benderly was tall, charming, and intelligent. He spoke in a way that was impressive, persuasive, and very convincing. He told her he had grown up as an only child, but his parents had died when he was young, leaving his grandmother to raise him. After high-school he went to college and received a master's degree in business.

It didn't take long before Loretta had fallen in love with her new room-mate. In the following years, Loretta continued to work with her daughter while Benderly tinkered in the garage. He had convinced himself that he could become an inventor and was full of ideas that he claimed would be "the next big thing." He worked on projects such as a "revolutionary" lawn mower blade, a solar-energy unit, and a shield to keep cars cool in the Arizona heat. Unfortunately, none of his ideas ever seemed to work out.

Loretta combed through garage sales and estate sales. She looked for watches and jewelry that she could refurbish and resell at a profit. Meanwhile, Benderly toyed with his inventions, cooked, and cleaned the house. Although he didn't bring home any income, from the outside it seemed that the couple were fine that way. In reality, however, it was far from okay.

By the early nineties, Benderly convinced Loretta that she was entitled to a much larger stake in Terri's furniture business and encouraged her to sue her daughter. The lawsuit took years and drove a wedge between the mother and daughter team. The dispute was eventually resolved, but it had been a very difficult time for Loretta emotionally.

As the years pressed on, Benderly became condescending towards Loretta. He constantly put her down and made her feel inadequate. The abuse crumbled her self-esteem. Her bookshelves were filled with self-help books and video recordings of Oprah and Dr. Phil episodes about how to save a relationship and domestic abuse.

Loretta had confided in her daughter and sisters that her life with Taw Benderly wasn't ideal. However, as a woman in her sixties, she believed it was too late to leave him and start anew. She and Benderly had promised each other early in their relationship that they would grow old together; she was intent on keeping that promise.

Benderly talked incessantly at family get-togethers about the income potential of his pet projects. Terri was receptive and for years gave him $20,000 to $40,000 per year to help get his inventions off the ground. She had no idea that other friends, neighbors, and relatives were loaning him money too.

At 6:00 p.m. on December 14, 2004, Taw Benderly walked up to the security desk at the Park Place Mall in Tucson, Arizona, in a frenzy. He told mall security that he had dropped Loretta off at the Dillard's

Department Store at 2:00 p.m. that day. He had planned on picking her up at 4:00 p.m., but had spent the last two hours walking through the mall looking for her. She was nowhere to be found.

That evening, police searched through the Dillard's store, the mall, and the surrounding neighborhood, but found no sign of Loretta. The police were familiar with Loretta's name because they had seen her and Terri on their television commercials. Initially, they thought she had possibly been abducted and was being held for ransom.

Benderly explained to detectives that he and Loretta Bowersock, his partner of eighteen years, had planned on coming to Tucson for a five-day vacation and to do some Christmas shopping. He claimed that he and Loretta left Tempe at 10:00 a.m. and drove to Tucson. They checked into the Tucson Residence Inn at 12:30 p.m. before he dropped her off at the mall at 2:00 p.m.

It didn't take long for police to find holes in his story. The mall security tapes were the first inconsistency. After poring through the security tapes of both Dillard's and the rest of the store, there was no trace of Benderly looking for Loretta for two hours as he said. Instead, he had parked his maroon mini-van in the parking lot at 6:00 p.m. and walked straight to the security desk. There was also no footage of Loretta in the mall at all that day.

With a warrant, police searched Benderly's hotel room. Inside they found various valuables: expensive watches, necklaces, and rings. He had also brought several guns and ammunition. He packed eight suitcases for the five-day trip, but only one suitcase contained any of Loretta's clothes. The rest were his own belongings.

However, what troubled police the most was what they found when they searched his maroon mini-van. In the back of the van was a pickaxe and shovel, both caked with dirt. They also found a box of miscellaneous pieces of rope and a map of the desert area between Phoenix and Tucson. This discovery was more than just a red flag.

Tucson detectives contacted Tempe police for a warrant to search Benderly and Loretta's home. Inside their garage was another minivan. In the back of the van police found a purse containing Loretta's identification, checkbook, and credit cards. In a trash can outside of the house was a paper towel with a small amount of blood on it. It was clear to Tucson police that Loretta never made it to Tucson alive.

Taw Benderly & Loretta Bowersock

With good reason, police didn't believe Benderly's story and brought him in for questioning. During the interview he was combative and showed more concern for the accusations against him than finding Loretta:

 "You need to respect that the fact that I'm trying to give you information in as clear a form as I can. I was not prepared to have to account minute for minute for my time."

Tucson detectives were convinced that Benderly had killed Loretta and most likely buried her in the desert somewhere between Tempe and Tucson. Benderly eventually refused to speak further with police and, without a body, they were unable to charge him for anything. They were forced to release him.

Investigators began backtracking Benderly's movements of the day Loretta went missing. He claimed they left Tempe at 10:00 a.m. that day and checked into the hotel at 12:30. At 2:00 p.m., he dropped her off at the mall. Hotel records at the Residence Inn, however, showed the check-in at 2:48 p.m. – and the hotel staff said Benderly checked-in alone. There was no record of Loretta in the hotel.

Benderly's credit card and cell phone records also told a different story of the day. He had used a credit card to purchase two baseball caps at 11:00 a.m. at an outlet mall in Casa Grande, just south of Phoenix. At 12:30 p.m. he returned a cell phone call to his dentist. The call used a cell phone tower near exit 199, also near Casa Grande. Finally, at 1:15 p.m., he purchased two sandwiches at the Love's truck stop just a mile further down the interstate.

The time between 11:00 a.m. and 1:15 p.m. remained unaccounted for. Police believed that after he left the outlet mall, he buried Loretta in the desert somewhere nearby before continuing down to Tucson.

Terri Bowersock was distraught at the disappearance of her mother and confronted Benderly personally. Despite the inconsistencies, he insisted he had nothing to do with Loretta's disappearance.

Terri didn't know what to think. Having had close contact with the Phoenix area television stations and newspapers, she turned to them for help. The story of Loretta's disappearance became front-page news. The media attention incited friends and strangers to help her search the area between Phoenix and Tucson. Although Benderly's call had bounced off of a particular cell phone tower, the area covered by that tower was an enormous area of desert; finding a body in that large of an area was highly unlikely.

The story also attracted psychics who claimed they could help. Terri was a believer in the supernatural and hired eight different psychics for advice. The psychics provided her with tips that were mostly available to anyone that read the newspapers. One particular psychic, however, convinced Terri that she could talk to the dead. The clair-voyant told her she needed to check on the whereabouts of Taw Benderly.

Tucson police were building their case against Benderly and were close to having enough evidence to arrest him. They had gone through his and Loretta's financial records and found that he had taken out several large loans using her name. He had also embezzled money from her company and hadn't been making the mortgage payments. Together, they were tens of thousands of dollars in debt and Loretta's beautiful Tempe home was just days away from foreclosure. Phone records showed she had made seventeen calls to the bank the day before she disappeared.

Terri hadn't spoken to Benderly in the past few days and went to check on him. After there was no answer at his door and he wasn't answering phone calls, she called the police.

On December 22, just eight days after Loretta went missing, Tempe police entered Benderly's home to find him dead. He had hanged himself using an extension cord tied to rafters in the garage. Benderly had left a suicide note, but it said nothing of Loretta's whereabouts or how she died. It only said,

"Loretta and I vowed over the years that we would spend eternity together, and so we shall."

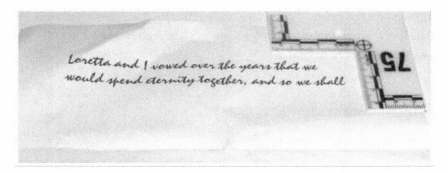

Taw Benderly suicide note

Though Loretta and Terri had been told by Benderly that his parents were dead and he was raised by his grandmother, Terri soon found out this story was a lie. Benderly not only had a brother, but his mother and father were still alive. He also had an ex-wife and two children that he hadn't spoken to in over eighteen years. His story of having a master's degree in business was a lie too. In fact, when he showed up at Loretta's doorstep eighteen years earlier, he had only recently been released from prison for theft.

It appeared that any hopes of finding Loretta's body had vanished with the death of Taw Benderly. The only remaining clues came from psychics with vague descriptions like; "look for something red in the dirt," "she's in the desert," or "she's buried next to something blue." But Terri still put her faith in the psychics, even inviting one to help her hike through the desert looking for her mother.

Six months after she went missing, police called off the official search for Loretta Bowersock. Nonetheless, Terri continued to spend her weekends hiking through the desert south of Phoenix.

Just over a year after she went missing, two hikers kicked at a rock in the desert and uncovered part of a human skull. When police dug just eighteen inches below the surface, they unearthed a complete female skeleton wrapped in plastic bags. One bag covered her head, another was shoved down her throat.

Loretta Bowersock's remains found in the desert

Dental records proved that the body was that of Loretta Bowersock. A forensic examination determined that she most likely died of asphyxiation by placing a bag over her head. The body was buried without shoes, leading police to believe that she had died at their home in Tempe.

Terri Bowersock found solace in the discovery of her mother's body and that she could give her a proper burial. Rather than the police work involved, she credited the clairvoyant with finding her mother's remains. Today, the same psychic can be found on social media websites spouting dozens of unsubstantiated and easily debunked conspiracy theories.

The economic downturn wasn't kind to Terri Bowersock and her consignment stores. Three years after her mother's body was found, her multi-million dollar empire came crumbling down. The Better Business Bureau received 188 complaints in a matter of thirty-six months. Google and Yelp were filled with negative reviews of her businesses from people who put their furniture on consignment and never saw a dime in return.

The business she started with a $2,000 loan – which had grown to seventeen stores, employed 300 people, and made $36 million a year – eventually filed for bankruptcy protection. Terri Bowersock also filed for personal bankruptcy.

CHAPTER 2
CONSUMED BY DESIRE

Eighteen-year-old Heather Gibson was in her senior year at Loy Norrix High School in Kalamazoo when she first met Chadwick "Chad" Wiersma. The young and naive girl was thrilled that an older boy liked her, but it was his "bad boy" nature that intrigued her the most.

Chad was a stocky blonde that grew up in a middle-class family just outside of Kalamazoo, but he had a knack for getting into more trouble than his siblings. At twenty years old, although he had a job and an apartment of his own, he'd had a few brushes with the law which eventually resulted in a felony conviction.

When Heather and Chad first began dating in 1993, she lived with her parents and younger sister in a quiet neighborhood on the south side of Kalamazoo, Michigan. Though Heather was smitten with him, her parents could tell that the young man was trouble. Her father, Robert Gibson, knew Chad wasn't an ordinary kid. Robert tried to convince his daughter that she should avoid Chad and concentrate on school, but it was too late. Like any teenage girl, she was deep into her schoolgirl crush.

However, her father was right. It only took a few months before Heather realized that the relationship with Chad wasn't going to work.

When she told him she thought they should start seeing other people, Chad became enraged. He forced her into her car and told her to drive. They drove to a remote location where he berated her.

Chad exploded in anger, telling her she absolutely couldn't leave him. He threatened her and told her he would kill her and her family if she ever left him. Heather pleaded with him for hours before he eventually calmed down, but it was only temporary.

Heather reluctantly agreed to continue dating Chad, but his obsessive jealousy continued. He constantly watched every move she made. He repeatedly accused her of flirting with other young men. The couple constantly argued and it all came to a boiling point in December 1993. She told him it was over, turned her back on him, and walked to her car.

In a rage, Chad pulled his own car in behind hers in the parking lot so she couldn't drive away. He got out of the car and stomped over to her driver side window and screamed at her through the glass. Although Heather tried to calm him down, it was no use. His mind was gone in a testosterone-fueled rage. Using a large rock, Chad smashed her driver's side window and dragged her out of the car, onto the pavement.

After a crowd of witnesses gathered around, she managed to calm him down. She screamed at him that it was over for good this time. He eventually moved his car and Heather drove away. At home, Heather's father was livid and stressed his point that Chad was trouble. She really needed to end their relationship for good.

Chad Wiersma & Heather Gibson (high school photos) / Chad Wiersma (mugshot)

For the next four months, Heather managed to stay away from Chad – but he was persistent and persuasive. By the spring of 1994 they'd made up and she had moved in with him. She was convinced he had really changed this time. Heather's father, however, wasn't as forgiving. He made it clear that Chad was never to be welcome in their home.

Over the next two years, Heather and Chad's relationship was a yo-yo. They broke up, got back together, and broke up again so many times that their friends lost count. But finally, in February 1996, Heather broke it off with him one last time. She moved out of his apartment and back home with her parents. This time it was for good.

Chad was not one to accept rejection. Over the next month, he obsessively asked friends if she was dating someone else. He asked them to spy on her and couldn't stand the thought that she could be with another man. Each time he called her at home, her father would answer and immediately hang up on him.

Chad grew frustrated that he couldn't talk to Heather and had heard rumors that she was dating someone new. His drug and alcohol use fueled his rage until, eventually, he couldn't take any more.

In late March he asked his co-worker, Robert Burr, multiple times to call the house, ask for Heather, and then hand the phone to him. When that trick no longer worked, Chad asked him to help him get a gun.

Robert knew that with Chad's prior felony, he couldn't legally possess a gun. He knew helping Chad get a gun was a crime and turned him down. Chad was desperate. He asked other co-workers, but all knew of his prior record and refused to help him.

On April 1, Chad visited with a friend, Eric Edgerson. Eric had been cleaning a 9 millimeter pistol that evening as the two of them drank gin and orange juice, smoked pot, and snorted some cocaine. When he finished cleaning the gun, he set it on top of a stereo speaker.

Later in the evening, Chad grabbed the gun off of the speaker and fired it inside the house. Eric screamed at him, "What the fuck are you doing?!" Chad only laughed and claimed it went off by accident. He set the gun back down and the two continued partying.

By the early morning hours, Chad was too drunk and high to go home so he slept on the couch. When Eric woke up the next morning, Chad and the gun were gone.

Eric drove to Kalamazoo to look for Chad and the gun. He too knew that Chad wasn't allowed to carry a gun. Eric drove to both his apartment and his grandmother's house, but there was no sign of Chad or the gun. Knowing of his felony conviction and his rage toward Heather, Eric drove to the police station to report his gun stolen.

Late that morning, Chad drove to another co-worker's house. When he arrived at Brian Kirsch's house, Chad immediately started complaining about Heather. He was convinced she was flirting with other men. He ranted about Heather leaving him and how she wouldn't take his phone calls.

Brian, however, didn't take him seriously when Chad said he was "thinking about killing someone." Unfortunately, that would soon become a reality.

In the early afternoon, Chad Wiersma left Brian's house and drove to Heather's parents' house at 4039 Duke Street. Robert Gibson was working in the garage when Chad drove up. Before Heather's father had a chance to speak, Chad pulled the handgun from his pocket and motioned for Robert to go inside the house.

Once inside the house, Robert tried to calm him down but Chad screamed, "Shut your fucking mouth! Just keep walking into the kitchen." Robert walked into the kitchen, pulled out a chair from the kitchen table, and sat down. Robert desperately tried to settle him down, but there was no use. Chad's brain was boiling. He walked behind Robert, put the gun up to the back of his head, and fired. Robert Gibson fell to the floor, his body curled in the fetal position under the kitchen table, and bled out.

With Heather's father dead on the kitchen floor, Chad ransacked the rest of the house, starting with Heather's room. He was looking for evidence that Heather had been cheating on him. They had been broken up for two months, but in his mind he still considered it cheating. He ran from room to room emptying drawers onto the floor, but found nothing to satiate him.

Consumed with adrenaline, Chad sat behind the front door in the living room with the gun in his hand, waiting for Heather to get home from work.

A little after 3:00 p.m., the door opened – but it wasn't Heather. It was her younger sister, Rachel, with her friend Melanie. The two fourteen-year-old girls had recorded the latest episode of X-Files and were excited to watch it after school, but their plans came to a screeching halt. Chad pointed his gun at them as soon as they walked in the door and forced them to the floor. "Keep your eyes down! Don't look up!"

he screamed. Chad didn't want them to see that Rachel and Heather's father lay in a pool of blood in the kitchen.

Chad screamed at Rachel, "I'm waiting for your mother to get home so I can kill your family all at once!" He then pushed the two young girls onto the living room couch and forced one to perform oral sex on him while training the gun on the other. For several hours Chad sodomized and tortured the two girls as Rachel cried for her father. All the while, he shielded the girls from seeing into the kitchen.

After almost two hours of abuse, Heather walked in the front door to a gun in her face. Chad immediately grabbed her and shoved her over by the two younger girls, then took all three girls into the front bedroom—away from the kitchen.

His jealousy took over and he screamed at Heather, questioning her about her social life and accusing her of flirting with other men. He and Heather argued for almost an hour when there was suddenly a knock on the door. Chad pointed the gun at the girls and told them to keep quiet. It was another friend of Rachel's that had arrived to watch X-Files with the other girls.

Eventually the knocking stopped and the young girl luckily escaped the ordeal. Chad told Heather that if she didn't go back with him, he would kill her entire family. Little did she know that her father was already dead.

Heather had a knack for calming Chad down and eventually bargained with him. She offered her own life for her family's. She told Chad she would go with him and he could kill her if he wanted to, but to spare the life of the rest of her family.

Chad placed the gun at her back and directed Heather toward her burgundy Pontiac Grand Prix. With Heather in the passenger seat, Chad drove down the street. Heather took her first opportunity to escape when he stopped at a stop light. She opened the door and ran as fast as she could, screaming at the top of her lungs. Chad panicked, stepped on the gas, and took off in her car.

When Heather ran back to her house, she and the other two girls discovered the body of Robert Gibson in the kitchen and called police.

Ninety minutes after Heather escaped, police received a call from Chad Wiersma. "I shot somebody and I don't know what to do," he told police dispatch. Chad told them he was at a convenience store and ready to give himself up. He reassured officers that the gun was in the trunk and the ammunition clip was in the glove box.

Police arrested Wiersma and put in the back of the squad car, where he immediately confessed that he had stolen the gun from a friend and had killed his ex-girlfriend's father.

At the murder scene, police collected the 9 millimeter metal-jacketed bullet and a shell casing. After test firing the gun retrieved from the trunk of the car, the ballistics test was a match. Police also obtained fingerprints from a drinking glass at the Gibson house that was a match to Chad Wiersma.

Wiersma was charged on twelve counts. One count of open murder, seven counts of first-degree criminal sexual conduct, assault with a dangerous weapon, two counts of committing a felony with a firearm, and being a felon in possession of a firearm.

After a psychiatric examination, it was determined that Wiersma was competent to stand trial. However, despite giving a full account of what happened during the questioning, he later claimed that he had no recollection of the events or anything that happened over the days prior to the murder.

The trial of Chad Wiersma began in October 1996. He pleaded guilty to seven of the charges, including all the sexual assault charges. This was good news for the prosecution, as the two fourteen-year-old girls could limit the amount of detail they would have to tell the court about the traumatic events.

Before Heather and Rachel Gibson testified about the ordeal, the judge ordered all spectators and media from the room. Only their mother was allowed to remain for support.

Heather explained how Wiersma was consumed by desire. She detailed his abuse dating back to the early days of their relationship, when he broke the car window and dragged her through it. She went on to explain the events of the day and his threats to murder her entire family.

Rachel told the court of the torture and abuse she endured as Wiersma threatened to kill her entire family while he raped her and her friend.

His defense attorney asked to have Wiersma's confession removed from the record, claiming that he hadn't been read his Miranda rights at the time. In court he changed his story and claimed that he hadn't told police that he shot anyone, but the Kalamazoo arresting officers testified that he voluntarily gave the statement about the killing.

The dispatch officer that took his phone call before his arrest also testified that he said, "I shot somebody and I don't know what to do."

Wiersma's friends also testified against him; his two co-workers and the friend from whom he stole the gun.

Regardless of his denials, Wiersma was going away for life no matter what. On November 19, 1995, Chadwick Robert Wiersma was found guilty of the remaining two charges, resulting in his guilt on all twelve charges.

Three of the rape charges received a sentence of 60 to 90 years. He received a life sentence each for the remaining four charges. The murder charge carried yet another life sentence. All of his sentences were harsher because of his habitual offender status.

CHAPTER 3
GAY PANIC

G wen Amber Rose Araujo was born in 1985, but she wasn't born with that name. She was actually born Edward Araujo, Jr.

When he was just ten-months-old, Eddie Araujo's father disappeared after his parents divorced. Eddie spent his early childhood years like a normal kid in the Bay Area of California: he was into baseball, fishing, and camping. But his mother and sister both knew early on that Eddie was different. They didn't understand it… but they knew it.

Eddie never had a masculine side. Instead, he was extremely feminine in everything he did. At school he was ridiculed by many classmates, but despite it all, he was outgoing and had many friends that accepted him for who he was.

By the time Eddie was fourteen, he knew it was time. He couldn't pretend to be a boy any longer. Eddie let his mother know he was transgender and wanted to become a girl. From that point on, she asked to be referred to as Gwen after her favorite musician, Gwen Stefani. Although Gwen's mother accepted her new identity, she initially refused to call her by her new name.

Gwen proudly wore girl's clothes and makeup. Though the bullying at school increased, she still had plenty of friends who accepted her new look. It took immense courage to dress as she did in a suburban town. However, Gwen just felt so natural as a girl. She took such pride in playing the part that someone who had just met her would have a hard time realizing she was born male.

Gwen Araujo

Despite the support of her friends, the bullying got worse and worse. As a result, her grades suffered and eventually she dropped out of school. She was an expert at applying her makeup, so much so that many of her female friends regularly asked her to do their makeup for them. She had hopes of going to cosmetology school, moving to Hollywood, and becoming famous.

Finding a job proved difficult as well. Gwen looked convincingly like a girl. When the name on her job applications didn't match her appearance, she was usually turned down. By the time she turned seventeen, Gwen had planned to begin hormone treatment and undergo surgery to become a woman.

Gwen liked to party and, in the late summer of 2002, met several young men that enjoyed the same. José and Paul Merél were two brothers that rented a house in Newark, California, a small residential town midway between San Jose and Oakland near the south end of the bay.

José and Paul's house was known as a party house where teenagers and young adults would regularly drink alcohol and smoke marijuana. In late August, Gwen partied with José and his friends Michael Magidson, Jaron Nabors, and Jason Cazares.

All four men were in their late teens or early twenties and found seventeen-year-old Gwen to be an attractive young girl, albeit with a bit of a deep voice. She drank, smoked pot, and flirted with the young men throughout the night. When she left, Jaron turned to the other three, noted her deep voice, and jokingly said, "Could this be a dude?" All four laughed off the comment and didn't take it seriously.

During subsequent nights, Gwen returned to the house and continued partying and flirting with the young men. One evening she performed oral sex on Michael Magidson. On another night, during an encounter with José Merél, she told him she was having her period and pushed him away from her genitalia and toward her anus. They had anal sex without José realizing she was a man.

———

José's older brother, Paul, had been dating a girl named Nicole Brown who often partied at the house too. Nicole was a tomboy—a tough girl that liked to fight. She had never lost a fight to another girl... until she met Gwen.

Toward the end of a night of drinking, Nicole challenged Gwen to give the men in the room a striptease. The young men gathered around, but Gwen wanted no part in it. As Nicole egged her on, the challenge had escalated into hair pulling, shoves, and eventually a full-fledged fistfight.

In the end, the men pulled them apart. But Gwen had gotten the best of Nicole. Shocked that she received such powerful blows from a girl that was much smaller than her, Nicole told the men,

 "She fought like a guy."

That night was the beginning of much speculation between the four men; José, Michael, Jaron, and Jason. Over the next two weeks, the men debated whether Gwen could actually be a boy. José and Michael, both of who had sexual encounters with her, were especially concerned. They questioned their own manhood. The four concluded that if she was indeed male...

 "something bad could happen."

Two weeks later, on October 3, 2002, the four men were at a nightclub early in the evening. "I swear, if it's a fucking man, I'm gonna kill him. If it's a man, she ain't gonna leave," José told the other men. Michael replied, "I don't know what I'm gonna do." Jaron added, "Whatever you do, make sure you don't make a mess."

Gwen was back at the house drinking and smoking with Nicole and José's brothers, Paul and Emmanuel, when the four young men returned home from the club after midnight. Michael and José were obsessed with the possibility that Gwen was male. They could think of nothing else.

A little after 3:30 a.m., Paul and Nicole were preparing to go to bed in the back bedroom when they heard a commotion in the kitchen. When Nicole came out she heard Michael confronting Gwen,

 "Are you a man?! Are you a man?!"

Gwen stood in silence.

Nicole encouraged the confrontation and said, "Why don't one of you guys find out?" Michael's heart raced. He grabbed Gwen by the arm and pushed her into the bathroom. The others waited patiently in the kitchen while Michael and Gwen talked in the bathroom. But Nicole was an instigator - she couldn't wait any longer and went into the bathroom. Gwen was sleepy and drunk, sitting on the bathroom counter when Nicole grabbed Gwen's knees and spread her legs open. "It's a man! Oh my God!" she screamed.

When José heard those words, his stomach churned. He started crying and vomited near the bathroom while the other three men stormed out the door of the house to smoke cigarettes. "I can't be gay!" José repeated, over and over. Nicole tried to console him, but he was lost in a world of self-pity.

Nicole could see the blood boiling in the other three men and pleaded with them, "Let her go. Just let her walk out the door." Feeling a bit of remorse that she encouraged all of this, Nicole went back to the bathroom and told Gwen, "You better run as fast as you can."

Gwen ran for the door, but Jaron blocked her path. Michael grabbed her, threw her to the ground, and sat on her chest, pinning her down. He screamed at her for a moment, then let her up.

Nicole knew something seriously bad was going to happen. Her boyfriend, Paul Merél, was on probation. She knew that if he was involved in anything that was about to happen, he would go back to jail. Nicole ran to the back room, grabbed Paul and his younger brother Emmanuel, and the three of them left before the situation spun further out of control.

Michael yanked down Gwen's skirt to show her genitals, then started punching her in the face. When she fell to the ground, he put her in a chokehold, but Jaron and Jason pulled him off.

When Gwen stood up, she said, "Please don't. I have a family." But José became enraged, grabbed a can of food from the kitchen counter, and struck her in the head with it. Gwen fell to the floor again, then he took a frying pan from the stove and swung it, hitting her in the head.

Emotions were raging all around. Jaron and Jason knew what was inevitably going to happen. "They're going to kill that bitch," one of them said to the other. The two left the house, went to Jason's house, and returned with a pickaxe and shovels. They knew they would have a body to dispose of.

When Jason and Jaron arrived back at the house, Gwen was still alive and conscious, but bleeding profusely from the head and sitting on the couch. Worried that she would stain the couch, José ordered her off. Michael wasn't finished with her yet, though. He grabbed her and continued beating her.

Gwen lost consciousness when Michael hit her with his knee, smashing her head against the living room wall, cracking the plaster. Jason then joined in and started kicking her while José continued crying and tried to clean the blood from the couch and carpet.

With Gwen unconscious, Michael tied her ankles and wrists with rope and wrapped her in a comforter in an attempt to stop the blood from spreading throughout the house. He then dragged her into the garage.

Jaron watched as Michael placed a rope around her neck. Michael twisted the rope around her neck. He twisted and twisted until it eventually strangled her. Jason then hit her in the head twice with a shovel. Jaron wasn't sure if the strangling or the shovel had killed her, but it was clear—Gwen was dead.

The men put her body in the back of Michael's pickup truck, smoked cigarettes, and discussed what they should do. All four men drove east throughout the night. They drove for four hours, deep into the El Dorado National Forest in the Sierra Nevada mountains. As the morning light poked over the mountains, they dug a shallow grave.

José told the others, "I'm so mad I could still kick her a couple times more." The men put her in the ground, covered her up, and had breakfast at a McDonald's on the way home.

It wasn't unusual for Gwen to stay out all night. But when she didn't return home on the second night, her mother called police to report her missing. Initially, police didn't take her disappearance seriously. She was transgender and was known to stay out late.

It's hard enough for two people to keep a secret, but seven people knew this secret. Keeping it that way would prove to be impossible. Within two days, Jaron Nabors was noticeably stricken with guilt. He needed to let his secret out. When a friend confronted him about his melancholy, he confessed what he and the three other men had done.

Jaron's friend went to police with the information and agreed to wear a wiretap. The friend's next conversation with Jaron was recorded; he incriminated himself and was quickly arrested. On October 15, eleven days after they buried Gwen, Jaron Nabors led police to the gravesite.

Michael Magidson, José Merél, and Paul Merél were initially arrested. However, when Nicole Brown and Emmanuel Merél informed police that Paul had left the house before the killing and took no part in the violence, he was released.

As Jaron sat in jail, he wrote a letter to his girlfriend. In the letter he described a "Soprano-type plan to kill the bitch and get rid of her body." Detectives, however, intercepted the letter which also implicated Jason Cazares, who at that time had only been considered a witness. Jason was subsequently arrested as well.

Jaron Nabors was the most willing of the four to speak to police. After four months behind bars, Jaron pleaded guilty to voluntary manslaughter. The conviction came with an eleven year prison sentence as long as he agreed to testify against the other three during their trial. If he didn't testify, the charge would be changed to murder and his sentence extended.

At the trial, the prosecuting attorney referred to Gwen using her birth name, Eddie. He argued that the three men had acted as a jury of their own:

 "the wages of Eddie Araujo's sin of deception were death."

The defense attorney argued for a defense known as "gay panic." He claimed his clients were "shocked beyond reason" when they realized that they'd had sex with a man. He claimed that California law calls for a charge of manslaughter at most, rather than murder.

Although Jaron Nabors testified against his friends, he added that he felt that Michael and José had been raped. Araujo "didn't come clean with being what he really was. I feel like he forced them into homosexual sex, and my definition of rape was being forced into sex." When the prosecution asked him how Gwen had "forced" them, he replied, "Through deception."

After nine days of deliberation, the jury couldn't decide if the murder was premeditated. Although most of the jury wanted to convict Michael of first-degree murder, some wanted to acquit the others. Ultimately, because they could not unanimously decide, the trial ended in a mistrial.

The second trial began more than a year later in May 2005. By that time, Gwen's mother was granted approval to have her name posthumously changed, requiring the defense lawyers to refer to her as Gwen rather than Eddie. Also, all three defendants had the charge of hate-crime added to their first-degree murder charge.

During the second trial, all three defendants blamed each other, including Jaron Nabors. José claimed Jaron was the one that hit her in the head with the shovel, while Michael had strangled her. Michael admitted to strangling her, but also said Jaron hit her in the head.

After over three months of testimony, Michael Magidson and José Merél were both found guilty of second-degree murder and received a sentence of fifteen years to life in prison. On the hate crime charge, they were both found not-guilty.

The jury, however, was again undecided on Jason Cazares. To avoid a third trial, he agreed to plead no contest to a lesser charge of manslaughter and was sentenced to just six years in prison with credit for the time he had already done.

In the years after Gwen's death, her mother suffered from Post-Traumatic Stress Disorder and was unable to return to work as a legal assistant. As of 2016, she was homeless.

The murder of Gwen Araujo resulted in changes in California laws. The change limited the use of gay or trans panic as a defense; defendants may no longer claim they were provoked to murder a person based on their gender or sexual orientation.

By 2016. Jason Cazares, Jaron Nabors, and José Merél had all been released from prison. Michael Magidson, however, told his parole board that he was not ready to be released in 2016 and his parole was denied. In 2019 he was denied parole a second time.

CHAPTER 4
SAVING A SOUL

On a crisp October night in 1958, fifteen-year-old Carl Eder threw a rope out of his second-story bedroom window, quietly climbed down, and disappeared into the dark suburb of Rochester, New York.

Eder spent the next month hitchhiking his way across the country, eventually ending up in the San Diego area. As the child of a first-generation German immigrant family, Eder had experience making cabinetry for his father and looked for work in the area, but had trouble because of his age.

The six-foot-four boy crossed the southern border of the United States into Tijuana, Mexico, where he found a shop that would make him a fake identification card. Eder paid for his ID card, called himself "Charles Harrison", and crossed back into San Diego.

Still unable to find work, Eder slept in a coat closet in the Mission Beach Ballroom. That was when he first met thirty-nine-year-old Tom Pendergast.

Tom Pendergast was a religious man. As a youth, he spent time in reform school after he and some friends were caught stealing a car and taking it for a joyride. After that experience, he made it his life's mission to help young boys find their way in life and avoid a life of crime.

Throughout the years, Tom had tried to help four young boys. He brought them into his home in El Cajon, just east of San Diego, and introduced them to his wife and children. He gave them food and a place to sleep and helped them try to find work. His efforts, however, hadn't always worked. On one occasion a boy that he let into his home robbed him and was never seen again – but that didn't deter Tom. He believed God had a task for him and he was determined to follow through.

On a stormy Southern California night, Tom Pendergast was driving home from work when he saw the pimply-faced Carl Eder hitchhiking on the side of the highway. He felt sorry for the boy and knew right away that he was homeless, headed for a life of crime, and needed help. Tom offered the boy a ride and Eder introduced himself as Charles Harrison. By the end of the drive, Tom invited Eder to his family home for dinner and a place to sleep for the night.

The Pendergast family embraced Eder and were more than happy to let him stay in a cottage they had on their property while he looked for work. Lois Pendergast made dinner every night for Eder, Tom, and their four young children; Diane, Allen, Thomas Jr., and David.

Six weeks had passed and Eder still hadn't found work. During the day he sat at home while Mrs. Pendergast watched after the two youngest children and Tom worked as an aircraft mechanic. The two oldest boys were in school.

In the early afternoon of December 15, 1958, Eder was annoyed with four-year-old Diane Pendergast. She was being a typical hyper girl and wanted to play. When Eder told her it was time to take a nap, she protested as any four-year-old would. She jumped up and down on the bed, ran around the room, and screamed. But Eder had had enough.

He grabbed the girl and threw her to the floor. When the small girl's head hit the hard floor, it cracked her skull. She was killed instantly.

Thirty-nine-year-old Lois Pendergast ran into the room and screamed, "You killed her! You killed her!" Eder was in a panic. He ran to the garage where he kept his suitcase, grabbed his .38 caliber pistol, and put shells in it. He then ran back into the house and shot two warning-shots into the wall. When Mrs. Pendergast screamed, he shot her in the left side of her chest. As she lay on the floor, he put the gun to her left temple and shot again.

Eder ran back into the garage, reached back into his suitcase, and removed a ten-inch hunting knife. He returned to the house to find two-year-old Allen Pendergast screaming on the floor. He took the knife and slashed his throat, then slashed the throat of Diane to make sure she was dead. Eder pulled Diane and Allen's bodies into the bathroom and piled them on top of each other. He then dragged Mrs. Pendergast's body into the bathroom and lay her next to her children.

For the next hour, Eder sat in the front bedroom of the home and waited for the two older boys to return from school. Six-year-old Thomas Jr. got home first. When he walked in the front door, Eder grabbed him, but the boy wiggled free and ran into the garage. Thomas Jr. was no match for the tall, lanky Eder. He caught Thomas in the garage bathroom, slit his throat, and disemboweled him as if he were gutting a deer.

Soon afterwards, nine-year-old David walked in the front door to find a knife at his throat. Eder quickly sliced his throat and cut his torso from his navel to his breastplate. He left the five dead bodies inside the house, walked out the front door, sat on the front steps, and waited for Tom to get home from work.

When Tom Pendergast drove up to the house, Eder didn't give him time to exit the vehicle. He pointed his pistol at him, got in the passenger side of the car, and told him to drive. For two hours, Eder forced Tom to drive randomly through the streets of San Diego without telling him what he had done to his family.

When they reached the Mission Beach area, Eder told Tom to stop at a gas station and forced him into the men's bathroom at gunpoint. He instructed Tom to take off his clothes. He had no choice but to comply. As Eder removed his own clothes and put on Tom's, Tom attacked him and wrestled the gun away from him. Tom managed to get the gun, but Eder fled out of the bathroom door and ran down the alley.

Tom had escaped with his life, but he had no idea the shock he was in for when he would return home. When he opened the door to his home, he first found his oldest son, David, eviscerated on the living room floor. Then he found his wife and two youngest children piled on top of each other on the bathroom floor. Tom screamed and lifted his wife's body, pulling her into the hallway. In shock and disbelief, he cradled her in his arms and cried. Lastly, he found Thomas Jr. butchered in the garage.

When police arrived Tom was crying in the front yard, still in shock, and covered in blood. He was calm enough to tell detectives about Carl Eder, who he knew as Charles Harrison.

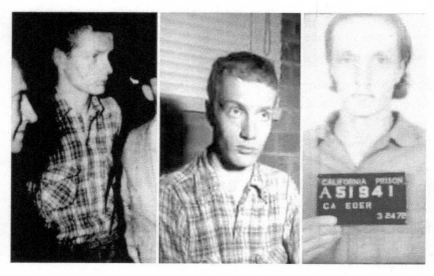

Carl Eder

Police didn't know whether or not to believe his story. Tom had the gun and it was covered in blood. His story seemed too extreme to be true, but police noticed the trousers he was wearing were far too large for him. Tom Pendergast was only five-foot-ten, while Eder was six-foot-four. Police thought there could be some truth to his story, so they alerted all law enforcement in the area and the media to be on the lookout for a suspect that matched Eder's description. They also knew that he would be wearing Tom's clothes, with trousers that would have been much too short for him.

Tom was taken to the psychiatric ward of the county hospital for fear that he may be suicidal. When doctors cleared him, he was brought to the police station where he was given multiple lie detector tests and questioned. Tom told investigators, "I was trying to save a soul" when he took Eder into his home. After seven hours of interrogation, detectives finally believed his story and stepped up the search for Carl Eder.

Police searched the canyons around San Diego on horseback and in helicopters, while members of the public called in hundreds of tips. It seemed likely that Eder may have crossed the border again and escaped into Mexico. Detectives had another theory that he may have taken another family hostage in the area and conducted hundreds of door-to-door searches looking for him. The only clue they had was his bloody t-shirt, found a mile from the gas station that he fled from.

Three days after the murders, Eder was in Mission Beach again trying to hide from authorities. He managed to buy a loaf of bread and a hamburger without being recognized, but when a man saw him walking in front of his house, he instantly recognized the short-legged pants he was wearing. The man ran next-door to his friend's house, who was a San Diego police officer.

Still wearing his pajamas, the officer hopped onto his bicycle and rode in the direction that Eder had been walking. The officer caught up with Eder at a Mission Beach amusement center that had been closed for the winter. Eder had been sleeping in the bathroom there for the past three days. When the officer confronted Eder, he claimed he didn't have any identification, but handed him a jury summons with the name Max

Turner. The officer didn't believe him and said, "You are Carl Eder," to which Eder offered no resistance and said, "Yes, I am."

Tom Pendergast was at the police station when Carl Eder was arrested and brought in. Tom yelled, "Why did you do it?! Why did you do it?!" After a brief silence Eder quietly said, "I didn't want to, Tom."

When questioned by police, Eder easily admitted to killing the family, "Yes, I killed them all. The noise of the kids annoyed me. I must have flipped my lid." Eder explained how he butchered each member of the family, but when asked why he didn't kill Tom Pendergast, he replied, "I didn't want to kill him. He was really good to me."

Despite being sixteen years old at the time of the murders, Eder was tried as an adult. Because he was still a juvenile, however, he was not eligible for the death penalty. Initially he pleaded innocent, but after persuasion by his lawyer he changed his plea to guilty.

At sentencing, his lawyer explained his client was eager to start psychiatric treatment, hoping that this would add some leniency to his sentence. Eder was given five life sentences, three concurrent sentences and two consecutive. He would be eligible for parole after only seven years.

As he left the courthouse, Tom Pendergast said to him, "Rest in peace there, Carl. Remember that."

Tom addressed the media and said, "I don't think he should ever be released. I don't consider him excused for killing my wife and four children because of any mental condition. He's just wicked. It was premeditated murder. Carl doesn't feel any remorse."

Carl Eder spent the next fifteen years moving from prison to prison throughout the California Department of Corrections. At one point he was just a few cells down from the notorious glamour girl slayer, Harvey Glatman (featured in True Crime Case Histories Volume 2).

In 1971, Eder was sent to the California Correctional Institution in Tehachapi, a minimum security prison with a population of 1,200 inmates. Tehachapi allowed him the freedom to work outside of the prison for periods of time without supervision. Eder had been working on a farm work detail for three years without incident until, one day, he vanished.

In October 1974, when he was thirty-two years old, Eder was on farm detail working completely unsupervised when he simply walked away. Personnel working at the farm didn't notice he was gone for at least seventy-five minutes.

Still wearing his prison denims, Carl Eder was on the run. When prison officials searched his cell, they found a note reading, "I've done enough time and I'm leaving."

While in prison, Eder had contact with several extremist groups including white supremacists, outlaw motorcycle groups, Venceremos Brigade, and the Symbionese Liberation Army. It's believed that any of these groups could have been involved in assisting his escape.

Throughout the years authorities tried to locate Carl Eder, including featuring him on America's Most Wanted and offering a $20,000 reward, but he seemed to have completely disappeared. There were reports he was spotted in Calistoga and St. Helena, California, but police had no luck in apprehending him. As of this time of writing, Eder would be approaching eighty years old; police speculate that he either left the country or was killed by one of his own extremist groups.

CHAPTER 5
THE JACKSONVILLE MONSTER

On a Sunday morning in 1992, thirteen-year-old Kerri Anne Buck walked toward her friend's house through her suburban neighborhood in Jacksonville, Florida, when she heard the low rumble of a vehicle pulling up behind her. Kerri Anne turned around to see a white van with tinted windows slowing down beside her.

The passenger side window of the van rolled down and the driver, a man in his thirties, called out, "Do you know Susie?" Kerri Anne replied "No" and continued walking. Slowly rolling beside her as she walked, the man then said, "Do you go to Southside Middle School?" His voice sounded angry to the young girl. She replied, "No," which was a lie.

The man was a stranger. Kerri Anne knew better than to talk to strangers. The man then stopped the van and commanded her to,

 "Get the fuck in the van!"

Kerri Anne ran down the street as fast as she could. When she reached her friend's house and pounded on the door, there was no answer. She knew the neighborhood well and continued running around the corner

to a large park as the man ran after her. In the park, Kerri Anne found a playground which had a children's slide shaped into a tube. She climbed the ladder, slid halfway down the tube, stopped, and wedged herself against the walls of the slide.

Kerri Anne could hear the man entering the area around the playground as she pushed harder and harder against the walls, trying not to slip out the bottom of the tube. She heard him grunt

> "I know you're in there, you little bitch. I'm going to find you."

She waited for what seemed like an eternity and eventually got up the courage to peek out. He was gone. For the time being, Kerri Anne was safe. She ran back home as fast as she could.

Kerri Anne and her parents were on edge for several days afterward and Kerri was frightened to step foot outside their home. A few weeks after the incident, Kerri Anne's mother saw a strange white van parked outside their house. Mrs. Buck called her daughter to the window and Kerri Anne confirmed that it was the van of the man that tried to abduct her. Kerri's mother took down the license plate and called the police.

The owner of the van was thirty-six-year-old Donald Smith – and it wasn't his first brush with the law. Smith had been in and out of prison for sex crimes since the 1970s. As a registered sex offender, Smith was quickly arrested and sentenced to six years in prison for the attempted kidnapping of Kerri Anne Buck.

Prison was no deterrent for Smith. When he was released in the late nineties, he continued to prey on children. His obsession was insatiable. He was in and out of prison for the next fifteen years for crimes ranging from selling obscene material, voyeurism, and public masturbation, to felony child abuse.

In 2009 Smith was charged with impersonating a public employee and aggravated child abuse by willful torture. He had posed as a child welfare case worker, got a ten-year-old girl on the phone, asked her sexually explicit questions, and threatened to harm her.

After serving less than fifteen months in Jackson County Jail for the crime, the repeat sexual offender was released once again on May 31, 2013.

Rayne Perrywinkle had fallen on hard times – but then again, times were always hard for Rayne. Although she had given up her first-born daughter twenty years prior to relatives in Australia, she was doing her best to raise her three youngest daughters by herself in Jacksonville.

Eight-year-old Cherish Perrywinkle was the oldest of the girls living with Rayne. Rayne had had a very brief relationship with Cherish's father, Billy Jarreau. To put it bluntly, it was a one-night-stand. In 2003 she had been a stripper, Billy a recently divorced Navy officer, when they met at a Jacksonville strip club. After several nights of lap dances, Billy convinced her to go home with him. Nine months later, Cherish was born.

Initially Billy contested his paternity. He was willing to provide support for the girl, but needed proof that he was the father. Eventually a court-ordered paternity test proved he was indeed Cherish's father, so he accepted her with open arms and financial support.

Despite the financial support, Rayne continued to struggle to get her life on track. She had two more girls with another man but never married, while Billy believed Cherish would be better off living with him in California. He tried several times to get custody of the girl, but each time failed. Instead, Rayne agreed to let Cherish spend summers with her father in California.

On June 21, 2013, Rayne was reluctantly getting ready to send Cherish to California for the summer. The flight was scheduled for the next day and Rayne took her three girls to the Dollar General store to get Cherish some clothes for the trip. They shopped in the store for over an hour, unaware that sixty-one-year-old Donald Smith was watching them from afar.

Cherish Perrywinkle

Rayne and Cherish found a little black and white dress with hearts that they liked, but when Rayne asked the cashier the price of the dress, she realized she didn't have enough money to buy it and still pay for a taxi to the airport the next day.

Donald Smith had come into the store just minutes before and asked the cashier if they had any adult magazines. When Smith overheard Rayne explain to the cashier that she couldn't afford the dress, he took notice. He could tell that Rayne was frustrated and struggling to provide for her young girls.

When Rayne and the girls left the store, Smith approached Rayne outside of the store and said, "If you really want that dress, I'll get it for you. You look like you really have your hands full. I have a couple of little ones myself."

At first glance, he seemed harmless enough. Just an older gentleman – a good Samaritan. Rayne had no way of knowing he was a deranged predator that had been released from prison only three weeks earlier.

Smith introduced himself as Don and explained to her that he was waiting for his wife to arrive. He claimed his wife had a Walmart gift card for $150 that he was willing to give to her to help buy Cherish some clothes. Rayne was apprehensive about talking to a complete stranger, but he spoke at length about his own young children and wife—none of which existed. He told her he worked for the charity Habitat for Humanity—another lie.

When Rayne informed him that she needed to get home and get Cherish ready for her flight, he told her to be patient and encouraged her to wait. His wife would show up any minute and she would be driving a gold car. He then reached into his pocket, opened his phone, and pretended to talk to someone on the other end. After the call he said, "That was my wife. She's just going to meet us at Walmart."

Walmart was ten minutes away and Rayne didn't own a car. She had no way to get there other than by taxi, but of course, Smith offered to take them in his van. Still feeling uneasy, she declined at first, but he insisted he was no threat. "Do you want to see my driver's license or something?" He did his best to make her feel foolish for being paranoid, so eventually she accepted the ride.

When they arrived at Walmart around 9:00 p.m., Rayne and the girls entered the store while Smith faked another phone call. He then told Rayne that his wife had called and the two of them would like to take them out for dinner after shopping, but Rayne had no intention of going out to dinner with them. Her only concern was getting the gift card for her kids and going home.

Cherish tried on clothes for over an hour and a half while Rayne put the girls' items into her push cart. The only item Smith put in the cart was some rope that he picked up in the hardware department. As he watched the girls shopping, Rayne was shocked when Cherish brought a pair of women's high heel shoes to her and asked if she could try them on. She immediately told her, "No, those aren't kids' shoes! Where did you get those?" Cherish replied, "Don wanted me to try them on." Rayne told him, "Those are women's high heels! I wouldn't even wear heels that high!"

After shopping for almost two hours, Smith's wife still hadn't arrived. Each time Rayne asked where she was, he just replied that she was "on her way." At 10:30 p.m., Walmart announced that the store would be closing in thirty minutes. The girls were getting tired and hadn't had any dinner yet. Smith held his hand up next to his face imitating a sock-puppet and said to the girls, "I'm going to McDonald's. What do you want to eat?" All the girls screamed "cheeseburgers!"

Smith started walking toward the McDonald's restaurant located within the Walmart store near the front entrance and Cherish followed him. Rayne was initially concerned, but Smith had spent the entire night making Rayne feel over-protective. She knew there were security cameras all over the store and believed there was no chance he could disappear with her daughter. Ignoring her better judgement, Rayne let her daughter follow the man she had met only hours ago.

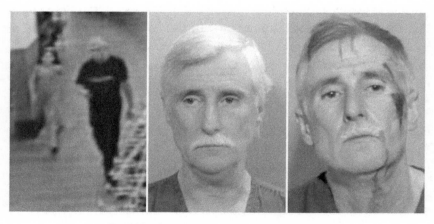

Donald Smith (Walmart security footage & mugshots)

Knowing the store was closing soon, Rayne and her two girls finished up their shopping and pushed their cart toward the front of the store. When they got to the McDonald's, Cherish and Donald Smith were nowhere to be found. Rayne pushed her cart with a quickened pace back and forth along the front of the store, looking down each aisle for her daughter. As she passed each empty aisle, she felt her heart beating harder and harder. With each step, she became more and more panicked.

When Walmart announced they were closing for the night and she couldn't find her daughter, terror overwhelmed her. Rayne was frantic and asked for help from Walmart employees, "Call 911, my daughter's been taken!" Rayne didn't have a working phone of her own and asked them to call, but the Walmart employees didn't take her seriously. The store was massive and the employees just assumed the young girl was lost.

Rayne continued to panic. She looked through the store and in the parking lot, but there was no sign of her daughter or Smith's white van. After 11:00 p.m., the store had closed and Rayne hadn't seen her daughter for a full thirty minutes before a Walmart employee finally let her borrow a cell phone.

During the heart-wrenching 911 call, Rayne explained the events of the day as police rushed to the scene:

 "… I had a bad feeling, I thought, well, I feel like pinching myself cause this is too good to be true, so I got to the checkout and he's not here and I'm hoping he's not raping her right now, cause I've had that done to me. I don't understand why he would leave right now unless he was gonna rape her and kill her - that's the only reason. And I'm wasting my time standing here!"

Rayne was so distressed she couldn't even remember what her daughter had been wearing that day. Throughout the night Rayne described the van and Smith's appearance to police. Using the description and checking the local sex offender registration, police quickly knew they were looking for Donald Smith. By 4:00 a.m., police had issued an Amber alert. By morning, the entire area of Jacksonville was looking for Cherish, Smith, and Smith's white van.

Just after 7:00 a.m., police received a call from a woman in north Jacksonville. She had seen a white van parked in an odd spot. It was discreetly parked in some bushes behind a church. It seemed suspicious to the woman because it was wedged deeply into the bushes. The woman suspected that someone in the van had dumped something in the bushes, but when police arrived and did the initial search of the area, they found nothing.

Smith lived with his mother. The police had already been to her house looking for him, but she claimed she had no idea where he was. After they left the house, police received a call from a man that rented a room at the Smith home. He told police that the prior afternoon, he had helped Smith remove the middle row of seats from his van. He also said that Smith had told him that if he ever had to run from the police, he would hide in the woods near a homeless camp in the area. Smith had told the man that he knew someone that had lived at the camp for twenty-eight years without police ever bothering him.

Every division of law enforcement in the area was on the lookout for Smith's 1998 white Dodge van. It didn't take long to find him. Before noon the morning after the abduction, Smith was pulled over and arrested... but there was no trace of Cherish. When the arresting officer noticed his pants were soaking wet, he yelled to the other officers, "Oh my God, she's in the water!"

Police rushed back to the Highlands Baptist Church. The earlier caller's suspicions were correct. The same officer that arrested Smith found the body of eight-year-old Cherish Perrywinkle wedged under a tree in a marshy wetland behind the church. Her body had been weighed down with chunks of asphalt and hidden with grass and branches. She was still wearing the bright orange dress with a fruit pattern on it, but naked beneath it. Her underwear and purple flip-flops were never found.

The sixty-seven pound girl had been gagged, raped, and sodomized for hours before she was strangled to death with a piece of clothing. The massive force of the trauma caused her gums, nostrils, and eyes to bleed. A forensic pathologist that examined Cherish's body would later tell the court, "She had so much trauma, her anatomy was totally distorted by the trauma she suffered."

The trial of Donald Smith didn't begin until February 2018, almost five years later. Smith faced the death penalty if found guilty. The trial was incredibly emotional as Rayne Perrywinkle recounted the horrifying evening. The jury was shown photos of the young girl that made them gasp out loud and cover their eyes. Some cried out loud. Even Smith turned his back and couldn't look at the autopsy photos of Cherish.

The Walmart and Dollar General security camera footage evidence against him left very little doubt of his guilt. When asked if the defense wanted to cross-examine Rayne, Smith said,

> "I don't want her to go through anything she doesn't have to go through. I'm done."

The jurors took only fifteen minutes to convict Donald Smith of kidnapping, rape, and murder. The week following his conviction, the jurors were asked if he should spend life in prison or be executed. New constitutional guidelines required a unanimous decision; every juror chose the death penalty.

At sentencing, Judge Mallory Cooper's voice cracked with emotion when she told Smith,

> "Donald Smith, you have not only forfeited your right to live among us, you have forfeited your right to live at all. May God have mercy on your soul."

After suffering the loss of her daughter, Rayne Perrywinkle's troubles were not over. The public condemned her, blaming her for leaving her daughter alone with Smith. Some went so far as to speculate that she was somehow involved in human trafficking. It didn't help matters when it came out during a deposition that Rayne claimed she was a clairvoyant and had a vision that her daughter would be dead by the time she was eight years old.

After the death of Cherish, Rayne was unable to shake the extreme grief of the traumatic event topped off with the blame from the public. She couldn't keep a job and was often turned down because everyone knew her name.

The state of Florida gave her twelve months to show that she could provide for her two remaining daughters, but it wasn't enough. Nine-year-old Destiny and seven-year-old Nevaeh were inevitably adopted by Rayne's sister and now live with their older sister, Lindsay, in Australia.

CHAPTER 6
DEAD IN THE WATER

To say life on their 300-acre dairy farm was "busy" was a gross understatement. It was exhausting. Hal and Jo Rogers spent excruciatingly long hours working their northwest Ohio farm for nearly every day of their adult lives. They were a hard-working family, to say the least.

Hal and Jo were high-school sweethearts who married just a few months after graduation and immediately started a family. Michelle was born first. Three years later came Christe.

As the years passed, they gave the girls chores on the farm such as working in the barn and looking after the cows. Christe was a daddy's girl and followed her father around the farm as often as she could. Although the young girls grew up loving life on the farm, over the years the day-in-day-out monotony and hard work wore on their mother, Jo.

Hal owned and worked the farm jointly with his younger brother, John, who lived in a small trailer on the same property. But John was a little odd. He wore military fatigues and often told tall tales of his non-existent work with the CIA and Secret Service.

In March 1988, however, John was accused of rape by a woman that lived with him in his trailer. The woman told police he wore a mask, bound her arms with handcuffs, blindfolded her, and raped her while holding a knife to her throat. Although he wore a mask, she told police she recognized his voice. She also said that he had videotaped the rape.

When detectives entered the trailer with a warrant, they found a briefcase with a videotape of the rape, just as the woman had claimed. The briefcase contained more than just the rape video, however.

Detectives found photos of Michelle, who was sixteen at the time. She was naked, blindfolded, and her hands and feet were bound with rope. They also found cassette audio tapes of Michelle screaming for John, her uncle, to let her go.

When confronted, Michelle confirmed the rape and told police that John had been raping her for more than two years. He told her he would kill her if she ever told anyone.

Before Hal knew about Michelle's accusation, he had promised his brother that he would post his $10,000 bond. But, despite posting the bond, the news destroyed the Rogers family. Hal and John's mother refused to believe her granddaughter and stood by her son, John. This drove Hal away from his mother.

Initially, John denied the rapes. Michelle was embarrassed and traumatized and had no intention of testifying against him. She just wanted it all to go away. In the end, she didn't need to testify. John pleaded guilty to raping the first woman and was sentenced to seven to twenty-five years in prison.

With the rape of his daughter and the loss of the relationship with his mother and brother, Hal fell into a deep depression. He became despondent and would sometimes disappear for days at a time, locking himself in his brother's trailer. The small town gossip weighed on the entire family.

The following year, Jo and the girls thought it would be good to get away for a while. Hal couldn't leave the farm, but at least the three girls could get a respite from the small town. Michelle and Christe had never had a real vacation. They had never even left the state of Ohio. Even Jo had only left the state once, for her and Hal's honeymoon, to spend a night in a hotel in Fort Wayne, Indiana.

Christe, Michelle, and Jo Rogers

The three girls planned a trip to Florida, where they could leave behind the gossip, the farm, the counselors, and the detectives. They wanted to meet Mickey Mouse and go to every theme park they could think of. What they really needed was some sunshine and sand in between their toes. Although none of them even knew how to swim, they needed to feel the warm ocean waters. Just a week away would do a world of good, they thought.

Michelle's only hesitation was being away from her boyfriend, Jeff Feasby. Although they had only been dating for less than a month, she was smitten and they spoke on the phone every night. Jeff had heard rumors of Michelle's troubles with her uncle, but he didn't know details. He didn't care to know. It was her own business and she clearly didn't want to talk about it.

Although they were only leaving for a week, Michelle and Jeff's final goodbye was emotional for the young couple. They kissed on their front porch while fourteen-year-old Christe watched. Still, all three of the women were excited to get started on their journey and packed the car the night before the trip. At the break of dawn on May 26, 1989, they left Willshire, Ohio, and headed south.

The first day of driving was both exhausting, yet exciting. Jo was known for driving fast and Michelle had only recently got her driver's license, so Jo drove most of the way. The first night they stayed in a hotel just across the Georgia border, then continued on to their first stop the next day: Jacksonville, Florida.

After a day at Jacksonville Zoo, they headed inland to Silver Springs where they took a tour on a glass-bottom boat. The family was finally having a proper vacation and filled rolls of film with snapshots along the way.

After Silver Springs, they moved toward the Atlantic coast and drove down Highway 1 toward Cape Canaveral. Jo sent a postcard to Hal, while Michelle sent a postcard to Jeff. She was feeling a bit guilty for being on vacation during the week of Jeff's birthday, so she got him a trashy joke postcard – it had a bikini-clad woman rolling in the sand on the Florida beach with an alligator snapping at her bikini bottom. The postcard read:

 "Hi! How is everything with you? I'm doing great. Yesterday we went to the Zoo in Jacksonville. I was visiting my relatives, and we found Geoffrey (you). Later we went to Silver Springs and rode on a glass-bottom boat. Today we are going to a beach and then to Sea World. You have fun at work and behave yourself. Have a great birthday. I'll be thinking of you! I miss you!

Love ya,

Chelle"

The girls had no intention of slowing down. The following days they went to Sea World, Epcot Center, and Disney's Hollywood Studios. By Thursday, they were ready to explore the bay side of Florida and headed to Tampa.

Just after noon, the three girls checked into their hotel overlooking Tampa Bay and snapped a few photos as they unpacked their suitcases. Michelle called Jeff for his birthday while Jo and Christe looked at brochures they had picked up in the hotel's lobby. The Busch Gardens brochure seemed promising. Jo called Busch Gardens for more information and wrote directions on the brochure so they could go the next day.

That evening, the three girls were seen having dinner in the hotel restaurant. However, this was the last time they were seen alive.

Jo and the girls were due back at the farm that Sunday, June 4. Jo was scheduled for work and Michelle's summer school started on Monday, but there was no sign of them. Hal hadn't heard a word.

That same Sunday morning, a sailboat was passing under the Sunshine Skyway Bridge, where Tampa Bay opens into the Gulf of Mexico. As the boat lumbered toward the gulf, the captain noticed something floating in the water. He slowed the boat and it gradually became clear that the floating object was a body.

The captain of the boat called the Coast Guard to report what they had found. It was the body of a female. She was floating face-down and naked below the waist. Both her legs and feet were bound with yellow rope. The same type of yellow rope was tying her neck to something beneath the water, partially weighing her down. The Coast Guard, however, couldn't lift the object that was tied around her neck. They cut the rope, let the object sink, and lifted the body aboard. As they headed toward the marina, another call came in. Someone had found a second body.

Not far north of the first body was another similar site. A female, face-down, bound with the same type of yellow rope and naked below the waist. A rope around her neck was tied to a large object beneath the water. Minutes after finding the second body, another call came in of a third body.

When the Coast Guard retrieved the bodies, they realized that all three had been weighed down by a large concrete block tied to the rope around their necks. The bloating caused by decomposition, however, had caused the bodies to float to the surface despite the heavy weight.

Each of the bodies had been bound in the same manner with the same type of rope, but one of the girls had managed to get a hand free. All three were also gagged, with duct tape over their mouths.

Although decomposition had made it difficult to determine with certainty if they had been sexually assaulted, the fact that they were all naked from the waist down seemed to point to that conclusion. There were no defensive wounds and no evidence that a knife or gun was used against them. However, the evidence indicated that they had been alive when they entered the water with concrete tied around their necks.

Although Jeff had barely known Michelle's father, he repeatedly called Hal at the farm asking if he had heard from them. Both of them were getting worried. Hal had called Jo's friends and relatives, but nobody had heard a word. By Wednesday, the girls were three days late and Hal had worked himself into a panic. He went to the bank to withdraw $7,000 in cash with a plan to hire a private plane. He thought he could search the route from Ohio to Florida from the air.

Although the Rogers party was due to check out of their hotel almost a week prior, the maid at the Tampa Days Inn noticed the suitcases hadn't moved from room 251. The beds had never been slept in, the soaps were still wrapped in paper, and a purse lay on the table. Each day she walked in to clean the room, but nothing had been touched.

The news of the three female bodies was on the television news in Tampa every night. On Thursday, June 8, the hotel management called the Tampa police. When detectives arrived, they thoroughly examined the room. Fingerprints lifted from a tube of toothpaste matched fingerprints from one of the bodies. Using the hotel registration, they were able to identify the female victims as the Rogers girls.

Hal Rogers had already been in a deep depression dealing with the rape of his daughter by his brother. When the local Sheriff told him of the rape and murder of his wife and both daughters, it was more than he could handle. Television cameras and reporters were at his door almost immediately after the news became public. He fell apart emotionally, but kept working. The farm still needed to be run.

Police found the Roger's car parked near the Courtney Campbell Parkway at a boat ramp just a few miles from their hotel. Nothing seemed out of the ordinary. Christe's stuffed cow toy was still stuck to the back window with suction cups. On the front seat police found a sheet from a Days Inn notepad where Jo had written directions to the boat ramp:

 "turn rt (w on 60) - 2 1/2 mi - on rt side alt before bridge"

Below that was:

"blue w/wht"

It appeared that someone had given them instructions to the boat ramp. Detectives assumed they were told to look for a blue and white boat.

Also on the front seat of the car was a brochure for Clearwater Beach, Florida. Written at the bottom of the brochure were directions back to their hotel. The handwriting on the brochure, however, wasn't the same as the handwriting on the Days Inn note paper. Someone other than Jo had written it.

During their investigation, detectives learned of Michelle's rape by her uncle. Although John Rogers was in prison at the time, police needed to eliminate the possibility that John had somehow had something to do with the girls' death. Both incidences involved being bound with rope – had he somehow arranged to have them killed from behind bars? To find out, detectives flew to Ohio.

When detectives interviewed John Rogers in prison, they quickly realized that he had nothing to do with the murders. There was no way he could have arranged something from behind bars. Even within the prison, John was a loner and had few friends. He had no packages delivered and the only phone call or visitor to the prison had been his mother.

Hal Rogers was having trouble making sense of his life. The constant badgering by news crews drove him crazy. To cope, he kept working on his farm. At the funeral, he fought back the urge to punch his own mother. He couldn't believe she had the nerve to show up at her granddaughter's funeral after calling her a liar and saying she had made up the rape charge. While the entire congregation sobbed, Hal was more angry than sad. He was mad at his mother, mad at God, mad at the killer… he sat behind his tinted glasses, silently showing no emotion. After the funeral, he went straight back to working the farm.

Detectives took notice of Hal's behavior and, for a brief time, considered him a possible suspect. It seemed suspicious that he had paid his brother's $10,000 bond after his arrest. Then, just days after the murders, he made a $7,000 cash withdrawal from the bank. His actions definitely raised questions, but in the end Hal was able to account for the cash he withdrew and police confirmed he had never left the state of Ohio.

Investigators used a forensic handwriting expert to analyze the brochure they found in the Rogers' car. They knew it wasn't any of the girl's handwriting. Right away, the examiner noticed two unique characteristics about the handwriting: the person who wrote the note had a peculiar habit of capitalizing T's in the middle of words. There were also four Y's in the note, each written in a different style.

The brochure was also analyzed for fingerprints. There were several fingerprints on the brochure, but all belonged to the Rogers girls. Only one print was unidentified—a partial palm print. But until detectives had a suspect to match it to, the print was useless.

Hundreds of tips came in from the public throughout Florida, but one in particular seemed to be relevant. A twenty-four-year-old woman named Judy Blair was visiting from Canada and told police she was approached by a man just two weeks before the murders in the same area. The man offered to take her out for a sunset cruise on his blue and white boat. Once they were out in the open water and away from other boats, the man sexually assaulted her.

Judy told police he had approached her one evening at a 7-Eleven store. He was a white male in his mid-thirties with reddish-blonde hair, about 5 foot 10 and 180 pounds. She mentioned he was friendly and drove a dark color Jeep Cherokee with tinted windows.

He took her out on a sunset cruise, but once the sun had set, he tried to have sex with her. When she refused, he got angry and attacked her. He screamed at her,

"What are you doing? Nobody's going to hear you. What are you going to do? Jump out of the boat? Is sex something worth losing your life over?"

She pleaded with him, telling him that she was a virgin, but that seemed to excite him more.

Once he was finished, the man seemed to have immediate regret for his actions and apologized for what he had done.

 "I've taken something from you that you can never get back,"

he told her before vomiting over the edge of the boat.

As he drove the boat toward the shore, he threw up several more times. The man took her camera, pulled the film out, and threw it overboard. When the boat reached the shoreline, he spared her life and let her swim to safety.

Judy told police that he had completely removed her shorts and bikini bottoms during the rape, just like how the Rogers girls were found. She said she noticed rope on the boat that was similar to the rope used in the murders and he had threatened to tape her mouth with duct tape.

Detectives knew this had to be the same man. Using the girl's description, police created a composite drawing of the man which was released to the public. The sketch was aired on the television news, printed in the newspapers, and used for posters distributed through the area. More and more tips poured in, but most were dead ends.

Over three years had passed since the murders. Investigators believed their best hope was the unique handwriting on the brochure that was left in the car. Maybe if they released it to the public, someone would recognize it. Police placed five billboards throughout the Tampa area near the boat ramp. The billboards featured a large image of the hand-writing and asked the question "Who wrote these directions?" It was a long-shot, but they hoped for the best.

The day after the billboards went up, Jo Ann Steffey did a double-take. Her heart skipped a beat when she realized that she knew the hand-writing. She had just seen the composite sketch of the suspect in that morning's paper and rushed home to look again.

The description of the suspect seemed to match a neighbor that lived just two doors down. Forty-three-year-old Oba Chandler was an aluminum siding contractor that had done some work on her house. He was married and had eight children from seven different women. As she read the story in the paper, everything seemed to fit together.

His reddish-blond hair fit the description, as did his size and weight. He resembled the composite sketch. He drove a dark blue Jeep Cherokee and his house backed onto a canal where he had his own boat. A blue and white boat. The canal he lived on led to the bay, just a mile from the boat ramp.

Jo Ann then remembered that she still had the invoice Chandler had written for the work he had done. When she looked at the handwriting on the invoice, she noticed right away that he had the habit of capital-izing his T's in the middle of a word. She immediately called police.

Billboard and matching handwriting

Oba Chandler was born in 1946 and had grown up in Cincinnati, Ohio. When he was five years old, one of his brothers died. His father never recovered from the loss. Five years later, his father hanged himself in the basement of their home. According to one of his cousins, Oba jumped into the grave as the gravediggers shoveled the dirt over the coffin. He stomped the dirt with each shovel full.

In his early teenage years, Oba was arrested for stealing cars. By the time he reached eighteen, he had been arrested twenty times. Throughout his adult life, he constantly found trouble. He had been charged with loitering, burglary, possession of counterfeit currency, armed robbery, and kidnapping. In one instance, he was caught masturbating as he looked through the ground-floor window of a woman's home. On another occasion, he and an accomplice robbed a Florida couple's home. He tied the man up and made the woman take off her clothes. He tormented her by slowly rubbing his gun across her naked stomach.

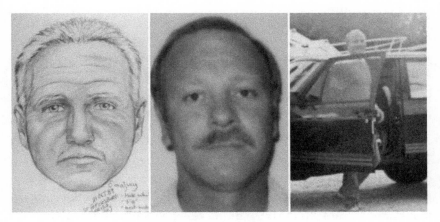

Police sketch and Oba Chandler with Jeep Cherokee

Oba Chandler was arrested on September 24, 1992. When placed in a police lineup, without hesitation Judy Blair identified him as the man that had raped her. Additional samples of his handwriting were analyzed and matched the handwriting on the brochure exactly. The palm print on the brochure also matched his left palm print.

While building the case against Chandler, detectives gathered ship-to-shore phone records from the night of the rape and the night of the murders. On both occasions he placed phone calls to his wife that put him in the location of the crimes during the times that they happened.

At trial, Oba Chandler was advised by his lawyer to not testify in his defense, but he did so anyway. He insisted that he met the Rogers girls, gave them directions, and never saw them again except in the newspapers and the billboards. He claimed that he was in his boat on Tampa Bay those nights, but he was fishing by himself. He said he had engine trouble with his boat, asked the Coast Guard for help, but ended up fixing the problem himself.

During the trial, Judy Blair flew down from Canada to testify that Chandler had raped her on his boat just two weeks before the Rogers murders. A former employee of Chandler's testified that the morning after the murders, Chandler boasted that he "dated" three women on the bay the night before.

Two of Chandler's daughters and his son-in-law all testified against him. His daughter, Kristal Sue Mays, told the court that while he was visiting family in Ohio just after the murders, she overheard her father saying, "I can't go back to Florida because police are looking for me because I killed some women." She continued, telling the court that her father had also told her that he had raped a woman near Madeira Beach, Florida.

Two of Chandler's cell mates from jail also testified against him. One claimed that Chandler said, "I'm not the only one that ever uses duct tape, but it's easy to tie someone up with." The second told the court that Chandler said, "If the bitch didn't resist, I wouldn't be here in jail."

Oba Chandler was found guilty of all three murders and was sentenced to death on November 4, 1994. At his sentencing, Judge Susan F. Schaeffer told him,

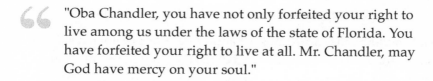

> "Oba Chandler, you have not only forfeited your right to live among us under the laws of the state of Florida. You have forfeited your right to live at all. Mr. Chandler, may God have mercy on your soul."

In an interview, Judge Schaeffer later described Chandler as

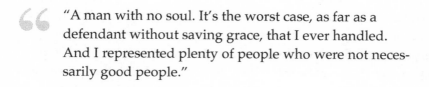

> "A man with no soul. It's the worst case, as far as a defendant without saving grace, that I ever handled. And I represented plenty of people who were not necessarily good people."

Since he was already on death row for the murders, prosecutors spared Judy Blair the emotional heartache of going through a rape trial.

Although he was suspected of several more similar murders, no additional charges were ever brought against him. On November 15, 2011, Oba Chandler was executed. His last words were

> "Kiss my rosy red ass."

His written statement wrote:

 "Oba Chandler LasT StatemenT

You are killing a innocent man Today

Nov. 15th 2011

Oba Chandler"

He had capitalized every T.

Three years after his execution, DNA evidence proved that Oba Chandler had murdered twenty-year-old Ivelisse Berrios-Beguerisse. Her body was found in Coral Springs, Florida, in 1990. Chandler lived just a mile away at the time.

CHAPTER 7
THE CARNIVAL CULT

In the early nineties, police in Johnson County, Indiana, noticed a surge of graffiti on walls and abandoned barns in the rural area. The vandalism seemed to be concentrated in the area around Whiteland, a small town of about 2,500 people.

Police were familiar with the symbols spray painted on the walls: pentagrams, upside down crosses, the numbers "666", and the letters "COS." The symbols were satanic. "COS" referred to the Church of Satan, while 666 referenced the "Number of the Beast" from the book of Revelations in the Bible.

The spray paint was a nuisance, but the police believed it was just the work of harmless kids. Many of the local kids were into heavy metal music, which used macabre theatrics and many of the same satanic symbols. However, police soon realized that the kids creating this graffiti were anything but harmless.

As a young teen, Mark Goodwin was a heavy metal kid. His favorite artist was Ozzy Osbourne, the former singer of the band Black Sabbath. Like thousands of other kids, the dark lyrics and eerie symbolism of the records he listened to intrigued Mark. Although the music was mostly dramatization, these records were his first introduction into what would become an obsession. For a seventh-grade school assignment, Mark was required to write a report on the meaning of Halloween. He checked out books about Satanism and the occult from the library, discovered *"The Satanic Bible"* by Anton LaVey, and wrote his report about demons and spirits. By the time he was fifteen, Goodwin was obsessed with Satanism and had started his own satanic cult he called "Satan's Disciples."

Satan's Disciples consisted of six or so like-minded kids in the Whiteland and Franklin area of central Indiana. At first, their meetings would consist of reading passages and chants from various satanic books and walking through graveyards late at night. Over time, however, the group were butchering small animals as a sacrifice to their lord Satan.

While many of the members were only part of the cult as an excuse to rebel against their parents and drink alcohol, Goodwin took it seriously. He wore a black robe and stayed sober as he killed the small animals. He drained the blood into a small chalice and drank from it, passing it around for everyone to sip. Afterwards they would play music, smoke pot, and dance like they were possessed. There were rumors that they would sometimes have both heterosexual and homosexual orgies.

Goodwin had his limits, however. When one member of his cult suggested they kill a baby as a sacrifice, that was too much. At eighteen years old, he walked away from the cult he had created, but his interest in Satanism never waned. He was still obsessed and read everything he could find on Satanism and the occult. Two years later, he met Keith and David Lawrence while working at a fast-food restaurant.

At eighteen years old, Keith Lawrence was three years younger than his brother David, yet the dominant sibling. Like Goodwin, Keith started listening to heavy metal music at an early age and listened to every word carefully. To Keith, every album became like a Bible to him. He read the same books on Satanism that Goodwin read. Around his neck he wore an upside-down cross necklace and a pentagram medallion with a goat's head, all symbols of Satanism.

Keith had been a troubled kid and a bully his entire life. In the eighth grade, his teachers recommended psychotherapy. As a result, Keith's parents sent him to boarding school - but that experience only seemed to strengthen his hatred of all people. It was during those years that he found Satanism.

The older brother, David Lawrence, wasn't as intrigued by Satanism. Keith, however, intimidated his older brother, bullying him into giving his life to Satan. In one instance, Keith chased his brother through the house with a knife, threatening to kill him if he didn't become a Satanist. David, however, didn't get along with the other members of his family. He respected his little brother and spent most of his time with him, regardless of his beliefs.

Mark Goodwin and Keith Lawrence had a lot in common; Keith's views on Satanism intrigued Mark. The young men became inseparable and eventually Mark and Keith drew up a twenty-year written contract devoting their lives to Satan. They both signed it in their own blood. Each believed the contract would provide them with anything they wanted for the next twenty years. "After twenty years are up, Satan can do what he wants or kill us. At the time we really didn't care," Goodwin later recalled.

In May 1991, all three boys had troubles with home life and were days away from being thrown out by their parents. David suggested they all work as carnival workers with a company that travelled throughout Ohio and Indiana during the summer for local county fairs and carnivals.

The Lawrence brothers had worked for a similar amusement company the previous winter in the Bahamas. When they crossed back into the United States that January, US Customs noted that Keith had seventeen books on Satanism, witchcraft, and the occult.

The three young men got jobs as traveling carnival workers, also known as "carnies." While traveling throughout Indiana that summer, they met another worker named Jimmie Lee Penick while working in Brownstown. Twenty-four-year-old Penick fit right in with the other three. He was also a practicing Satanist.

The four men were outspoken about their involvement in Satanism and openly spoke to other carnival workers about random crimes that they had committed throughout their lives. It was okay for them to talk about their own crimes, but when eighteen-year-old Andrew Wright repeated a story he had heard about a crime that Penick had committed in Ohio, Penick became enraged.

Just east of Toledo, Ohio, on August 30, 1991, the day before the start of the Fulton County Fair, Penick and Keith Lawrence stabbed Wright to death. They slit his neck and dumped his body in the woods off of the Ohio Turnpike near Wauseon, Ohio.

Even after killing Wright, Penick and Keith couldn't help but brag about their killing and told David and Goodwin what they had done. Four people knew about the murder, so the chance of it remaining a secret was slim.

During September 1991, the four men were working at the Dekalb County Free Fall Fair when they befriended another worker named Tony Ault. Twenty-one-year-old Ault had dabbled in Satanism as well and wanted to be a part of their cult. Eventually, one of them told Ault of the murder of Andrew Wright and asked if he still wanted to be involved. Ault was undeterred. He wanted to belong.

After the carnival closed on September 25, they told Tony Ault that they were going to have a satanic ritual that night and he was welcome to come along. Goodwin's girlfriend, Brenda Ferguson, drove the five young men out to an abandoned barn deep in the woods. She dropped them off and was told to come back later to pick them up.

Outside the barn, the five men built a large bonfire. Inside the barn, Keith asked Ault to lie down on an old unhinged door as part of an initiation ritual. The door was to be used as an altar. They tied Ault to the door and put a gag in his mouth. Once he was secure, Keith began reading a chant he believed could invoke Satan.

Penick then took Keith Lawrence's knife and made a deep cut, from Ault's neck to his pelvis. The cut was just deep enough not to kill him. Goodwin and the two Lawrence brothers then made additional cuts on his torso to make the shape of an inverted cross and several other satanic symbols. They then tried to cut his ear off before Goodwin attempted to cut out his heart while it was still beating.

With Ault still strapped to the door and clinging to life, Penick took the knife again, put his face to Ault's face, and asked, "Are you ready to die?" He then slit his throat from ear to ear as Keith chanted.

The four men had no intention of allowing Ault into their cult. Instead, they wanted to ensure he didn't tell anyone about the previous murder of Andrew Wright.

Penick, Goodwin, and Keith then cut off Ault's head and hands while David watched. Keith threw his head and hands on the bonfire. This dismemberment and burning of his hands was an attempt to thwart identity. Keith, however, said he cut off and burned his head because he wanted to come back later and collect the skull to give to a friend.

When Brenda Ferguson returned to pick them up, they took Ault's money from his wallet and used it to buy a meal at Arby's.

The four continued to work for the carnival company through the end of the season into late October. When their jobs ended at the end of the season, Penick returned to his parent's home in Shelbyville, Indiana. Goodwin and the Lawrence brothers drove to Florida in Goodwin's van, which he had nicknamed "Rigor Mortis," where they hoped to work the winter carnival circuit.

While working in Florida, Goodwin felt guilty for what he had done and called his father back in Indiana. He explained to his father that he had witnessed a murder in Dekalb County. Goodwin assumed his father wouldn't tell the police, but on December 12, that's exactly what he did. Police questioned Goodwin's ex-girlfriend, Brenda Ferguson, who led them to the barn where she had dropped off the five men. There, detectives found the decomposed remains of Tony Ault.

Goodwin returned to Indiana on December 13 and was immediately arrested and charged with conspiracy to commit murder. Penick was simultaneously arrested in Shelbyville on murder charges.

The Lawrence brothers had been working in the Bahamas again with the carnival and had no idea that Goodwin and Penick had been arrested. When they returned to the United States on January 10, 1992, their plane landed in Miami, Florida. US Customs agents arrested the brothers at the border and returned them to Indiana.

David Lawrence was both the first to show signs of remorse and the first to plead guilty. He was only charged with assisting a criminal. David insisted that he was never really a Satanist, but was intimidated by his brother into following his lead. In April 1993, David Lawrence was sentenced to eight years in prison.

At his sentencing, the judge commented,

 "Although the older of the two brothers, David Lawrence was led and manipulated by Keith. David, in your sentence there's a good deal of punishment, but there's also a good deal of rehabilitation. In the end, it's up to you how to deal with this. I want you to be a law-abiding citizen, a good husband, and a good father. I think you can do it."

David's brother, Keith, was sentenced the same day. Keith, however, had been a much more active participant in the murder and his history of prior criminal activity was well documented. Keith was initially charged with murder and faced eighty years in prison. Eventually, he and his defense made a deal with prosecutors to have the charge dropped to conspiracy to commit murder if he agreed to a guilty plea.

At sentencing, Keith's lawyer argued,

> "No question Keith used poor judgement in picking Jimmie Lee Penick as an acquaintance. Not a friend, an acquaintance. Keith is a person who studied religions. Not a person involved in religions himself."

His lawyer went on to claim that Keith was not solely interested in the occult, but also studied the Greek and Hebrew versions of the Bible, as well as the Quran. His plan, however, failed to impress the judge. Keith was sentenced to thirty years in prison plus twenty additional years of probation. The sentence was the maximum allowed with a guilty plea.

The judge said of Keith,

> "In his home community of Whiteland, Indiana, Keith had a reputation as an intimidating and dangerous character. Although Keith Lawrence did not inflict the fatal wound on Ault, he did carve an inverted cross onto the victim's torso. To sentence Keith Lawrence to less than the maximum would depreciate the seriousness of the crime."

Mark Goodwin, too, was deeply remorseful for his role in the ritualistic murder. He pleaded guilty to assisting a criminal and battery by means of a deadly weapon, but pleaded not-guilty to the charge of helping to conceal a body. As he awaited trial, he spoke to the press about the dangers of Satanism and met with a chaplain on a daily basis.

At sentencing, Mark Goodwin told Tony Ault's mother, "Mrs. Givens, I never really knew your son. Whatever I know, I do know he was a good-hearted person. I am shameful of what I did to your son." Mrs. Givens had anything but sympathy for the twenty-year-old Goodwin and cried, "You damn well should be. What chance does he have now? What am I supposed to feel... sorry for you? What? You should've never done it!" Goodwin was sentenced to eight years in prison.

In January 1994, Jimmie Lee Penick faced the death penalty in Indiana for the murder of Tony Ault. He also faced life in prison in Ohio for the murder of Andrew Wright.

To avoid the death penalty in Indiana, Penick pleaded guilty to murder. The maximum allowed for a guilty plea of murder in Indiana was sixty years, which was exactly what he got. The sentence, however, was to be served consecutively to the Ohio sentence, for which he was given twenty years to life. As of this time of writing, Jimmie Lee Penick is still serving his twenty years to life sentence in Warren Correctional Institution in Ohio. If he is ever released from the Ohio facility, he'll go straight to Indiana to start his sixty year sentence.

Mark Goodwin and David Lawrence each fulfilled their eight-year sentence long ago. Keith Lawrence served only eleven years of his thirty-year sentence. His original sentence included the first five years of probation to be on home detention, but upon his release the home detention was erased. While in prison, Keith Lawrence acquired a significant amount of good-time credit for earning two college degrees.

Keith Lawrence was arrested in 2006 for public intoxication, battery, and criminal confinement which violated his parole. The criminal confinement and battery charges were dropped, but the public intoxication charge remained, which landed him in jail for 180 days.

CHAPTER 8
THE MOUSSE CAN KILLER

R obert Mark Edwards didn't stand a chance in life. Born in 1961, his father didn't believe that Robert was his child and began beating him daily when he was just six months old. His abuse wasn't just directed at Robert, however—he beat Robert's brother, sister, and mother as well. His father's nickname for Robert and his brother William were "SFB1" and "SFB2" — Shit for brains 1 and 2.

Robert's father worked as a bartender and his mother was a nurse. Both were alcoholics and by the time he was eleven, his mother had a drug problem. She was addicted to Valium.

The family lived in Florida and moved briefly to Puerto Rico. When he was thirteen years old, Robert's mother finally divorced his father and moved the family to California. Shortly after their arrival in California, she was run over by a car while on a drug and alcohol binge. She lived, but her drug and alcohol habits eventually rubbed off on the kids.

Just a year after their arrival in California, Robert and his brother began breaking into homes and stealing items to pay for their own drugs and alcohol. They drank, smoked pot and hashish, and took LSD, cocaine, peyote, methamphetamines, barbiturates, heroin, and anything else they could get their hands on. His sister, Elena, wasn't immune and developed an addiction to Valium. Even both of Robert's grandmothers were addicts, one to Lorazepam and the other to Valium and oxycodone.

Robert dropped out of school in the eighth grade and soon after started selling fake LSD to kids in Long Beach, California. He and his brother sold little tabs of paper with designs on it, claiming it was LSD, but it was nothing more than printed paper.

Robert's alcohol abuse became a serious problem when he experienced his first alcoholic blackout at sixteen. He drank so much and took so many drugs that he found himself wandering the streets of Long Beach the next morning with no idea how he got there. On one occasion, he woke up under a kitchen table in a house he wasn't familiar with and had no recollection of anything from the previous night.

In March 1986, Robert met Kathryn Deeble while he was selling fake LSD near a Long Beach bus stop. He had crashed his motorcycle a few months earlier and his leg was in a cast. As Kathryn drove by the bus stop in her pickup truck, she saw Robert, felt sorry for him hobbling around in his cast, and offered him a ride. From that point on, they were a couple. Kathryn invited him into her life and introduced him to her mother, Marjorie Deeble.

Fifty-five-year-old Marjorie was a strong-willed woman. She had been a successful real estate agent living in nearby Los Alamitos, California, just inland from Long Beach. One afternoon while her mother was at work, Kathryn brought Robert to her mother's apartment. Robert took note as Kathryn retrieved a key hidden in a nearby drain pipe to get into the condo. The couple then went inside to have sex.

Kathryn and Robert had been dating for two months when she and her mother took a trip to Palm Springs together in early May. Robert helped them load their suitcases into their car and he borrowed Kathryn's truck while they were away.

The alternator in the truck, however, failed while they were gone and Marjorie blamed Robert for the problem. She became upset with Robert and demanded that he get the truck fixed before they returned.

Robert agreed and took the truck to the dealer, but later it became clear that he harbored some resentment at Marjorie's harsh words towards him.

Kathryn and Marjorie returned from their trip on the morning of Monday, May 12. Kathryn dropped her mother off at her apartment and headed home. That would be the last time she saw her mother alive.

The morning of May 13, Kathryn noticed something strange. She normally parked her truck in the driveway with her driver's side door either before or after the juniper bushes so she could open the door without hitting them. That morning, however, it was parked with the door directly against the bushes, causing her to stand in the bushes as she got in.

Kathryn knew that the only other person that had access to her truck was Robert. Although she thought it was strange that he had borrowed the truck in the middle of the night, she thought little of it at the time.

Three days later, Marjorie's co-workers at Great Western Real Estate were getting worried. The sparky, petite woman that had won Salesperson of the Year in 1985 hadn't been to the office in days. That was completely out of character for her, so they called Los Alamitos Police.

The afternoon of May 16, police arrived at Marjorie's apartment for a welfare check only to find her front door cracked open. They could hear loud music playing in the bedroom, so knocked and called her name but got no answer. When they entered her bedroom, they found Marjorie Deeble dead, face-down on the floor.

She was naked from the waist down and her nightgown had been torn and pushed up to her torso. Her hands were tied behind her back with a piece of her nightgown and a telephone cord. A thin belt was tightened around her neck and the end of the belt was tied to the handle of the dresser, suspending her neck eight inches above the floor. Her legs showed signs that they had been tied at one time as well.

The bedroom was covered with blood. Drawers were open, her jewelry was missing, clothes were thrown all over, and the telephone had been ripped from the wall. A bloody pillowcase had been used as a hood over her head. Marjorie had lost a lot of blood from her ears, mouth, and nose. Her nose was broken and her face had the residue of an adhesive, indicating that she had been gagged. She had been beaten, raped, and strangled. On the bed was a bloody can of hair styling mousse that had been used to sexually assault her.

Robert was with Kathryn when the Los Alamitos Police called her into the station. He sat in the waiting room and could hear her crying in a nearby room when they told her that her mother had been brutally murdered.

During Kathryn's grief, Robert continued to date her for a few more weeks, but eventually they drifted away and lost contact. The police, however, considered him a potential suspect. They asked him for a DNA sample, but he refused.

Seven years went by with no leads in the case of Marjorie Deeble's murder, but Los Alamitos Police Detectives kept track of Robert's every move. Although they had no physical evidence linking him to the murder, they patiently waited, knowing he would eventually slip up.

During the years following the murder, Edwards couldn't seem to stay out of trouble. He had been arrested in 1984 for vehicle burglary, again in 1987 on a weapons charge, and in 1988 for receiving stolen property and vehicle theft. In 1992 he moved to Hawaii and was again arrested in 1994 for kidnapping, sexual assault, robbery, and burglary.

In the summer of 1996, Robert Edwards was working as a roofer in the south Maui town of Kihei. He lived just a block from the beach with his girlfriend, Janice Hunt, and her twelve-year-old daughter. From the window of their second-story apartment on Kanoe Street, Janice could watch whales breaching using a pair of binoculars that she kept on a table below the window. Edwards, however, was more interested in using the binoculars to watch the neighbors.

Peggy Ventura was from Alaska and spent a few months every year vacationing in south Maui with her mother, sixty-seven-year-old Muriel Delbecq, a successful real estate agent. Peggy rented a condo about a half mile from the beach, while Muriel rented a ground-floor apartment on Kanoe Street, just one block from the beach—and directly across the street from Robert Edwards.

On January 25, 1993, after an evening out, Peggy dropped her mother off at her apartment and drove home. Across the street, Robert Edwards had just learned that his dog had been hit by a car. Robert sobbed and cradled the dog in his arms, but it was too late. Just a month earlier, he had learned that his step-father had been killed in a plane crash. He'd spent the past month numbing his pain with excessive alcohol and cocaine. The sudden death of his dog compounded his sorrow.

That night, Robert carried his dog's body to his kayak and paddled out into the ocean for a burial at sea. When he returned to shore around 11:00 p.m., he went to a friend's apartment, injected a half a gram of cocaine, and drank himself into a blackout.

The next morning, Janice Hunt woke to a commotion on the street outside. Police cars had gathered at the Kanoe Apartments across the street from their apartment. She walked outside and spoke to neighbors who informed her that a murder had occurred during the night.

At 7:30 that morning, Peggy Ventura went to her mother's apartment so they could go to the beach together for their morning walk. When she knocked on her door, however, there was no answer. A pair of flip-flops that she didn't recognize sat outside the front door. Using a key that she knew her mother had hid under a rock, she entered the apartment and immediately noticed blood on the floor. In a panic, Peggy tried to open the door to her mother's bedroom, only to find it locked. She reached for the phone in the kitchen, but it had been ripped from the wall.

Peggy ran outside to a neighbor's apartment, screamed for them to call the police, and ran to the side of the apartment to try to get in through the window. When she crawled through the window, she couldn't see. A comforter covered the window, leaving the room pitch black. In the dark, Peggy found her way to the bedroom door and opened it to let light into the room.

She could see the bedroom had been ransacked and there was more blood on the floor and walls. Beneath a pile of blankets in the middle of the bed was her mother. Muriel laid face-up, completely naked, bruised, bloody, and lifeless. She had been beaten viciously about the head, sexually assaulted and strangled to death.

When police arrived, there was evidence that Muriel's arms and legs had been bound at one time, but whatever the killer had used to bind her was gone. Her wedding ring was missing from her ring finger and other items were missing from the apartment.

Her body was sprawled on the bed with her legs open and a mousse can was still inserted into her vagina. The medical examiner said the mousse can had been inserted into both her vagina and her anus. It had been inserted so far that it protruded into her abdominal cavity. Her breasts were cut and bruised and her pubic hair had been cut or shaved off.

The killer had left behind plenty of evidence. On the wall near the bed was a bloody palm print. A white t-shirt on the floor had a bloody foot impression. There were cigarette butts on the floor and the killer had spit into the bathtub.

A bent window screen told investigators that the killer had most-likely come in through the window and unsuccessfully tried to replace it. On the windowsill and the floor near the window were pieces of dried grass that the killer had left behind.

In a dumpster near the crime scene, police found a bloody pillowcase that matched the pattern of Muriel's bedding. Inside the pillowcase was her checkbook, traveler's checks, two telephones, and two pieces of telephone cord tied together. It was obvious that the cords were used to bind her wrists and ankles. They also found a bra with the tips of the cup cut out, a pair of panties that were cut open, and several random household items from her apartment.

When Janice Hunt was interviewed by police, she reported that when she told Robert Edward of the murder across the street, he seemed genuinely surprised. She also claimed, however, that while they were dating Edwards liked to tie her up and had twice tried to sodomize her with a bottle. Detectives also learned that, using the binoculars near the window in their apartment, Edwards had a clear view to the front door of Muriel's apartment.

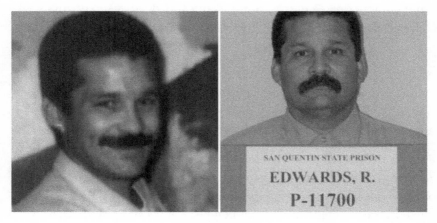

SAN QUENTIN STATE PRISON
EDWARDS, R.
P-11700

Robert Mark Edwards

It wasn't hard to tie Edwards to the crime. The bloody palm print was a match for his palm and the glob of spit in the bathtub contained his DNA. When Maui police pulled his California police record, it was nine pages long and he had been wanted in California for the past eighteen months for parole violation. When Los Alamitos detectives heard of Edward's arrest, they knew they could now link him to the murder of Marjorie Deeble as well.

At trial, Edwards blamed his frequent alcoholic blackouts. He told the court, "It's hard for me to understand that I could do something so horrible." Blackouts were, of course, no excuse for such a heinous murder. After only two hours of deliberation, a jury found him guilty. Maui county court sentenced him to five life terms plus twenty years.

Edwards was then transferred to California where, if convicted, he faced a possible death sentence for the murder of Marjorie Deeble. The two murders had astonishing similarities. Both women were near the same age, both were real estate agents who lived alone in a ground-floor apartment, both had their limbs bound with telephone cords, were strangled, and were violated with a mousse can. They even coincidentally shared the same three initials—M.E.D.

In California, Edwards didn't deny that he murdered Marjorie Deeble, but claimed he had no memory of the event. He was again found guilty of first degree murder, but the jury was deadlocked during sentencing.

His lawyers argued that his struggles with drugs and alcohol, along with the abuse by his father, contributed to his crimes. However, prosecutors pointed out the excessive nature of how the victims were tortured and mutilated before death. The second jury was unsympathetic and, on September 9, 1998, Edwards was sentenced to death.

Due to a moratorium on the death penalty in California, Edwards has spent more than twenty years on death row and, as of this time of writing, resides at San Quentin prison north of San Francisco. He writes poetry and short stories. The following is a short story by Robert Edwards.

 As I stepped off the bus at 3:45 a.m., the cold, wet coastal air stung my face.

I inhaled deeply. Freedom! For years, I'd yearned to smell the sea air of my home city.

There was nothing open but a twenty-four-hour restaurant a mile down the road. I had no money. The manila envelope in my hand held all my worldly possessions. Tucking the envelope under my arm and thrusting my hands deep into my pockets to keep them warm, I started walking. Maybe I could wait out a night in the restaurant's foyer before being run away as a vagrant.

By the time I got there, my clothes were damp with dew, and I sat shivering on the bench in the entryway. I thought of what the morning would bring. Would my ex-wife let me see my son? Would I get any support from my family? Should I go find my old crew? No, I thought, that's what got me sent up in the first place. It wasn't going to be easy, but this time I would try to make it on my own.

The waitress inside the restaurant kept looking at me through the inner door. Finally, she opened it. I felt sure I was about to be booted out, but instead she smiled politely and said, "Sir, there's a gentleman inside who says that, if you'd like some breakfast, he's buying."

I was instantly suspicious. But it was also an opportunity to stay inside until sunrise. "Sure," I said, and I stood and followed her to the booth where the man was sitting.

I took a seat across from him, and he smiled and shook my hand. While the waitress went to get my coffee, I said, "Look, dude, I'm gonna tell you right now, if you're looking for some action, you're looking in the wrong place. I don't play that shit."

He chuckled softly and said, "I'm not sure what you're talking about, but I don't want anything. I saw you walk by the window all hunched over, and when you didn't come in, I figured you could use some grub, or coffee, at least. Order anything you want. No strings attached, OK? My name's Steve."

Reaching out to shake his hand again, I said, "I'm Rob."

Then I took the menu and ordered an especially large breakfast, so that, if he left, I'd still have some food on the table and be able to stay until I finished.

I noticed the faded US Marine Corps tattoo on Steve's forearm and asked if he'd been in long. It turned out he'd served in Vietnam at the same time as my father. We talked about our children. Finally I admitted that I'd just got back into town after doing some time, and every-thing I owned was on my back or in the envelope on the table.

"Listen," Steve said, "why don't you let me get you a room for a couple of days?"

"No way," I said. Why was this guy doing this? "Whats your trip?" I asked him.

"There was a time when I was in a situation like yours," Steve said, "and someone helped me out. I wanted to pay him back, but all he said to me was 'if sometime in the future you can help someone who is down and out, then do it.' Simple as that."

I was moved by Steve's story, but I didn't take the room he offered. That was twenty-two years ago. I never got my son back. Life on its own terms proved too much for me. I'm back in prison, this time on Death Row.

CHAPTER 9
A GLITZY COWBOY TALE

Benny Binion was born in 1904, just north of Dallas, Texas. As a young boy, he traveled with his father, a horse trader, to county fairs throughout Texas rather than attending school. It was during these early years with his father that Benny learned to gamble. Although he didn't know how to read or write, Benny knew numbers. Despite it being illegal, he played poker with the farmers with whom his father did business.

In 1920, the sale of alcohol in the United States had been banned, beginning the thirteen year Prohibition Era. But Benny saw an opportunity. At just eighteen years old, he began distilling his own illegal "moonshine." He sold his spirits throughout the Dallas area, which landed him in jail a few times but didn't slow his pace.

At twenty-four years old he combined the sale of his alcohol with illegal gambling. He ran a no-limit craps game in the back room of a downtown Dallas hotel, where he catered to big spenders who had made their money with the Texas oil boom. With the odds in his favor and the local Sheriff in his back pocket, Benny made a fortune.

Benny was very unforgiving and had killed two men that crossed him by the time he was thirty-three. The first was a rum-runner named Frank Bolding. Bolding had tried to attack Benny with a knife, but

Benny rolled backwards over a crate and came up shooting. His style of shooting earned him the nickname "Cowboy." The second man he killed was Ben Frieden, who ran a rival gambling hall. Benny ambushed him while he sat in a parked car and shot him three times in the heart. Although Benny was convicted of the first murder, he only served a two-year suspended sentence. When he killed Frieden, however, he purposely shot himself in the shoulder and claimed that he had acted in self-defense.

Over time, Benny acquired opposing gambling rackets from other mobsters that mysteriously died. The FBI suspected Benny of killing several other mobsters, but could never prove it. However, when the Dallas County Sheriff that had been helping him was voted out of office, Benny lost his government help. At the same time, World War II had ended and the Chicago mob had moved into the Dallas area. Benny Binion took his wife, two sons, and three daughters to Las Vegas to start his next empire.

In 1951, Benny Binion opened Binion's Horseshoe Casino on Fremont Street in Las Vegas and changed the face of gambling. His was the first casino to install carpeting on the casino floors instead of sawdust-covered wood. He offered high limits in his casino, which attracted the high rollers. His casino was the first to offer free drinks to players, $2 steaks, and give complimentary hotel rooms to high rollers.

Benny redefined Las Vegas casinos, but after only a few years in business, he was convicted of tax evasion and sold the majority of the Horseshoe. It took eleven years for the Binion family to regain control of the casino, but with his conviction Benny was no longer allowed to hold a gaming license. His five children took over the casino, one of which was his son, Ted Binion, who took the role of Casino Manager.

Ted Binion became the new face of the Horseshoe Casino for the next thirty years. Like his father, Ted considered himself a cowboy. As a boy he had spent his summers on the family's 85,000 acre ranch in Montana working with the ranch hands.

Although a cowboy at heart, Ted was eccentric and loved the glitzy life of Las Vegas – partying with celebrity guests, showgirls, strippers, and members of organized crime. He also had an affinity for drugs.

The Nevada Gaming Commission knew of Ted's drug use and association with organized crime, so they watched every move he made. When they asked Ted to submit to drug testing, he was livid. Knowing that drugs would stay in his hair much longer than in his bloodstream, Ted showed up for the drug test with his entire body shaved so they couldn't sample his hair.

Ted was inevitably arrested on drug trafficking charges. The conviction and his association with organized crime was too much for the Nevada Gaming Commission; in 1986 he was permanently banned from his management role at the Horseshoe.

Losing his role in the casino and the death of his father in 1989 weighed heavily on him. Having lost his livelihood, Ted relied more on drugs to occupy his time. He smoked marijuana and took Xanax, but his drug of choice was tar heroin. Ted, however, knew the dangers of drugs. His sister Barbara, who had similar drug problems, had committed suicide in 1977. Ted made a point to only smoke his heroin rather than inject it, reducing the chance that he could overdose.

Eventually Ted's wife took their daughter and left him. After she left, he spent more time in Las Vegas strip clubs where he met a young dancer named Sandy Murphy.

Sandy Murphy was a young, fit, strawberry-blonde beauty from Southern California. She had dropped out of high school and lived with an older man near the beach just south of Los Angeles, where she loved to surf. But in 1995, when that relationship fell apart, she and a girlfriend packed their bags and moved to Las Vegas.

At just twenty-one, Sandy arrived in Las Vegas with $15,000 and had never gambled in her life. By the end of the first night at Caesar's Palace, she had lost everything at the blackjack table.

Sandy's friend was a lingerie designer and the two girls started a business catering to Las Vegas strippers. The girls set up a table at a club called Cheetah's, where her friend sold the outfits and Sandy modeled them. When Ted saw Sandy modeling the Dallas Cowboys cheerleader outfit, he was hooked. That night he asked her to sit with him for a drink and they instantly hit it off.

Ted and Sandy started dating, but she didn't really know what he did for a living. Ted surely didn't look the part of a millionaire. He drove a pickup truck and wore cowboy boots and Levi's. So, when he took her to the Horseshoe and told her he owned it, she had her doubts. It didn't help his story when he explained that he couldn't go inside his own casino.

Although Sandy was less than half his age, she and Ted eventually fell in love and he moved her into his 8,500 square foot home. He bought her a convertible Mercedes and gave her a credit card with a $10,000 limit. She was thrust into a life of luxury.

Their relationship, however, didn't sit well with the rest of the Binion family. The family, particularly his eldest sister, considered Sandy a gold-digger who was only out for his money. His new relationship, coupled with his inability to be a part of the family business, drove a further wedge between Ted and his family.

Ted's excessive drug use fueled his paranoia. He didn't trust his family and he didn't trust banks. Since he could no longer enter the Horseshoe, he needed to move his belongings from a floor-to-ceiling vault that he kept in the casino's basement. The vault housed his massive silver collection that would need to be relocated.

On a small piece of land that he owned in the desert sixty miles west of Las Vegas, Ted had an underground concrete bunker built to house his valuables. The vault was built twelve feet below the surface of the desert floor. Inside he stored six tons of silver bullion, paper money, Horseshoe Casino chips, and over 100,000 rare coins, including extremely rare Carson City silver dollars. Those alone were believed to be worth as much as $14 million.

The construction of the bunker was extremely secretive. Only a few in Ted's immediate circle knew of its existence. He had commissioned a trucking company, MRT Transport, to build the huge bunker and secretly transport his collection from the Horseshoe to the new location. After the valuables were moved, only two people had the security code to enter the underground vault: Ted Binion and the owner of MRT Transport, Rick Tabish.

Ted had met Rick Tabish at a urinal, of all places. They struck up a conversation about Montana, where both men had spent time in their childhood. Although Tabish had previously been convicted of theft, he was a handsome smooth-talker and they developed a friendship. Rick quickly became an integral part of his life. Ted hired Rick to do odd jobs, which eventually led to the construction of the desert vault.

By mid-1998, Ted's drug use had escalated and his relationship with Sandy was going south. He became abusive and she was often seen with bruises – and, on one occasion, with a clump of hair missing. His paranoia was out of control; he took more drugs and carried a gun with him everywhere he went.

In early September, Ted got his next-door neighbor, a medical doctor, to write him a prescription for the anti-anxiety drug Xanax. The following day, Ted picked up the prescription himself at a nearby pharmacy. Then, on September 16, 1998, Ted bought twelve balloons of tar heroin from a dealer on the streets of Las Vegas.

Just before 4:00 p.m. the next day, Sandy Murphy walked into the home she shared with Ted Binion to find him lifeless on a yoga mat in the middle of the living room. An empty bottle of Xanax lay on the floor next to him. She frantically called 911, but he was gone. The medical examiner determined that Ted had overdosed on heroin and Xanax.

When police arrived, Sandy was crying over the death of Ted so hysterically that she had to be wheeled out of the house on a stretcher and taken to the hospital. Nurses at the hospital, however, noticed that her crying seemed overly theatrical. At times it seemed as if she were literally crying the words "boo hoo, boo hoo."

When she was allowed to go back into the house, she brought her attorney with her and videotaped the house. She believed that either the Binion family or the police had stolen many items from the house. Her intention in making the video was to take an inventory of the house, but this would later come back to bite her.

The news of Ted Binion's death was immediately on the television news. When Ted's lawyer heard the news, he contacted police. The lawyer said that Ted came to him just the day before his death and asked to have Sandy taken out of his will. The lawyer claimed that Ted no longer trusted her. Ted told him, "Take Sandy out of the will. If she doesn't kill me tonight. If I'm dead, you'll know what happened."

Las Vegas Police Sergeant Steve Huggins also had a strange conversation with Ted just before his death. Ted called the sergeant and told him that if he died, he should go to a small piece of land that he owned in Pahrump, Nevada. He told him that he had buried millions in silver and he wanted to make sure that it was given to his daughter.

Two days after Ted's death, police arrived at the desert vault at 2:00 a.m. to find Rick Tabish and two other men with a backhoe and a semi-trailer. They were digging up the vault. Tabish claimed that he was digging it up at Ted's instruction, to make sure that it got to his daughter Bonnie, but police didn't believe a word of his story. Tabish was arrested and charged with grand larceny. In an interesting twist, the following day Sandy Murphy paid his bail. It became clear that Sandy and Tabish had been having an affair.

Five months had passed since Ted was buried with his cowboy boots and hat on top of his coffin. The Binion family didn't accept the coroner's report and pressed the police about Ted's official cause of death. They insisted that the medical examiner had made a mistake and Ted had not overdosed or committed suicide. They believed he was murdered by Sandy Murphy and Rick Tabish.

The Binion family had massive amounts of influence in Las Vegas and hired Tom Dillard, a former homicide detective turned private investigator, to look into Ted's death. In his opinion, everything pointed towards murder. With persuasion from the influential Binion family, the coroner reclassified Ted's death as a homicide. One month later, the Las Vegas police arrested Sandy Murphy and Rick Tabish and charged them with first degree murder, conspiracy, robbery, grand larceny, and burglary.

The Las Vegas district attorney hired a new medical examiner, Michael Baden. Baden was a celebrity among medical examiners, known for his high-profile work on the cases of OJ Simpson and Phil Spector. His more recent work included the autopsies of Jeffrey Epstein and George Floyd.

Baden disagreed with the original medical examiner's report. He believed that the red marks on Ted's chest were indentations from the buttons of his shirt. His theory showed the possibility that someone had sat upon his chest, depleting his air supply. He also pointed out that more red marks around Ted's mouth showed that he could have been smothered with a hand or a pillow. Baden hypothesized that he had been killed by a process called "burking."

Burking is when a victim is killed by someone sitting on the person's chest and simultaneously smothering them with a hand or pillow. This is usually while the victim is intoxicated. The process is known for leaving minimal evidence of a homicide.

Burking borrows its name from William Burke, who used the method to kill women in the late 1700s with his partner, William Hare. The duo sold the corpses for dissection at anatomy lectures.

At trial, the prosecution piled up the witnesses against both Sandy and Tabish. Baden presented his theory that Ted was killed by burking and claimed that almost no one dies from smoking heroin. The forensic pathologist testified that both heroin and Xanax were found in Ted's stomach, meaning that he had to have ingested the heroin rather than smoking it. It was an extremely unlikely way of consuming heroin which Ted had never done before.

A childhood friend of Rick Tabish testified that Tabish contacted him and asked him to help kill Ted. He claimed that Tabish offered him payment in silver and diamonds once the job was done. Another associate of Tabish claimed that he had bragged to him that he was Sandy Murphy's lover and was in the process of stealing Ted's buried treasure.

One of the most damning witnesses was Sandy's manicurist. She claimed that while getting her nails done three weeks prior to Ted's death, Sandy told her that Ted had a drug problem and he was going to overdose on heroin soon. She claimed that Sandy confided in her that after Ted's death, she would be rich and could be with her boyfriend.

The video that Sandy and her lawyer filmed of the house after Ted's death was brought into evidence by the prosecution. They claimed that the video showed Sandy taking a wine glass during the filming and placing it in her handbag. They hypothesized that the wine glass must have had evidence of a Xanax and heroin cocktail that she was hiding.

Murphy and her lawyer claimed the opposite - that the video showed proof that the house was not treated as a crime scene by the police and any evidence was either not preserved or had been contaminated.

There was no doubt that Ted Binion was a paranoid drug addict, but that didn't prove that he'd overdosed or committed suicide. After a two month trial and eight days of deliberation, both Tabish and Sandy were found guilty on twelve counts. At just twenty-eight years old, Sandy Murphy was sentenced to twenty-two years in prison; Tabish was sentenced to twenty-five. But that's not the end of the story.

Sandy didn't go to prison without a plan. Immediately after her sentencing, she wrote a thirty-page letter to Alan Dershowitz and asked if he would manage her appeal. Dershowitz was known for his work with the OJ Simpson case and got several letters every day from convicts around the country. However, Sandy's letter was convincing. After reviewing the evidence, he responded and took the case. He believed that Baden's evidence of burking was flawed.

All of Sandy's legal bills were paid for by a benefactor named Bill Fuller. The eighty-two-year-old was one of the most well-known music promoters in history. Throughout his career, he ran some of the most successful music venues in the world. He worked with a long list of musical acts including Johnny Cash, Patsy Cline, U2, Oasis, The Sex Pistols, and countless others. In the seventies, the eccentric Irishman moved to Nevada to prospect for gold. When he heard Sandy's story, he was intrigued. He said he was drawn to her because he believed in her innocence and her surname was Irish.

Sandy Murphy had spent four years in Florence McClure Women's Correctional Center, reminiscing her days surfing at Dana Point, when her conviction was overturned by the Nevada Supreme Court in July 2003.

Although both Sandy and Tabish had been convicted on twelve counts, the Judge had erred in deliberation. Tabish should have been tried separately for the assault and blackmail charge. Those charges were against another Las Vegas businessman and completely unrelated to the Ted Binion murder case. The judge also allowed testimony about Ted's will into evidence. The judge didn't inform the jury that the information was only a representation of Ted's state of mind—not as evidence that Sandy intended to kill him. Because of these errors, both Sandy and Tabish were granted a new trial.

At the second trial, Sandy didn't mess around. She and Tabish hired flamboyant civil rights attorney Tony Serra. Serra pointed out that the marks on Ted's chest could have been anything from dermatitis to skin cancer to even cigarette burns. Baden hadn't even examined Ted's body, only hypothesized based on photos from the original autopsy. To further disprove Baden's original testimony, the defense brought in nine medical experts who testified that his theory of burking was illogical.

During the second trial, Sandy's manicurist that had testified against her during the first trial admitted that the Binion family had paid her off. She received $20,000 from Ted's estate after her original testimony. Tabish's childhood friend whom testified in the first trial returned as well. This time, he claimed that Tabish was only kidding when he offered to pay him to kill Ted.

Their defense worked and both Sandy and Tabish were found not guilty of first degree murder charges. On the remaining cases of burglary and grand larceny, however, both were found guilty. Prosecutors hadn't claimed that she was with Tabish when he was digging up the silver, but charged her as a co-conspirator because she had paid Tabish's bail. Sandy was sentenced to time-served and was immediately released from jail.

Rick Tabish was also convicted of an additional charge of use of a deadly weapon and returned to prison. His original sentences were to run consecutively, but in 2009 his three convictions were reduced to run concurrently. In 2010, he was granted parole and released from prison.

Tabish moved to Butte, Montana, where he founded a startup providing services to the oil fracking industry. Years later, he founded and now manages a $100-million bitcoin mining operation. Besides a DUI conviction, Tabish has managed to stay out of trouble. In early 2020, however, his cryptocurrency business was temporarily shut down after a colleague of his was indicted for running a $722 million Ponzi scheme.

Sandy Murphy moved back to California, where she works as an artist and manages an art gallery with her husband in Laguna Beach. She has two children and goes by her married name, Sandy Pieropan.

CHAPTER 10
BLUE MIST #22

On a snowy January morning in 1972, eight-year-old Shelly Mickelson grabbed her coat and walked with a friend from her fourth-grade classroom at Marshall Elementary School toward her home in Flagstaff, Arizona. Like any other day, her mother expected her home for the lunch hour. But before Shelley made it past the baseball field between the school and her home, a familiar green Chevy Chevelle pulled up beside them. It was her neighbor, twenty-three-year-old Robert Moorman.

Moorman had received treatment for an intellectual disability and worked bussing tables at a nearby restaurant. He lived with his mother just a few blocks away from the Mickelson home and was known by Shelly's family. Earlier that week he had been to their home to ask what toys Shelly liked so he could buy something for her.

Moorman rolled down his passenger side window, called to Shelly, and told her that he was there to take her to lunch. "It's okay with your mom," he lied. Shelly had no reason to not trust him, got into his car, and the two drove off as the other girl continued her walk home.

It didn't take long for Shelly's mom to know something was wrong. As soon as she didn't show up for lunch, her mother called the school. One of the school officials had seen Shelly getting into the car, but thought nothing of it at the time, as Moorman was known by the school staff as well.

When she reported Shelly missing, a full-scale police manhunt was initiated and the media were immediately alerted. That evening, the story of the kidnapped girl was the lead story on the local television news channels.

Backtracking Moorman's movements, police learned that earlier that day he had asked for a $10 advance on his paycheck at the restaurant and cashed a $5 check at a local bank. He then borrowed a .22 pistol from a friend. At a local gun shop, he pawned two rifles for $60 and purchased ammunition for the handgun.

Late that evening, a motel manager in the tiny town of Ash Fork, Arizona, called the police. He had seen on the evening news that Moorman was wanted for kidnapping. The news piece showed photos of him, the young girl, and his green Chevy Chevelle. Although he hadn't seen Shelly, the motel manager recognized Moorman and the car. Moorman had checked into the motel using his real name and had told the manager that he was staying there with his niece.

Police instructed the motel manager to quickly move his own car behind Moorman's so he couldn't leave, but by the time he got off the phone, Moorman had disappeared with the girl. Moorman had seen the same nightly newscast. When police arrived and entered the motel room, all they found was the baseball hat he had been wearing earlier in the day, a section of rope, and pawn tickets for the two rifles.

Moorman had taken the girl to another motel near Kingman, Arizona. The next night they continued north to yet another motel in Lake Mead, on the border of Arizona and Nevada. Police and FBI meanwhile went from motel to motel throughout Northwest Arizona, but just missed him at every step.

The following morning Moorman was frustrated. He was running out of options and knew the police were onto him. It was only a matter of time before he would be apprehended. His frustration escalated when his Chevelle broke down on the side of the road. Furious, he got out and started walking away, leaving the young girl alone inside the car. January in northern Arizona was well below freezing. He knew Shelly would freeze to death in the abandoned car, but Moorman couldn't take Shelly's cries, eventually turning back and letting her out of the car.

He took her by the hand, put his thumb out, and walked with her down the side of the frozen highway. Although he felt sorry for the girl, he pitied himself more and wanted out of the stupid situation he had gotten himself into. If they didn't get someone to pick them up, Moorman's intention was to kill the girl and dump her body on the side of the road.

Mr. and Mrs. Swanson were traveling the country in their motor home when they saw Moorman and Shelly on the side of the road and offered them a ride. Shelly was cold and shivering – the couple could tell from her red eyes that she had been crying. Mrs. Swanson made them both some food in the back of the motor home as Mr. Swanson drove north toward Las Vegas. When Shelly had finished her food, Mrs. Swanson laid her on the bed in the back and told her to get some rest.

When she returned to the front of the motor home, Moorman had removed the bullets from his pistol, set it on the table, and asked if they had a drawer he could store his gun in. As they drove toward Las Vegas, the Swansons successfully persuaded him to surrender to the police. Moorman agreed and Mr. Swanson drove to the nearest police station.

Robert Moorman walked into the Las Vegas police station and placed his handgun and a pair of handcuffs on the desk in front of the desk sergeant. "I'm wanted for kidnapping a little girl," he said. The officer asked where the girl was and Moorman pointed below the edge of the officer's high desk. When the officer peered over his desk, he saw Shelly Mickelson.

Except for some light rope burns, Shelly seemed to be physically unharmed and the Mickelson family thought the horrible ordeal was over. When questioned by police, however, Shelly told them that she had been molested by Moorman. It was far from over for Robert Moorman, who faced kidnapping charges and was returned to Arizona.

Moorman had come to the attention of Flagstaff police in the past, but had never been arrested. Their first encounter with young Robert was when he accidentally shot and injured his mother. The second occasion was when he set their house on fire. Again, his mother covered for him and told police it was an accident. When he was sixteen, police were called to the Moorman house after he had used rope to tie up an eight-year-old girl. Claiming they were only playing "cowboys and Indians," Moorman was released without charges. His mother wasn't going to be able to get him out of the kidnapping charge, though.

During questioning after the kidnapping of Shelly, Moorman denied molesting the young girl, claiming he had blacked out and couldn't remember anything like that happening. He admitted that he intended to kill Shelly. He also initially intended to kill the Swansons, but when asked why he didn't, he replied, "Because they were nice to me."

Moorman's lawyer argued that he was mentally disabled and didn't understand the charges against him, but two psychiatrists provided by the prosecution disagreed. After examining him, both psychiatrists found that he was indeed mentally sound and able to stand trial.

 "His intelligence deficiency is so slight as to not be classified as mental retardation."

Both psychiatrists agreed that Moorman was neither a sociopath nor a psychopath; his only "illness" was a predilection for young girls.

Although he had been prescribed medication to control his sexual appetite, Moorman had stopped taking it days before the kidnapping.

The judge agreed with the psychiatrists and concluded that Moorman was competent enough to stand trial and fully understood the charges against him.

In June 1972, Moorman pleaded guilty to the kidnapping charge. Before his sentencing, he gave a brief statement expressing his remorse and asked for another chance to begin a new life. But, despite his plea, Moorman was sentenced to nine years to life in prison.

Robert Moorman was born Robert "Bobby" Conger in 1948. His biological mother was just fifteen years old when she gave birth. She had been working as a prostitute, which left the identity of his father unclear. When his mother was seventeen, she broke her neck and died in a car crash. Two-year-old Robert was handed over to his grandparents, but life with them was no better. His grandfather was a violent, abusive alcoholic and Robert was inevitably sent to foster care.

Eventually he was adopted by the Moorman family just before his third birthday and renamed Robert Moorman. His adoptive father, Henry Moorman, was a successful businessman and ran a well-known taxi service in the Flagstaff area. By the time he was five years old, however, his adoptive father had passed away and Robert was left to be raised alone by his adoptive mother, Roberta "Maude" Moorman.

Growing up in Flagstaff, Moorman was a chubby boy who wore large, thick glasses and spoke in a childlike voice. Making friends was difficult and the other kids called him "slow" or "retarded." Relatives would later say that his mother was the only real friend that Robert ever had.

Maude Moorman insisted that Robert wasn't "retarded", but only a "slow learner in book matters." He had successfully completed high school and a course at a barber school. However, when he couldn't find work as a barber he enrolled in another course to become a hospital orderly. His mother claimed that before the kidnappings, Robert had never done anything violent in his life.

Maude supported her son and stayed by his side all throughout his life, including during his incarceration. For eleven years she took a bus more than 200 miles every month to visit her son in Florence, Arizona, a small town about an hour south of Phoenix that was home to the state prison.

In January 1979, after serving only seven years in prison, Moorman was paroled. However, his freedom didn't last long. He quickly returned to prison after he violated parole for possessing a weapon. Back in the Florence prison, Maude Moorman continued her routine of taking the bus regularly to visit her son.

Throughout the years Moorman continued to apply for parole, but was repeatedly denied. In lieu of parole, however, the prison had a program called "Compassionate Leave", in which well-behaved prisoners were granted temporary leave outside of the prison walls for short periods of time. Moorman had spent his time in prison being obedient and productive, so in 1983 was allowed compassionate leave three times. He used each opportunity to meet with his mother for 72 hours at a time.

On Thursday, January 12, 1984, Robert Moorman was granted compassionate leave a fourth time. He was allowed through the prison gate and walked to the Blue Mist Motel, just a quarter of a mile west of the prison. It was a small mid-century motel known for its bright blue paint. It resembled something straight out of an old movie, with the motel doors opening directly to the parked cars and a gated outdoor pool. As she had in the past, Maude Moorman was waiting for him in room 22.

Just before 7:00 a.m. the next morning, Moorman walked to a nearby convenience store where he purchased a folding buck knife, a steak knife, and some food. On his walk back to the motel, he stopped by a pizza parlor that was owned by a former prison guard that he knew. He told the owner that he was on furlough visiting his mother at the motel and they planned on coming back that evening for dinner, but she wasn't feeling well.

Blue Mist Motel and Robert Moorman

When Moorman returned to the Blue Mist Motel, he stopped by the office and spoke to the owner. He told Mr. Patel, who ran the motel with his wife, that his mother wasn't feeling well and there was no need to clean the room that day. As he left the office, he ran into Mrs. Patel who usually cleaned the rooms. Moorman told her that the room had a strange smell and asked to borrow some disinfectant spray. However as Mrs. Patel handed him the spray, she notice that it was Moorman that smelled putrid. He also seemed to have some spots on his face that looked like tiny drops of blood.

Later that morning, as Mrs. Patel cleaned the adjacent rooms, she noticed that Moorman had dropped several dirty towels outside the door. As she picked up the towels, she noticed they smelled worse than he did. The towels were ruined. There was no way that smell was coming out. Rather than wash them, Mrs. Patel threw them in the trash.

Later that afternoon, a friend of Maude's stopped by the hotel room looking for her. Marianne Southworth lived in Florence and visited with Moorman's mother every time she came down to see her son. When Robert answered the door, however, he claimed that his mother had gone to lunch and he wasn't sure where she was.

Marianne thought it was odd that Maude's purse was clearly visible on the table in the room. Even stranger was the temperature of the room. Despite the cold January afternoon, the air conditioner was running full-blast.

Later that afternoon, Moorman asked Mr. Patel if the dumpster behind the motel would be picked up in the morning. He explained that his mother had brought some meat with her from Flagstaff, but it had spoiled and he needed to get rid of it. Mr. Patel, however, explained that the garbage wasn't due to be picked up until the following Monday—three days later.

That evening, Moorman asked the owners of the pizza parlor and a nearby liquor store if he could use their dumpsters to get rid of "cow guts" that a friend had given him. It was an odd request to say the least and both business owners refused.

The pizza parlor owner had worked in the prison and was familiar with Moorman. He could tell that Robert looked nervous and worried. He knew something was wrong. On a hunch, he called the Florence police, who checked in on Moorman at 10:30 p.m. The officers knocked on room 22 of the Blue Mist Motel and told Moorman that they had heard that his mother was not feeling well and they were there to check in on her.

Wearing only a pair of unzipped pants and a belt, Moorman explained that his mother had left around 6:00 p.m. that evening with a Mexican woman and he didn't know where she was, telling them, "I'm getting worried about her because she didn't take her medication with her."

When the officers asked why he was trying to get rid of "cow guts," he replied, "A friend gave them to me. But I got rid of them. I just flushed them down the toilet." Before the officers left the motel, they peeked into the dumpster behind the motel to make sure Moorman wasn't lying. Nothing seemed out of the ordinary, but they felt he was hiding something. The officers then drove to the prison to ask the guards for a description of Mrs. Moorman.

Late that night, Moorman was troubled. He really needed to get rid of that "meat." Moorman called the prison and spoke to a guard he knew, claiming he had twenty-five pounds of dog bones that he thought the prison dogs would like. The prison guard thought it was strange, but agreed to help him. He showed up at the motel a few minutes later with his truck, took the box of bones, and drove back to the prison.

Not long after the guard arrived back at the prison, he received a phone call from the officers that had spoken to Moorman earlier that evening. When they mentioned that Moorman's mother was missing and Moorman had been acting suspiciously, the guard told them about the box of bones he had just picked up.

When the officers arrived at the prison and opened up the box, they found trash bags filled with bones, but the officers thought they were too big to be dog bones. They believed they were human. The officers took the box and drove to the hospital - medical staff would know for sure.

While they waited for results, the officers drove back to the motel and found Moorman using the payphone near the office. As he walked from the payphone back to his room, they told him they would wait there with him until his mother arrived home and suggested that he wait with them in the squad car.

The three of them sat in the car for over an hour until two officers from the prison arrived and parked next to them. The results had come back from the hospital and the bones were indeed human.

Moorman was handcuffed and said to the officers,

 "I wonder if I need a lawyer. I'll leave it up you guys whether I need a lawyer."

When police entered room 22 at the Blue Mist Motel, the bath towels, bedding, bathroom walls, tub, and bathroom floor were all covered in blood. A buck knife, a steak knife, and a scouring sponge still had human tissue on them. Strangely, his mother's bra hung in the closet with $500 in cash pinned to it.

Although there was no question he had butchered his mother in the room, there was no sign of her body. It didn't take long, however, to find her remains. In a dumpster behind the motel police found Maude's head, torso cut in two pieces, feet, and hands. Each were wrapped in plastic bags. The hands were missing their fingers. They also found the packaging for the knives, a pair of his mother's paja-mas, and a razor. Another bag was filled with random bits of muscle, skin, and tissue. Only one finger was recovered from the sewer.

In Moorman's personal belongings in his prison cell, they found a notebook with odd writings such as instructions on how to train a dog to make deposits at a bank. However, investigators were most concerned with a document entitled "last will and testament."

Maude Moorman had already written a will that left everything to her son, but her assets totaling approximately $200,000 were to be put into a trust in his name. He would only have access to the interest it created. She didn't believe he was mentally or fiscally able to handle that much money all at once.

Robert didn't like that idea and had drawn up an amendment to the will. His amendment would have put the assets into a company called RHM Enterprises. RHM Enterprises, however, didn't actually exist and his mother hadn't signed the will. The amendment was dated January 13, the day he murdered her.

When Moorman arrived at the police station, he told detectives, "You can change the charge. She's dead." He told police that he "lost his cool" when his mother asked him to "take my father's place and do things I couldn't handle." He claimed that his mother had forced him to have sex with her ever since he was a child.

 "My mom and I had a... we had an argument, and during it I hit her a few times, and then it got worse and I... I lost my cool and I tied her up, and she kept on me, talkin' about things that, um… pertained to my real family and, I don't remember the exact time, and I suffocated her."

He explained that they were having sex and he put a pillow over her face to suffocate her.

 "Then I took the 409 (cleaning spray) and went into the wash room. I panicked, at which time I dissected her."

A postmortem examination of what was left of Maude's body, however, showed no sign of sexual activity. No semen was found on the sheets or clothes. The medical examiner noted that the dismemberment was meticulous. He had cut her feet at the ankles, hands at the wrists, and fingers at the knuckles.

Moorman told police that he had flushed nine of her fingers down the toilet. One finger had rolled away as he cut it off, and he lost it. He later flushed that one too, which was found in the sewer.

At trial, his lawyers again claimed that Moorman didn't know what he was doing and was mentally unable to understand the severity of his crimes. They argued that he had endured years of abuse from his adoptive mother, forcing him to perform sex acts on her which provoked his actions, but family members disputed his claim. By all accounts, his mother was loving and the best friend he ever had.

The jury agreed and found that he was sane. The way he dismembered the body showed that he knew the difference between right and wrong. Moorman was convicted of first-degree murder and was sentenced to death on May 7, 1985.

For thirty-seven years Moorman sat on death row awaiting execution, during which time his health deteriorated considerably. In the years leading up to his execution, Moorman suffered a stroke and received both an appendectomy and a quadruple bypass. Despite several appeals, he was finally scheduled for lethal injection with only two days' notice.

On February 29, 2012, Robert Moorman requested a double hamburger, French fries, two beef burritos, two 14 ounce containers of rocky road ice cream, and three RC Colas before his dose of pentobarbital. Because one of the drugs used for execution at the time had expired, his execution used only a single drug, rather than the standard three-drug cocktail.

His last words were an apology directed at the family of Shelly Mickelson, "I hope this brings closure and they can start healing now. I just hope they will forgive me in time."

CHAPTER 11
THE CRYBABY KILLER

Tami Engstrom had spent her entire life in the area around Youngstown, Ohio, midway between Cleveland and Pittsburgh. On a cold February evening in 1991, twenty-two-year-old Tami dropped her eighteen-month-old son off with her best friend, Sharon King, and drove to work.

Tami worked as a bartender at the Clover Bar in Hubbard, Ohio. Her shift started at 6:30 p.m., but she wasn't feeling well and called her mother at 9:00 p.m. and asked her to cover for her. Her mother, Elizabeth Heiss, worked at the same bar and came to cover the rest of her shift at 9:30 p.m.

When Tami left the Clover, however, she wasn't quite ill enough to go directly home just yet. Her friend was already watching her baby and there was a drinking event scheduled that evening at the Nickelodeon Lounge where her uncle, Daniel Hivner, was a regular patron. The Nickelodeon was another in a long list of dive bars in the area. It sat in Brookfield Township in the tiny town of Masury, Ohio, just a few hundred feet away from Ohio's border with Pennsylvania.

The Nickelodeon Bar and Tami Engstrom

Tami had several drinks with her uncle and showed off her new diamond ring she had purchased a few weeks before. It was a large ring with a cluster of diamonds that she had bought from her friend, Sharon, for $1,200.

Tami drank throughout the night with her uncle, a few other friends at the bar, and a man she met that night; thirty-two-year-old Kenneth Biros. Biros was a friend of her uncle. Although Tami didn't know him, Biros was well known in the bar and throughout the Youngstown area. He grew up and graduated high school in Youngstown before attending Youngstown State University as a geology major. Although it took him thirteen years, he finally got a degree. He had worked on an Alaskan fishing boat for a brief time, but most recently worked laying asphalt.

Despite feeling ill, Tami continued drinking. As midnight rolled around, she set her head on the bar table and, before long, she had completely passed out. When she fell off of her seat and onto the floor, Daniel helped her back into a booth and let her sleep for a bit. The bar was preparing to close at 1:00 p.m. and Daniel woke Tami and helped her out to the parking lot. He told her he would drive her home, but when he took her keys she became upset. She insisted she was fine to drive home, but she clearly wasn't.

That's when Kenneth Biros offered to take Tami to an all-night diner to get her some coffee with hopes that it would sober her up. He would then bring her back to the Nickelodeon Lounge and Daniel could decide if she could drive home herself. At 1:15 a.m., Tami and Biros left the bar in Biro's car as Daniel stayed after-hours with friends at the Nickelodeon.

That same evening, Tami's husband, Andy, had gone to the Clover Bar to see her. When Tami's mother told him that she went home sick, he drove to their house, but she wasn't there. He called her sister, who told him that she probably went to the Nickelodeon. Just after 1:00 a.m. Andy called the Nickelodeon and was mistakenly told that Tami and her uncle Daniel had left the bar and were on their way home. Andy wasn't worried and went to bed that night assuming she would walk in at any minute.

Daniel waited at the Nickelodeon, expecting Tami and Biros to return, but neither of them showed.

The next morning, Andy woke in a shock when he found that Tami never came home. He drove to the Nickelodeon to find Tami's car still sitting in the parking lot. Daniel informed him that Kenneth Biros had given her a ride the night before.

Andy showed up at Biros' home to ask where Tami was. Biros said that after they left the bar, he only drove about three blocks before,

 "I tapped her on the shoulder and she freaked out. She got out of the car and started running through people's yards on Davis Street."

Andy told him he was going to file a police report and,

 "If she don't turn up right fast, they are gonna come looking for you, and it's gonna be your ass!"

The area where Biros claimed that Tami had jumped out of the car was across the state line in Sharon, Pennsylvania. That day, Andy filed a missing person's report.

Biros was confronted by several members of Tami's family and friends. Each time he gave a similar explanation: she had jumped out of the car and he hadn't seen her since. He claimed that he chased her between houses for a while, but she was too fast and he didn't want to raise attention because he had been driving after having several drinks.

Tami's uncle, however, noticed that Biros had a scratch above his right eye that wasn't there the night before. There were also scratches on his hands that he didn't notice the night before at the Nickelodeon.

Biros claimed that he scratched his hand when he got home that night. He had locked himself out of the house and had to break a window. The scratch above his eye, he claimed, was from chopping wood early the next morning.

Both Tami's brother Tom and her father James didn't believe Biro's story. "If you put one scratch on my daughter, I'll kill you!" screamed her father. Tom told Biros, "I'll rip your heart out."

Biros reassured James,

 "Don't worry. Your daughter is going to be just fine. You wait and see."

That evening, Biros helped friends and family search the area where he claimed Tami jumped out of the car. After hours of searching, they found nothing.

When Biros returned home where he lived with his mother and brother, his mother had found a gold ring on the bathroom floor and asked him about it. "I have no idea. It looks like cheap gold," he told her. His mother disagreed. It was not a cheap ring. He told his mother that it could have belonged to the girl that jumped out of his car the night before. He took the ring and told his mother he would take it back to the Nickelodeon, but instead he hid it.

As Tami's friends and family continued the search, police called Biros and instructed him to come to the police station to give his statement. Except for an arrest for driving under the influence of alcohol, Biros had no prior police record. Police from both Brookfield Township, Ohio, and Sharon, Pennsylvania, were present at the interview since the disappearance happened literally on the state line.

During the interview, Biros gave a near identical story that he had told Tami's family, but this time he gave more detail. He claimed that Tami had passed out in the car. He stopped at a bank teller machine to get some cash and, when he returned to the car, she woke up and screamed at him. She wanted him to drive her back to the Nickelodeon. When he told her they were on their way to get some coffee, she jumped out of the car and ran.

The police Captain John Klaric from Sharon, Pennsylvania, had some doubts about his story. As the interview pressed on, Captain Klaric asked him if he had made sexual advances toward Tami. Biros had told Tami's husband that he only tapped her on the shoulder, but he told Tami's uncle that he accidentally touched her knee. Klaric knew there was more to this story.

Captain Klaric gave Biros his theories. He suggested maybe he made a sexual advance, she denied him, and then she ran out of the car. Initially Biros denied the idea, but when Klaric added that maybe Tami "accidentally" hit her head, Biros stopped him. Biros asked to speak to Klaric alone, then the other officers left the room.

Biros then told Klaric that his hypothesis was exactly what had happened. He added,

 "And I've done something very bad."

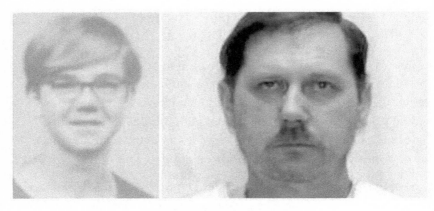

Kenneth Biros (high school & mugshot)

> "It's like you said. We were in the car together. We were out along the railroad tracks. I touched her on the hand. Then I went further. I either touched or felt her leg, but she pushed my hand away. The car wasn't quite stopped. She opened the door and fell and struck her head on the tracks."

Biros went on to explain that Tami had died next to the railroad tracks near his home on King Graves Road in Brookfield Township.

Biros was immediately arrested and he repeated the story for the other officers—Tami had hit her head and died along the railroad tracks. But when they asked where her body was, he asked for an attorney. After speaking to his attorney, he agreed to take police to the body, but they weren't quite ready for what they would find.

On Sunday, February 10, Biros took police forty miles east to Butler County, Pennsylvania. There they found parts of Tami's body. He then drove them thirty miles north to Venango County, Pennsylvania, where they found more body parts.

Biros had been busy that night. He had severed her head and right breast from the torso, while her right leg had been cut off above the knee. Her black leg stockings had been pushed to her ankles. Tami's torso had been butchered. Biros had cut her open and removed her organs. Her anus, rectum, and most of her genitalia had been removed and were never found.

After a search of the area next to the railroad tracks, detectives found massive amounts of blood on the gravel. In a nearby swamp they found pieces of her intestines, gallbladder, liver, and bowels. Later searches of the area uncovered her black leather coat with knife marks near the collar. Tami's black shoes were found with a single pubic hair inside that matched her DNA.

A search of Biros' home provided a pocket knife covered in dried blood. The long brown coat and tennis shoes that Biros had worn to the bar that evening were in his bedroom, also covered with blood. Tami's blood and pieces of her liver were found in the trunk of his car.

Despite the extensive butchering, sexual mutilation, and dismemberment of Tami's body, an autopsy revealed she died of strangulation. Biros had strangled her with his bare hands for almost five minutes before she finally died. The medical examiner counted ninety-one stab wounds, all of which were inflicted after she was already dead. There were also five blunt force wounds on the top of her head from the knife handle, or possibly his fist.

Kenneth Biros was charged with aggravated murder, attempted rape, aggravated robbery, and felonious sexual penetration. If found guilty, he faced a death sentence.

During his trial, Biros' defense told of how he grew up with a verbally and emotionally abusive father that denied him affection and constantly berated the entire family. They explained that until the murder, Biros had been a normal member of society with very little trouble with the law.

415

Biros testified on his own behalf and provided yet another scenario of what had happened that night. Throughout his testimony he wept profusely, garnering the nickname "The Crybaby Killer" from the press. During his testimony he claimed that, when he returned from the bank teller machine, he reached over and shook Tami, who had passed out in his car. When she woke up, she was too drunk to tell him where she lived, so he took her home to allow her to "sleep it off."

He explained that he parked within a few hundred feet of his home and tried to wake her again. When she awoke this time, she screamed at him,

 "I don't know you! Where are we?"

He went on to claim that she started hitting him and he hit her with his forearm. That was when she opened the door and started running along the railroad tracks. He explained that he tried to catch up to her with his car and inadvertently hit her. When she fell, her head hit the gravel.

Biros claimed he rolled Tami onto her back and saw that her head was bleeding. She had hit her head against the railroad track. He told the court that Tami screamed and threw rocks at him and he pulled out his pocket knife to "calm her down." Tami, however, was able to take the knife away from him, which scratched his hands. He then pinned her down and placed his hands over her mouth. He didn't realize until after he removed his hands that he had smothered her.

After realizing what he had done, he panicked, went home, and cleaned himself up. Twenty minutes later, he returned to the body. He was angry at himself and angry at Tami, believing that she had destroyed his life. He told the court that he then removed Tami's clothes because they were "in the way" and started stabbing.

He then dragged the body into the woods. As he grabbed her hands, he noticed her gold ring. He claimed he took off the ring and put it in his pocket to keep it from digging into his hands as he dragged her. When he tried to bury her, he realized that her body was too big for the hole he had dug. Rather than making the hole bigger, he cut off her head and leg. He then buried those parts in another location and buried her clothes separately from the body parts.

The next day, as Biros washed his car, he realized that Tami's purse was still in the car. He took it into his house and burned it in the fireplace. The following evening, after Tami's friends and family members threatened him, he got worried that the body would be found so close to his house. He dug up the body parts and buried them in two separate locations across the state line in Pennsylvania.

During his testimony, Biros denied that he had told police that he made any sexual advances toward Tami and had no excuse for removing her sexual organs, anus, and rectum. He told the court he had no recollection of where those parts were. He also denied hitting Tami on the top of her head with the knife handle or his fists.

The autopsy and testimony of a forensic pathologist, however, poked holes in Biros' new story. He claimed to have stabbed her using only a pocket knife, but evidence proved that a much larger knife was used. The incisions around the genitals were inflicted with much more precision than a pocket knife would have provided. Additionally, there was no evidence that the victim had been struck by a car. Finally, the autopsy showed that her hyoid bone had been fractured and there was damage to the tissue around her neck. This could only have happened by strangulation, not by suffocation, as Biros claimed.

It didn't matter what story he gave; he was going down one way or the other. Biros was found guilty on all counts, sentenced to death, and scheduled for execution by lethal injection.

A year before his scheduled execution, Tami's sister, Debi Heiss, urged the Attorney General to deny Biros' pleas for leniency:

 "Kenneth Biros beat, tortured, sexually assaulted, mutilated, dismembered, and robbed Tami with no remorse.

He has been given more humanity and mercy from the state than my sister ever had. It's time for justice to be served. Tami was my sister and my best friend. She was raped, she was tortured for hours. She had to be so scared that night."

Biros was eventually executed on December 8, 2009. He was added to the Guinness Book of World Records for being the first person in the United States to be put to death using a single-drug large dose of sodium thiopental, an anesthetic.

Twenty years after her death, Tami's friend Sharon King wrote about her theories that the murder was part of a still-continuing satanic cult in the area. She claimed that when Tami left the bar that night, her fingernails were painted red. However, when her body was recovered her nails had been painted black. She also claimed that Tami's corpse had been branded with the numbers 666, while her veins were completely dry when her body was found. Police records, however, mention none of those claims.

Additional unsubstantiated stories on the Internet claim that Biros had taken Tami to a shed behind his house where he butchered her. Because of these stories, some people believe the Biros' house – which has since burned down – is still haunted by the ghost of Tami Engstrom.

CHAPTER 12
THE DARLINGTON CANNIBAL

Julie Paterson had never really had it easy living in Darlington, in the northeast of England. When she was just an infant, her mother died of a brain tumor, leaving her and her three-year-old brother, Michael, to be raised by their father.

By the time she was thirty-two years old, she had four children but had lost custody of three of them. She shared the youngest child with her boyfriend, Alan Taylor. Throughout her life Julie had been prone to depression, which was amplified by her addiction to alcohol and Valium.

Julie Paterson and Alan Taylor

Alan knew Julie well and was used to her bouts of depression. He also knew that it wasn't unusual for her to go to a pub in Darlington and not return for a few days. She had been gone as long as a week in the past, but never longer.

In April 1998, Julie left for a pub and didn't come home the next day. As the days went by, Alan initially didn't worry. It wasn't the first time. However, when Julie missed an appointment to visit her eldest daughter, he knew something was wrong. That was one appointment that Julie would never miss.

He searched their local neighborhood, checked the local pubs, and called her friends and family. When nobody had heard from her, he called Darlington police to report her missing.

Since she had already been missing several days, police immediately started searching local parks, woodlands, rivers, and ponds. After days of searching, there was still no sign of Julie.

On May 16, 1998, a police dog picked up the scent of a human near a fence along a rarely travelled footpath. On the other side of a fence was a dilapidated house with an overgrown garden. The dog handler assumed the property was abandoned and entered the garden. The property wasn't abandoned, however, and a woman came out of the door to ask what he was doing. When he explained that his dog had picked up on a scent, the woman pointed toward the edge of the garden and explained that there was a garbage bag beneath a shrub. She said some boys had thrown it over the fence several days before. She told the officer she assumed it contained a dead dog because it had started to smell. As soon as the officer opened the bag, he knew it was the smell of decomposition. But it wasn't a dog. It was human.

A forensic examination determined it was Julie Paterson, but it wasn't all of her. The bag contained only a torso. Both legs, both arms, and the head were missing.

Before the news of Julie's death had hit the newspapers, a man named David Harker was in a local pub bragging to friends that he had "killed a girl called Julie." Twenty-four-year-old Harker, however, was a man known for telling tall tales and none of his friends took him seriously.

Harker had lived his entire life in the northeast of England and had trouble with the law at an early age. As a boy, he tortured and muti-lated small animals. At just sixteen, he attacked two men and their dog, resulting in the death of the dog. For this attack, he was sent to a young offender's institution for a brief time.

But there were two sides to Harker. To most of his friends and acquain-tances, he seemed like a good kid. He was charming, popular, and outgoing. His good looks made him a hit with the ladies, so he had no problem finding women to have sex with him.

In his later teen years, Harker sang for a punk band called Downfall and many young kids in the punk-rock scene admired and looked up to him. On the sides of his shaved head he had tattooed the names of his favorite punk bands: Disorder and Subhumans.

Harker spoke up against racists and sex offenders; he came across as polite and respectful. But when his girlfriend and the mother of his four-year-old son left him, he fell into a deep depression. His drinking increased and he became belligerent and angry. His anger issues got him banned from many pubs in the town. On one occasion, he got so angry that he put his fist through a pub window.

Harker was also an avid fan of true crime, reading every book about serial killers he could find. He often told his friends he would be a great serial killer because he knew so much about how to not get caught. His nickname for himself was "Devil Man."

Harker had bragged to no less than twenty-eight friends that he had killed a girl named Julie. Because he was usually drunk when he made the claim, none of his friends believed him. However, when the discovery of Julie's torso reached the newspapers, his friends reconsidered the possibility.

The evening after the news was released, several of his best friends speculated possibilities. Together, they read the article in the newspaper over and over. Could he have been telling the truth? Was he really capable of that level of mayhem? That night, Harker's best friend walked into a Darlington police station and told them of Harker's boasts.

Just days before his friends went to police, Harker had been arrested on a robbery charge and was awaiting trial at a bail hostel. With Harker already in custody, detectives obtained a warrant and searched his apartment. It was immediately obvious that his friends were correct; Harker was the killer.

The apartment walls and floor were literally covered in dark red, dried blood. It was clear that he had killed her in the apartment. He made no attempt to clean the crime scene. Bloody drag marks led from the hallway near the stairs to the kitchen. The kitchen had several large hooks attached to the ceiling and the whole place smelled dank and musky. The basement of his apartment was even bloodier than the main level. A forensic team matched the blood in his apartment to Julie Paterson and clothes found in the basement belonged to Julie.

The apartment itself was stark, yet messy. On the walls he had scribbled macabre lyrics to his favorite heavy metal songs. The floor could barely be seen through a layer of garbage and beer cans. His bedroom contained only an old mattress on the floor surrounded by various porn magazines. On his bookshelf police found several books about serial killers, a book about how to survive in prison, and another on how to dodge questions during a police interview.

Police arrested Harker at the bail hostel where he was being held. During questioning, he initially denied killing Julie despite the overwhelming evidence at his apartment and the statements of several close friends. Eventually, however, he confessed and told detectives the gruesome details of the murder.

Harker and Julie met one evening in April at a pub in Darlington. After a night of drinking, Harker charmed his way into getting her back to his apartment. Once there, they had consensual sex – but in the middle of intercourse, he claimed that he "got bored" and strangled her with one of her own stockings.

David Harker and his Darlington apartment

As her body lay there on the mattress, he had sex with her cold corpse. The next day, he cut a chunk of flesh from her thigh using a kitchen knife, placed it in a pan, cooked it with garlic, pasta, and cheese, and ate it. Harker then dragged her to the basement, where he wiped the body with bleach and kept her for several weeks. Using a saw, he cut off her head, arms, and legs. Detectives knew what he did with the torso, but Harker refused to say what he did with the head, arms, and legs.

During interviews with psychiatrists, Harker said,

> "People like me don't come from those films. Those films come from people like me."

He told them that his ambition was to become Britain's youngest and most notorious serial killer. He was destined to get caught, however, because he couldn't help but boast about his crime.

David Harker pleaded guilty to manslaughter on grounds of diminished responsibility. The sentence was essentially the same as a murder charge—life imprisonment with eligibility for parole in fourteen years. At his sentencing, one of the psychiatrists that analyzed

Harker said that he was pure evil; that no hospital treatment could be given for him. He suffered from multiple mental disorders and putting him in a mental institution would be a waste of time. The psychiatrist determined that he was in the top four percent of Britain's most disturbed men. As a result, he was sent to a high security prison rather than a mental hospital.

At sentencing, the judge told Harker,

> "You are an evil and exceptionally dangerous man. You killed her in the most terrible circumstances and dismembered her body. You glorified in her death and the manner of her death. I have no doubt that given the slightest opportunity you will kill again."

Even in prison, Harker basked in his depravity. Despite Julie's family's requests, he refused to tell what he had done with the rest of her body. Freddie Newman, the father of two of Julie's children, sent letters to Harker in prison, but he only replied with words of torment:

> "It's always good to know that people are thinking of me, especially those who suffer because of my actions.
>
> You are correct when you speak of decency, I have none. I have no inhibitions, remorse or regret, and therefore care not one bit if your wife has a full body burial or not.
>
> I hope you are happy in the knowledge that you don't suffer alone in your loss. Your wife was not the first or the last person I killed.
>
> You ask why I have done this evil thing. Well, I could intellectualise endlessly about murder, mutilation, decapitation and cannibalism but a man of your intellect wouldn't be able to grasp any of it.

So to give you something you could understand, I killed all the people I did because I enjoyed it.

Do you hate the evil man who chopped up and ate your wife? I am not evil Mr Newman but I am a monster.

Don't bother writing to me again or I will show you terror unbound. I do have your address now.

Goodbye Mr Newman."

Freddie Newman never recovered from Julie's death and eventually committed suicide in 2006.

Alan Taylor, the father of Julie's youngest child and her partner at the time of her death, suffered from the loss as well. It consumed him. Taylor became obsessed with trying to find the missing parts of Julie and spent years digging holes in the ground all over Darlington.

He would often weep over her gravesite and say,

  "How can she be at rest? She's not even here."

Like Freddie Newman, Alan Taylor also took an extreme measure. In 2006 he had given up all hope of finding Julie's remains and, in an alcoholic rage, strangled his best friend, John Morrison, with a belt.

When asked his motivation for killing his best friend, he told police that he wanted to commit a crime of the same level as Harker. He claimed that his alcoholism and post-traumatic stress disorder (PTSD) since Julie's death had left him a broken man. He felt that his only option was to be sent to the same prison as Harker so he could get his revenge.

At his sentencing, however, the judge realized that he wanted revenge and sent him to a different prison to Harker. Taylor was sentenced to life in prison and his hopes of ever finding the remains of Julie

Paterson were gone. Three months into his prison sentence, he committed suicide in his cell.

Nine years after the murder, the Darlington Police Chief Superintendent who worked the case made one last-ditch effort before his retirement. He visited Harker's prison with hopes of getting him to talk, but Harker refused to see him. He told prison guards,

 "If anyone from the Durham Constabulary comes to see me, I will tell them to piss off."

More than twenty years after her murder, Julie's family still struggles with the loss.

Online Appendix

Visit my website for additional photos and videos pertaining to the cases in this book:

http://TrueCrimeCaseHistories.com/vol4/

http://TrueCrimeCaseHistories.com/vol5/

http://TrueCrimeCaseHistories.com/vol6/

THANK YOU!

Thank you for reading this Volume of True Crime Case Histories. I truly hope you enjoyed it. If you did, I would be sincerely grateful if you would take a few minutes to write a review for me on Amazon using the link below.

https://geni.us/TrueCrime456

I'd also like to encourage you to sign-up for my email list for updates, discounts and freebies on future books! I promise I'll make it worth your while with future freebies.

http://truecrimecasehistories.com

And please take a moment and follow me on Amazon.

One last thing. As I mentioned previously, many of the stories in this series were suggested to me by readers like you. I like to feature stories that many true crime fans haven't heard of, so if there's a story that you remember from the past that you haven't seen covered by other true crime sources, please send me any details you can remember and I will do my best to research it. Or if you'd like to contact me for any other reason free to email me at:

THANK YOU!

jasonnealbooks@gmail.com

https://linktr.ee/JasonNeal

Thanks so much,

Jason Neal

More books by Jason Neal

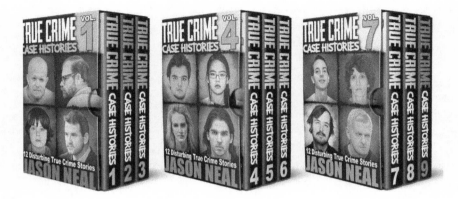

Looking for more?? I am constantly adding new volumes of True Crime Case Histories. The series **can be read in any order,** and all books are available in paperback, hardcover, and audiobook.

Check out the complete series at:

https://amazon.com/author/jason-neal

or

http://jasonnealbooks.com

All Jason Neal books are also available in **AudioBook format at Audible.com.** Enjoy a **Free Audiobook** when you signup for a 30-Day trial using this link:

https://geni.us/AudibleTrueCrime

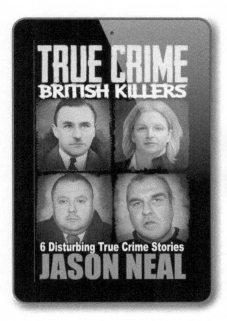

FREE BONUS EBOOK FOR MY READERS

As my way of saying "Thank you" for downloading, I'm giving away a FREE True Crime e-book I think you'll enjoy.

https://TrueCrimeCaseHistories.com

Just visit the link above to let me know where to send your free book!

ABOUT THE AUTHOR

Jason Neal is a Best-Selling American True Crime Author living in Hawaii with his Turkish-British wife. Jason started his writing career in the late eighties as a music industry publisher and wrote his first true crime collection in 2019.

As a boy growing up in the eighties just south of Seattle, Jason became interested in true crime stories after hearing the news of the Green River Killer so close to his home. Over the subsequent years he would read everything he could get his hands on about true crime and serial killers.

As he approached 50, Jason began to assemble stories of the crimes that have fascinated him most throughout his life. He's especially obsessed by cases solved by sheer luck, amazing police work, and groundbreaking technology like early DNA cases and more recently reverse genealogy.